The Gospel in the Anthropocene:
Letters from a Quaker Naturalist

Brian Drayton

illustrations by Darcy Drayton

INNER LIGHT BOOKS

Newberg, OR 97132

The Gospel in the Anthropocene

Letters from a Quaker Naturalist

©2026 by Brian Drayton

Inner Light Books
Newberg, Oregon
www.innerlightbooks.org

Cover art: Darcy Drayton

Author photo: Darcy Drayton

ISBN 978-1-59498-210-1

Printed in the United States of America.

Note: Translations herein are by the author, unless otherwise noted. Translations from the Jewish Scriptures ("Old Testament") and the Apocrypha are from the Septuagint (abbr. LXX), the version most often quoted by the Greek Scriptures ("New Testament"), unless otherwise noted.

For my children and grandchildren;
and for yours.

Contents

A Note to the Reader

The ecological, social, and political crises of the Anthropocene are multitudinous and pervasive: they already are affecting every corner of the world and at every level of organization, though in some cases the effects are barely perceptible.

Your response must grow authentically out of your situation, your worship, your love, your learning, and according to your measure of preparation and of faithfulness. This book, therefore, is not a "how to" book. It is intended to support, encourage, and perhaps goad you as you pray, observe, act, and learn from the doing. In writing, I have sought to do my work in such a way as to leave space for you to do your work. I am speaking as a Christian to other Christians, not to make barriers against those of other faiths or none but to help individual Christians see that the challenges of the Anthropocene require us to live up to the gospel of love we profess to follow. But I mind William Penn's comment, based on the confidence that the Spirit we call Christ is at work in all times and places:

> The humble, meek, merciful and just are everywhere of
> one religion; and when death hath taken off the mask

they will know one another, though the divers liveries
they wear here make them strangers.[1]

In what follows, you will find several elements that work best
together. Each needs its own kind of time. You, reader, are a compound—heart, soul, strength (body and action), and mind (knowing
and willing). Try to bring each of these elements in as view-ports and
also as sensors in your exploration of these materials.

Meditations

This element—mostly vignettes from nature or the boundary between
human life and the rest of nature—are not optional or superfluous to
the message. Indeed, as I suggest below, they are theology because
they reveal God's truth in ways that words alone cannot.

Though they are written in words, they will, it is hoped, move
you beyond words. Sit with each of them first as an exercise of the
imagination, in quietness and reverence of mind and body: give them
time. Bring to bear all your senses as you enter the scene. Be also alert
to responses from your heart (emotional self), your soul (your spiritual
commitments), as well as your mind. As with meditation on the words
of Scripture, try to see each scene from more than one point of view.
Do not worry about not knowing all the details. Let ignorance—like
reverence, beauty, fear, and delight—be one of the frontiers of wonder.

Make sure not to leave any of these times of meditation without
seeking beauty and love, for these are closely allied with knowing.

When some idea or image arises in your meditation that arrests
your attention or stirs your emotions, sit with that for a while, until
you feel released. So does *contemplatio* arise from *meditatio*.

This kind of seeing must be part of our spiritual practice in the
Anthropocene, and you are surrounded by an infinite host of materials. So think of these as samples to which you will add your own.

---

1   and Origen teaches "God is always giving a share of his Spirit to those who are
     able to partake of him." *Contra Celsum* vi : 70.

Drawings

The drawings are additional material for meditation and experience, helping to support the sense of immersion in the world, the book of nature.

Letters

I have written a series of letters to you, not a systematic treatise. The introductory letter explains the intent behind them all as well as the reason I wrote letters. The "Aphoristic spine" or "Overview of main points" may help make the underlying framework clearer.

In the searching that these letters draw from, I have read things. Short notes about references on particular themes appear at the end; a full bibliography is provided. In addition, there is an appendix briefly explaining the twin crises of climate change and biological extinctions.

Reflections

These are offered as seeds for reflection and discussion privately or in your community as you seek and follow your own path forward, doing your own work.

Overview or an Aphoristic Spine: The Gospel in a Time of Desolation

1. Creation is incarnation; incarnation is revelation; and revelation comes as nature, as the living Word experienced as the active Holy Spirit, and as words—in Scripture and other reports of encounter with the Holy One—no matter what your language, faith, or culture.

2. Life is process, including healing, growth, and death/transformation whether in individual organisms—in body or in spirit— or in communities. The creation is not finished; we say that the Divine Life creates and sustains, but these are different views from which to name the same process.

3. Worship is founded on encounter with the divine Presence. In it, we can find an increasing integrity among heart (desire and love), soul, strength (will and action), and mind (will and understanding).

4. The Presence is the love active in creation, transformation, and reconciliation; and it is also the truth and justice that dwell with love, as well as the suffering that love knows.

5. Encounter with this Presence leads to knowledge, grief, the taste of joy, and through them to *metanoia*.

6. We are always acting and taking action. *Metanoia* leads to clearness and whole-heartedness in action.

7. For Christians: if we are in Christ, we are one body, a body with diverse members that is always in process. So that each and all can stay attuned to the Presence, gospel community requires embodiment in forms and processes that facilitate tuning and re-tuning.

8. God in Christ is reconciling the world to Godself, and all creation waits for our reawakening into this wholesome, holy work. We are to participate in heart, soul, strength, and mind. Wonder and the reverence that follows are to be cultivated as indispensible roots of Christian witness. Wonder—delight at the givenness of the world and each individual—is a source of love; love sharpens the sight and casts out fear.

9. Reconciliation is a re-ordering of relationship and a kind of healing. It is thus an intentional, loving, and truthful transformation of understanding and of valuing. Reconciliation with nature and with other humans also requires our inward reconciliation. This inward work of Christ includes our daily living in the cross.

10. In this time of desolation, hope is in and takes the shape of this work of reconciliation. In this choosing of life, we receive power to act or to wait, to forgive and be forgiven, to mourn truthfully, and to discern the springs of joy. How and what we worship give formation for our actions on behalf of life—and bread for the journey. In true worship, we can feel the common life that all humans and all creatures share, and we learn how we may act in love to support that life.

Meditation: Devil's Hole Pupfish

You move across a semi-arid landscape, sparsely vegetated, punctuated by rocky hills and outcrops. You pull off the road at a sign and then climb up to an outcrop through warm March mid-day sun until you reach a simple metal platform from which you can look down into a cleft in the rocks. There's water a few yards below, much of it shadowed by the steep walls of the cleft. Sunlight happens to fall on a rock shelf that lies about a foot below the surface, about three yards wide by five yards long; beyond the edge of the shelf, the still water is black, the depth unguessable.

On the shelf, there is green algae fuzz, and a few dozen small blue fish, each perhaps an inch in length. They do not dart and school like some little fish do in the sun, but each moves about, foraging for tiny things, according to its own preference. Sometimes a fish swims off the rock and over the depths, but it does not dive nor stay there long, soon returning to the shelf and the sun.

You are seeing at a glance the entire population of the Devil's Hole pupfish. For them, the landscape, the subterranean water bodies, and the whole supporting earth are focused on the fluctuating conditions of water and sun as experienced on that fifteen square yards of rock, suspended over an inhospitable abyss.

Since you do not cast a shadow on their shelf, you don't exist for the pupfish. Though we are ignorant about fishes' mental powers, it is likely that their future, the time beyond sundown, casts no shadow on them, either.

Letter One: Introductory

Dear friend,

We have entered a time when global warming, the destruction of biological diversity, and other ecological crises are intensifying (and mutually reinforcing) in ways that will make the earth we have always known increasingly hostile to human society and life. Even though many refuse to accept what's happening, climate anxiety, even despair, are becoming widespread, and young people are especially affected. There is still time to avoid the worst futures, but even the least dire future will be transformational, dismaying, and grievous.

How can we live in this era, the Anthropocene, in durable compassion, prompt in doing well, steady in truth-telling, patient in disorientation or desolation, willing to serve, to wait, to suffer, and to enact mercy? How shall we seek and receive—like children—what we need for growth toward liberation? How shall we increase in clarity (to ourselves and others) about where our hope is founded? How shall we become ever more aware of and grateful for our place in creation and in harmony with the Creator?[2] How shall we remain spiritually

---

2 I use "Creator" and "creation" to indicate the world as experienced in prayer, poetry, or other states of wonder: direct encounter, with some of its transformations.

tender in the years that are coming? How shall each of us recognize what action is next called for from us, and how does our acting—and our way of acting—draw from and enrich our worship?

We humans are as subject to the laws of nature as any slime-mold, fish, or oak tree; yet we have fashioned cultural tools that, combined with our great numbers, make us a world-shaping force. Unlike the jet-stream or the landscaping beaver, we know and see in part what we do, how we choose, and what the consequences may be. In our knowing and choosing, we can feel grief, judgment, and remorse. These can embitter and dishearten to the point that survival in the face of harsh competition becomes the only imaginable reward.

The desolation of the Anthropocene is harder to bear as we come to see how we humans have inflicted it on ourselves and others of our kind; across several centuries, we have prepared a different and less welcoming world for future generations of humans and other species. Our culture, despite clear opportunities to take a different path, has helped ensure fear and loss for millions now alive and millions more to come. If we live in the arrogance of cultural amnesia, which is a product of our economic system, we will see nothing instructive in wisdom, let alone the resources that human experience and memory can offer for such times of desolation.

I ask myself and you: Does your worship, your spiritual practice, equip you to see truth, to accept the failure of conventions and systems that have been foundations of your world view? Does your worship support you in a time of catastrophe to respond reverently, constructively, advisedly, and with an enlarged charity? We shall have ever more need of such love!

Though every witness or storyteller sees meaning-rich events in their own way, we humans have enough in common that we enjoy or benefit from hearing or seeing what others make of things.

At least in part, this is why I am writing to you: I feel compelled to make something out of my experience of the early Anthropocene in case it may be of help to others. This event, still unfolding and gathering momentum, is so comprehensive and intense, so full of unrealized meanings as to challenge our minds, our emotions, our ethics, and our morality—our decisions and judgments about our doings and our relationships, now and in the future. Beyond this, the Anthropocene and its implications present a disturbing spiritual challenge—and, I have come to believe, a very great spiritual opportunity.

These letters are a report from my response to this challenge. They do not constitute a treatise but reflect my here-and-there search for opportunity. I did not seek to create a "how-to" manual with recommendations for specific actions you can take. Rather, as action is urgent, I am concerned to understand how recognizing our calling and taking action are inseparable today from becoming a more faithful follower and companion of Christ, who is alive and teaching among us.

Perhaps if I explain my title, you can get a glimpse of me as a companion—my point of view and my intent.

*   *   *   *   *

The Anthropocene

By the middle of the twentieth century, human activities began to leave a distinctive signature in the geologic record. The atomic bombs that devastated Hiroshima and Nagasaki opened this new epoch by initiating our ever-growing radioactive signal. As the century went on, however, the sheer number of individuals, the nature and scale of our environmental impacts, altered almost every aspect of earth's systems. We have worked lasting (and continuing) changes to the land, to atmospheric chemistry, and to the distribution and abundance of species. As our use of fossil fuels and of the land altered the earth's temperature regime, the durable ice on seas and land began its march toward effective extinction. Weather patterns have begun to change radically; so also the chemistry of oceans and of fresh water.[3]

As I am writing these letters, people on the whole have not changed their behaviors in ways that could prevent the world that supports us from becoming far less hospitable to *Homo sapiens* and many

---

3   Some geologists resist the declaration of an Anthropocene era, arguing that our impact will not be a truly distinguishable part of the geological record. See Brannon 2019.

other species as it has been for all of human history so far. It is true that many individuals understand what's happening and are working to respond, but large-scale action is so far wanting. After all, "behavior" includes politics and policy, commerce and agriculture, and all the other organized activities whose designs include the protection of participants from individual responsibility for negative effects that might be caused (note the use of the verbal voice that might be called "the impersonal of avoided culpability" so common in our public discourse). We have powers now that we cannot really control and that influence overwhelming natural processes that we hardly understand. We are like a child that has learned to use a match, a sliver of wood that makes a tiny fire—a child who then applies it to light a fuse that will eventually ignite dynamite. We have only a dim idea of what the next few centuries will be like, but science tells us that we have ruled out most comfortable scenarios, and it is very likely that we stand at the dawn of an epoch of upheaval, instability, and impoverishment.

A Naturalist

Just as a good cook is led by the flavors, textures, and meaning of food to take an informed interest in their craft, so a naturalist, out of delight and curiosity, pays increasingly informed attention to organisms and the lands or seas they inhabit. With this attention, this allowing oneself to be involved, come emotional and spiritual costs. As Aldo Leopold wrote:

> One of the penalties of an ecological education is that one lives alone in a world of wounds. Much of the damage inflicted on land is quite invisible to laymen. An ecologist must either harden his shell and make believe that the consequences of science are none of his business, or he must be the doctor who sees the marks of death in a community that believes itself well and does not want to be told otherwise.[4]

I can tell you from my own experience: a naturalist, watching and loving the natural world, holds this anguish alongside the deep,

---

4 *Round River.* New York: Oxford Univ. Press 1993, pg. 165.

renewing experience that comes from wonder and an engaged curiosity. A naturalist knows, indeed, the complexity of the world, the opening flower, the darting flight of bird and dragonfly, the wonderful contrivances of life, the grandeur of landscapes and heavens—and the dying prey, consumption, decay, the processes of generation and regeneration.

It is part of the naturalist's practice also to become familiar with unknowing, with waiting, with anomaly, with being wrong, and these are among the tools needed to riddle through the book of nature.

The Gospel

Many who have some awareness of the earth—farmer, fisher, birdwatcher, hiker, hunter, landscape-painter, gardener—are sharing in the dismay and feeling the wounds in the world. Treebeard speaks for them and for us when he says, as he takes leave of two representatives of wisdom, "...the world is changing: I feel it in the water, I feel it in the earth, and I smell it in the air."[5] The wounds and the fear of what is coming are the more bitter in the face of human indifference, misguidedness, and evil that are shaping the dawning epoch. Grief and rage are already abundant fruits of these times, and the burdens are falling most heavily on the powerless as well as on those whose power is not yet come—our children and grandchildren.

To mitigate the worst versions of the Anthropocene will require massive changes from us—changes in expectations, self-image, values, and ways of life. But the challenge of living with the world we have reshaped (in our own image?) will require resources of mind, emotion, will, and orientation. Here is where "gospel" enters the picture.

I know that some people, perhaps even you, will have been put off at first by the word "gospel" in my title, maybe because you belong to another faith community or to none. Others may take reassurance from it, at least at first; but the gospel is not a comfortable matter even though comfort can be found in it. Both the comfort and the discomfort stem from the demanding constraint of love, the love whose

---

5 In JRR Tolkien's *The Lord of the Rings: The Return of the King*, "Many partings."

momentum is toward wholeness, hoping "to outlive all wrath and contention, and to weary out all exaltation and cruelty, or whatever is of a nature contrary to itself."[6] It is a love that cannot exist apart from truth and courage. It means a recognition of woundedness, of failures, and of sin, as well as a growing experience of healing and power.

For the gospel is not a thing but a living process, a workshop, a place—God working within us for our liberation so that we are more and more available to that Spirit whose effects are joy, courage, peace, truth, and the heart and works of compassion. It is the continuing work of creation and, therefore, before and beyond any expression in words.

Through this gospel life, we come to understand that our own wholeness is not separate from the wholeness of the world. Just as the Anthropocene is an epoch that has to do with the state of the whole earth, not just the human part, so we also must recognize that our own wholeness or liberation is connected with that of the systems we depend on and have been reshaping. To put it another way, we must recognize that Christ's business is not now and never has been solely focused on human affairs (nor only on those who call themselves Christians). The incarnation gave the cosmic Lord a human face, but God did not thereby cease being Sustainer of Creation.

This realization entered Christian thought and piety from the beginning of the movement, and a central element of Christian apostasy has been the denial of this understanding. Here and there, from time to time, little groups or individual souls have been rooted in that broader understanding, but doctrine and worship have focused almost entirely on the "divine-human" relationship.

Now is the time to reclaim the early insight, the felt knowledge that the work of Christ in me or you, so intimate and individual, is continuous with the power that creates and sustains the cosmos. In so doing, we can (and must) learn to live in the spirit of love and justice that Christians call the spirit of Christ—in the Anthropocene—which otherwise seems more and more to be an insuperable challenge, for that Spirit is against despair and indifference or wrath and contention.

---

6   James Nayler *Works* vol 4, pg. 382

A Quaker

I am not writing about Quakerism, but as a Quaker, I will, from time to time, draw out some discoveries from Quakerism's traditional interpretation of Christian faithfulness, which has been described as "ethical group mysticism" and also as a kind of "nonverbal Christianity." It has led us to some specific practices and understandings of worship and its consequences in community and action that I believe offer resources to these times. Actually, some of what I write will be as unfamiliar to many Quaker readers as to non-Quakers, and this, I think, is a good thing if surprise encourages renewal.

Further, if anything I write can encourage open dialogue among groups or within groups (such as churches or Friends meetings), and if that dialogue opens any one toward a way of living more truthfully, justly, and hopefully in the Anthropocene, I will be very grateful.

Christianity in many forms, including Quakerism, has bred disunity within itself, with other humans, and with the earth; and in its perversions of the gospel, it has perpetrated great evils. It has often shown itself to be anti-Christ. Yet that despised and rejected One continues to call us to acknowledge our derelictions and come back to our right mind. It is still not too late.

> so far as [our gracious Creator's] love influences our minds, so far we become interested in his workmanship and feel a desire to take hold of every opportunity to lessen the distresses of the afflicted and increase the happiness of the creation. Here we have a prospect of one common interest from which our own is inseparable—that to turn all the treasures we possess into the channel of universal love becomes the business of our lives. (John Woolman)[7]

Reflection

What are you afraid of when you think of the next fifty years? For what do you grieve? How does your worship relate to these fears and griefs? Does your worship, your spiritual practice, equip you to see

---

7   *A Plea for the Poor.* in Moulton, P.P. *Journal and Major Essays of John Woolman*, OUP 1971 . pg. 241.

truths like this, to accept the failure of conventions and systems that have been foundations of your worldview? Does your worship support you in a time of catastrophe to respond reverently, constructively, advisedly, and with an enlarged charity?

Meditation: Spiderweb

Consider a spider web—a specific one.

1. Recall what you know about spider webs and what they are for, how they function. You may wonder how robust it is, how long it will last, what the limits of its strength or functioning life might be, how successful it is (how often prey is caught, whether it makes unsuitable catches, how long the spider needs to wait for its meals). You may well discover areas of ignorance, but don't worry about that! This is not that kind of science lesson.[8]

2. Focus first on function: call to mind what you know about webs and their uses by spiders; if other associations with "web" come to mind, note them, and then set them aside for later use. All the while, keep the image of the web clear in your imagination, and imagine it in operation—empty, moving with breeze or rain; with the proprietor waiting (whether hidden to the side or sitting motionless amidmost); as the scene of capture and struggle; as fraying and losing shape. Thus, into the web image, you incorporate its existence among the elements and in the life of its community.

---

8 For another time, and another kind of learning, see L. Brunetta and C. L. Craig (2010) *Spider silk: Evolution and 400 years of spinning, waiting, snagging and mating.* Yale UP.

3. Now allow your gaze to dwell upon the form, the construction of the thing, following the lines, just resting in the geometry of it, the shapes in it, some repeated, some not, at various scales. If you can, imagine the flow of contrary tensions that keep the web a functioning whole, perhaps recalling that these lines, so strong and functional, first were fluid until they froze into cables.

4. Transfer your gaze to the lines that anchor the web to the surrounding structures—trees, bushes, stones, building or fence, feeling how these anchoring points participate in the functioning of the web, the spider's purpose, and how, from the spider's point of view, all these are centered on her purposes.

5. Let your eye travel to one plant being used as an anchor point. (Let us say it's a tree.) Consider how the tree is the center of its world, as the spider is centered on the web. The tree is a light-catcher, wind-catcher, water-gatherer, shape-builder, habitat, and prey. Allow your imagination to surround the tree with its community—elements, soil, visitors and inhabitants, consumers and neighbors: you may find it useful to imagine a few hours or even a day in the life of the tree. Let your mind flow along the lines of it, and end by imagining the connections, through root or fungal net, between this individual and the vegetation around it.

6. Imagine the tree as it moves through time, as in a time-lapse moving picture: growing in stature over the years, its branches and roots stretching out through space above and below the ground with other roots reaching out toward it, the nets of root fungi appearing first as a faint fuzz but increasing in size and extent, spreading along the roots and outstripping them as connections are made. Imagine creatures coming to the tree (by air or land, below or aboveground), resting, hunting, eating, building, and passing away, as the seasons pass, and the leaves burst out, spread in sun and weather, and then fall away again.

7. Now follow a path from the web and its anchors to yourself. The path should be a physical one: imagine a specific physical way that you and the spider web connect—it will most likely be an indirect path, through the vegetation or some other element of the

landscape. Once you have the path in mind, hold it there firmly and concretely, following it back and forth until you don't need to "travel" the path to know it.

8. Each organism associated with the spider or the tree is the center of its own web, its own world—from the microbes in the spider's gut to the hawk that rests in the upper branches of the tree and from which it casts its net of vision. Each one also is woven into the fourth dimension, time, its integrity and its influence emerging, flourishing, and disappearing at its own tempo, with its own rhythms. Consider your own web and what its tendrils are made of, including those of memory, culture, behavior, and relationship. What are the boundaries of your being?

Part One:
The Worshipped and the Worshipper

In the next few letters, I invite you to consider what it is you worship and what it is to be a human being, a worshipper. We mean many things when we say "worship," and I should say here that I do not mean particular ceremonies. The ceremonies that have arisen in Christianity over the centuries have many purposes—re-enactment of sacred events, teaching, affirmation of community, the stirring up of emotions that motivate, comfort, or affirm.

But the essential root of living worship is an engagement with the living God, to be "subjected to [the object of worship] with total desire and zeal" in such a way that we are transformed into the image of the God we gaze upon (2 Cor. 3:18). This direct engagement, like all human experience, can be mediated by various helps, but it cannot be replaced or simulated by the results of art and invention, no matter how devout and beloved. Such worship will have consequences for our spiritual growth, for the formation of community, and for our action and service in the world.

So as I write to you about living the gospel in the Anthropocene, I find I have to start by exploring two ideas:

1. Our culture's idea of what a human being is is too small. We are not individuals in the sense of wholly autonomous actors. It can be useful to regard ourselves or others in that light, but we are dependent and interdependent ecological participants, not atoms. Much evil is perpetrated by adherence to the atomic theory of what it means to be a human. Some other cultures and some voices in our own have not made this mistake.

I have come to feel strongly that this understanding of the place of human beings in the world is an integral part of the gospel and related to our experience of mortality. This becomes most apparent and fruitful in light of the second point:

2. Our Christ is too small. Christ (who is the *Logos* and the wisdom of God) is a name for the creating, reconciling wisdom at work in, through, and around us, revealed in Jesus' life, teaching, crucifixion, and resurrection—and revealed also in many ways—from the beginning, before Jesus walked the earth, and ever since, too. Every revelation in nature, vision, and embodied action is a distinctive part of the message of love and truth that God has been preaching always to us in a thousand ways.

We cannot reconcile all contradictions that emerge from this revelation because, even as communities of ecological beings, we are too small to encompass the full story of our cosmos. The central message, however, entails love, which may also be called truth or justice. We can only receive the paradoxes and give thanks for being, with and in that love, growing as its vessels as we can. Jesus never said, "Blessed are those that have everything figured out."

His commandment to us (for we are his disciples as much as the twelve were) is to love one another as he has loved us, in the love of God that sends the sun and rain on just and unjust alike and enables us to bear his mild yoke, the daily cross, along his opening way.

His prayer is that we may be one in a unity by which we know ourselves to be bound intrinsically with the eternal/inexhaustible One, we who exist in and through the living, ever-changing fabric of the world.

Imperatives and prayers, love and unity, the starry mantle and the coat of many colors, yeast and Leviathan, Tyger and Lamb, the thief on the cross, the babe in every manger.

Meditation: By-the-Wind Sailor

When I first walked onto that Oregon beach, my attention was most with my companions, friends we'd joined for a Quaker weekend retreat. But the sea and the sea-wind and the life of the shoreline began to capture me, stealing in by way of every sense until, for a while, my friends and the good conversation faded into the background, and I was *located*.

At first it registered as a seashore such as those I'd grown up with, but gradually, its particular personality began to declare itself. Some of the sea-wrack and detritus under my feet was familiar to an East Coast beachcomber, but the shapes and colors of shells were pleasingly different, and the dried and drying weed was different, too.

Then my eye was caught by a pale blue spot nestled amongst the strands of seaweed. It was a blob, not a fragment of beach glass or plastic jetsam, and as I drew closer, I could see it was plainly organic, an organism that was just about a handfull. And then I recognized it as a by-the-wind-sailor (*Velella velella*), a beast which had been for me only a charming name in the caption of some childhood book about the wonders of life on earth.

Like its distant cousins, the Portuguese Man-of-War and other siphonophores, my little blue sailor was a colonial organism. Some of the individuals in these colonies are dedicated to capturing prey with little venomous harpoons, some to digestion and distribution of the results, some to reproduction. Some carry within them photosynthetic organisms (zooxanthellae), as corals do, which provide backup nutrition.

None of the colony members is devoted to locomotion except those that constitute the little air sac that floats the community and erects the little keratinous sail (right-handed or left-handed) that catches the wind. The sailors are pushed hither and yon across the pastures of the ocean surface, just as the wind listeth. Their blue colors (from pale to Prussian) provide both camouflage and protection against ultraviolet light but fade soon after the little craft is grounded on a beach; so I was lucky to have met my first sailor not long after they were cast away.

The sailors and siphonophores are weirdly beautiful and somehow challenging to the imagination: each component a creature of its own, a transform of a simple (?) two-layered polyp yet all cooperating as if a single being. Though not as wildly complicated as the mosaic creatures we call *Homo sapiens*, they are a unity-in-diversity whose unity is maintained, in a sense, by a common purpose, which lays down the lines along which their architecture is framed.

Letter Two: "We were never individuals"

Dear friend,

Let's start here: for too long, we have imagined individuals as atomic entities like automobiles, each with a hard case that defines its shape and protects the interior where all the important business happens. Inside, decisions are made, directions are chosen, space is allocated. The windows and vents let in sounds and light and smells or shut them out. Doors and hatches allow the passage of things in and out. Radios and cell phones enable the exchange of ideas and information among the human components of the various vehicles.

On a crowded highway of isolated individuals, there's also a lot of unspoken negotiation about space, speed, and location among the separate vehicles. Things outside (other cars, road conditions, pedestrians, signage) are either resources or problems, and values are assigned by the human components of the vehicles, most especially the one doing the steering. The culture within the vehicle is a matter settled by the human components among themselves. Things can be functional and happy, dysfunctional and happy, functional but unhappy, dysfunctional and miserable. I think I've experienced all these in road travel in my life. You can recall your own experiences of being in a module like this or of being one yourself.

Such an atomistic view of the individual is quite convenient for economists and policy-makers, who require simplified versions of reality for their arts and crafts. It narrows the kinds of motivations that you have to plan on or contend with. Values are mostly definable as inputs and outputs. Inputs are "consumed," the way a toad consumes a fly. For the purpose of planning and models, units ("humans," *Homo economicus*, the average person) can be treated as mostly uniform and can be trained (or coerced or "nudged") to want to consume some things rather than others. The units are components in a system, and the system is tuned to supply satisfaction—as the models define it—to enough of the units to make stability more likely.[9] In this framing, the idea of the commons fades away—every person and thing is available for competitive exploitation.

Such an idea of what it means to be a human being does not preclude some spiritual life, but it does not seem to me compatible with a spirituality adequate to the world-changes that are now gathering momentum. Indeed, you might wonder whether, if we could rerun the experiment with a different model of the individual, we might have avoided some of the current crisis. The triumph of the economic atom, the average person, has shown itself to be incompatible with the kind of resilience and reverence that will be necessary if humans are to live healthy and whole in the current age.

To be sure, in every culture, creation stories teach that humans arise from the stuff of the planet, its flesh and blood and desire—but it is a long time since our public culture has found this a reason for reverence. Rather, the continuity between our list of ingredients and requirements and what the world can give has introduced the commonsense notion that the world is our supply store from which we have every right to take what we "need" with no more thought or feeling than we feel when snagging a box of soapflakes or crackers off the market shelf.

---

9   It was not always thus, see works like B.M. Friedan's *Religion and the rise of capitalism*. The idea gained power in the modern era from Quetelet's idea of of *l'homme moyen sensuel*, followed soon by the rise of statistical methods for analyzing indivuals and groups.

From time to time, a poet or prophet will speak out against this idealized sovereign unit:

> No man is an Iland, intire of itselfe; every man is a peece of the Continent, a part of the maine; if a Clod bee washed away by the Sea, Europe is the lesse, as well as if a Promontorie were, as well as if a Manor of thy friends or of thine owne were; any mans death diminishes me, because I am involved in Mankinde; And therefore never send to know for whom the bell tolls; It tolls for thee.[10]

or even more radically,

> Then shall the King say unto them on his right hand, Come, ye blessed of my Father, inherit the kingdom prepared for you from the foundation of the world: For I was an hungred, and ye gave me meat: I was thirsty, and ye gave me drink: I was a stranger, and ye took me in: Naked, and ye clothed me: I was sick, and ye visited me: I was in prison, and ye came unto me... Verily I say unto you, Inasmuch as ye have done it unto one of the least of these my brethren, ye have done it unto me.[11]

This poetry and prophecy is still compatible with a human-centric view, which may keep all us "poor, forked radishes"[12] at the top of the ladder of nature, continuing an exploitive dominion of the globe.

We can acknowledge an ecological view that recognizes the limits to growth, the ways that energy is passed down from sun to tissue to soil chemistry and back to life again, pulling the elements around and around through their cycles, that knows the importance of biodiversity and the need for conservation. All this can proclaim our membership as one component in a council of all beings, yet it does not remove from us the assumption of our triumphal position at the apex of creation.

Though Solomon directed us to go to the ant to learn diligence, and Jesus pointed to ravens and lilies, I wish to point you to the

---

10 John Donne (1624) *Devotions on emergent occasions and severall steps in my sicknes* [sic].

11 Matthew 25: 34–46. KJV

12 *Henry IV* part II, Act III, scene 2

by-the-wind sailor as a hint of our true make-up. These little creatures and their more complex relatives can seem weird, possible models for sci-fi aliens. Yet other animals are just as weird, and none more than humans.

It's not just that we have bacteria in our guts and mites in our eyelash follicles. The majority of the cells in my body (or yours) are not human (only 55 percent or so). The nonhuman cells have roles in digestion, yes, but also hormone production, fetal and post-fetal development, in the immune system, and probably other activities not yet identified (science continues to explore this new region of ignorance). We have an internal ecology of as-yet unguessed complexity. As Gilbert, Sapp, and Tauber wrote in 2012, "We have never been individuals."

Our internal ecology is, in part, how we are intimately linked with what's outside. What we eat, breathe, and drink— as well as what we see, think, hear and feel—constitute signals to our persistent symbionts about the nature of the world we participate in, and in response, our whole selves respond from the genetic level up to the level of thought and choice. Moment by moment, we are actively interweaving with the winds and streams of life and material, receiving and giving, learning and teaching. We are legion, and the world's health and life is ours.

A meditation on this could be transformative. We could all be prophets, proclaiming with awe the ways—concrete, minute, and sensitive—in which the world's pulse and flow is united with our bodies, is part of our self in an active, measurable way—inside, outside, throughout. And when we formulate intents and take actions, we add new currents to the flow, shaping the world that shapes us. Reverence can be seen as an active and accepting response to the clearest possible understanding of who and what we are and what health can look like for us in our physical and social tapestries.

But almost all humans are many-minded. The prophet in us says, "Hear the truth! Live this truth henceforth!" but our culture and our history and our family and our temperaments then weigh in. "Not now. There's a job to do. What will my parents/partner/children/

neighbors think? It's hard. I'm tired, and I don't know how to do it, anyway." We all know the internal debates that go on within the council of all selves that resides in our heads and hearts. And so it's true, as Thomas Merton wrote:

> Here is an unspeakable secret: paradise is all around us and we do not understand. It is wide open. The sword is taken away, but we do not know it: we are off "one to his farm and another to his merchandise."
>
> Lights on. Clocks ticking. Thermostats working. Stoves cooking. Electric shavers filling radios with static.
>
> "Wisdom," cries the dawn deacon, but we do not attend.[13]

We are legion—indeed, legions within legions. Because of that, the work of gaining inward alignment and coherence, the work of reverence and spiritual formation, is an indispensable part of a constructive, wholesome encounter with the world now unfolding, our world (our body, our self) in catastrophe.

We have need of people who are free to love, to serve, to suffer, and to rejoice. Getting free is what the gospel is about, and gospel freedom comes through truth. One part of the truth is that we have never been individuals.

Reflection

What are the boundaries you most value? In what ways are they confining and in what ways liberating? What do they screen out, and what do they make possible?

In what ways are you divided within your self, and what are the effects of those divisions?

---

13 Thomas Merton, *Conjectures of a guilty bystander.*

Meditation: Warble

A deer mouse has found my live-trap, which I've baited with a little snack. There is also a twist of cotton batting so the mouse can make a bed in case things get chilly before I come along the trapline to weigh who's there and put a spot of color on its back, a tag so we can keep track of individuals.

The mouse—big soft ears, little hard hands, dark bright eyes—is gently poured into a baggy, which dangles from the field scales: hardly an ounce of mouse. Before I mark and free the captive, I look at it, really just look. It lies quiet in the bag's embrace, awaiting an unknown fate, not realizing that I intend no harm beyond this breach of privacy.

Amidst the lovely brown and white fur, I see a bulge, the fur looking thinner where the skin has stretched. It reminds me of how the trees thin out as you approach a mountain crown. The swelling seems almost a quarter of the mouse's size. What must it be like to haul that around?

A more experienced naturalist says, "Yeah, it's a warble. It'll be OK." Most mice we catch that day are bearing such a burden; squirrels and voles, too. The swelling is caused by a botfly larva.

A botfly lays its eggs on the ground near a tunnel, path, or run. An egg sticks to a passing rodent's fur and hatches, incubated by body heat. The tiny larva crawls about, seeking for an opening—orifice or wound—or creates its own entry. Eventually, it comes to lodge beneath the skin. Feeding from the host, it grows and eventually pupates, making a case within which it metamorphoses from maggot to short-lived fly. Transformed, it creates an opening to the outer world, hoping it is rich in botflies and in rodents, and departs, leaving the mouse to heal, as sometimes they do; or not.

This, too, is God's hand at work.

Letter Three: Death as Part of Life and the Gospel in Desolation

Dear friend,

I recently wrote to you with some reflections about our nature as composite beings, intimately woven—as a matter of everyday existence—with the whole web of life. But although in one sense one must say, "We have never been individuals," in another sense—just as undeniable—each of us is a single, unique constellation. You can't deny that each of us has a birth all our own and also a death equally unique. In between those two events, we accumulate a sense of our individual self. Part of being a human self is a recognition that the self will have an end, and for most of us, this is a disturbing thought no matter how buried under daily preoccupations (and a thick layer of denial). Yet our own unique death is a direct consequence of our unique self.

When we are reminded of this unavoidable event, it rouses emotional responses, often anticipatory fears—and many life events gain their intensity from the way that they remind us of the life-death transition that lies ahead (or all around us). **I believe that many of our fears and defenses, which inhibit us in our movement toward holiness, arise** from the need (often unconscious) to shield ourselves from one of two kinds of death.

The first fear is the death of not-being. The fundamental threat is of non-existence, physical death. Most of us, most of the time, don't encounter that level of threat in just such terms. However, I believe that more everyday concerns for health, for avoidance of poverty, etc., can be traced back to the basic desire to keep living. While the actual crisis (for example, losing a job) may be remote from the threat of actual annihilation, such incidents in our lives can engage basic, visceral reactions, the "fight or flight" responses that are instinctive in us for our bodily preservation. So, even minor threats in our material lives may feel urgent and desperate.

The other kind of fear, almost as significant, is the death of not-counting. As deeply social beings, we are programmed to care deeply about the good opinions of others. We may vary in how sensitive we are to whom—some people care about how almost anyone thinks of them, and some care only about the judgments of a few. Yet for almost all of us, the fear of being excluded, dismissed, or ridiculed is very real and shapes many of our actions.

Dealing with these fears is not a technical task, however, like eliminating weeds from the lawn, and we must beware of tackling them with the wrong tools or at the wrong times.[14]

Given the increasingly grave scientific news about climate change and the growing evidence of its deleterious effects on people's sense of well-being and hope, we are challenged to bring our fears of death and loss into our prayer work. Indeed, the invitation to despair—hopelessness—is a daily experience for many who are awake to the times; it has become a chronic, heavy burden for young people to carry.[15] I am grateful for the many wise people who are doing climate grief-work, who are helping make explicit some of the inarticulate groans of loss and anxiety that are echoing in many hearts.

14   B. Drayton *Getting rooted: Living in the Cross a path to joy and liberation.* Wslliingford, PA: Pendle Hill: Pamphlet 391. pp.15-16.

15   Whitlock, J. Climate change anxiety in young people. *Nat. Mental Health* 1, 297–298 (2023). https://doi.org/10.1038/s44220-023-00059-3

As I write to you this morning, however, I am drawn to some more particular reflections, stimulated by some recent reading, on the spiritual work that this loss and anxiety offers us—I would have said "demands of us," except that the Spirit reproves me and teaches that, for each of us, our personality and our times represent a gift, an opportunity to demonstrate that a soul living in the truth can be transformed by love and made fully available to the times. This is our opportunity.

Close to a Sword Is Close to God

Ignatius of Antioch's letters, written *en route* to his martyrdom in Rome, include some intense declarations of his eagerness for the martyr's death that awaits him (beasts will rend him to death in the gladiatorial arena). I have to confess that much of what he wrote feels foreign to me, but something clicked when I encountered this passage (§4 in his letter to the Smyrneans[16]):

> Why have I given myself freely to death, to fire, to the sword, to beasts? Well, close to a sword is close to God, and 'with the beasts' is 'with God.'

Now, as to martyrdom, I lean toward Erasmus's position: "Let others seek martyrdom; I don't think myself worthy of this honor."[17] Yet there is something further to be heard in these words of Ignatius, I think, beyond (and within) his obvious, fierce, self-surrendering witness.

In a close encounter with death, with the boundaries of our life as we know it, the many things that daily fill the foreground of our consciousness are pushed away, and we are confronted with mere existence. Our life is a mystery to us, and part of the mystery is the realization that death is a necessary and unavoidable part of the same fabric. To quote the Episcopalian *Book of Common Prayer* (1953), echoing Psalms and Ecclesiastes,

> Man, that is born of a woman, hath but a short time to live, and is full of misery. He cometh up, and is cut down,

---

16   Pp. 250–252 in Holmes, M. W. (ed). (2007) *The Apostolic Fathers*, 3rd ed. Grand Rapids, MI: Baker Academic.

17   Epistle #1167

like a flower; he fleeth as it were a shadow, and never continueth in one stay.

Meditation on death and upon its truth for one's own self was once recommended to everyone as an important—and indeed health-giving—practice. Socrates says (in the *Phaedo*) that the truest philosophizers should meditate on death, and it should be less fearsome for them of all people—precisely because it is the work of philosophy to figure out what is truly good and beautiful, what is of timeless value and what is perishable.

The acknowledgment of death, my own eventual death, brings a freedom into which grace can find entry. It is not, as I have experienced it, a counsel of despair or resignation in the face of ruin. It is a recognition of truth. In it, something fundamental is being revealed—about our material being, its life, its trials, its sufferings, and its end. In this recognition, we see how we participate in all the processes of the universe, from up-building to dissolution.

Thus much the ancient philosophers could teach and represent it with bleak grandeur: you have been born into this remarkable and abundant world and lived your span. It is only reasonable that you return to the state in which you were before becoming enfleshed. This participation in the great cycles of matter and energy can be beautiful to contemplate. As an Ursula LeGuin character says:

> "I think," Tehanu said in her soft, strange voice, "that when I die, I can breathe back the breath that made me live. I can give back to the world all that I didn't do. All that I might have been and couldn't be. All the choices I didn't make. All the things I lost and spent and wasted. I can give them back to the world. To the lives that haven't been lived yet. That will be my gift back to the world that gave me the life I did live, the love I loved, the breath I breathed."[18]

Now, the witness of Jesus—which is one with that of the Logos, the Christ spirit, that was before Jesus walked the earth and continues now—says something additional. Jesus shows us that in the

---

18 Ursula K. Leguin *The other wind.*

boundaries, limits, and extremities of our finite, mortal selves, God is to be found in ways not otherwise to be recognized or known—in our weakness, in our temporariness, in our vulnerability, and in our pain and grief. When we lose our certainties, our sense of safety, our sense of control—there is suffering there, fear, and anxiety: these are real. Yet many have found a way to live this desolation as a free gift: if you would be perfect, go, give up all that you have, and follow me.

Jesus does not demand this instantly of everyone, notably not those that he healed—after he restored them to health, Jesus admonished them to give appropriate thanks, do what was required under the law, and go on with life, taking care not to be alienated from God in future. Yet there can come a time—and this is a place I come most days, as I think about the condition of the world—when we recognize, with gratitude, the blessings we have received (and enjoy them), knowing that they will pass away. Even the blessing of life is not ours as we face soon or late our great change, "from works to rewards."

Yet Christ teaches that God has tasted and does now continually taste the bitterness of death and pain, and this does not negate the blessings of divine joy. Origen challenges us to recall that the risen Christ still bore the marks of torture and crucifixion when he ascended (as described in *Acts of the Apostles* ch. 1). We can know truth in these moments of spiritual poverty if we are willing to see that we are accompanied.

Thomas Merton conveyed something of the majesty of this vision in his *Hagia Sophia*:

> A vagrant, a destitute wanderer with dusty feet, finds his way down a new road. A homeless God, lost in the night, without papers, without identification, without even a number, a frail expendable exile lies down in desolation under the sweet stars of the world and entrusts Himself to sleep.

So this morning, I am able to see that it is in knowing the truth of our existence, its glories and its limitations, that we can grow to meet the challenges within and without. Amidst which we live and strive.

There was given to me a thorn in my flesh... to afflict me, in case I should take too much pleasure in my spiritual progress. Three times I asked God to take this away from me, but he said, 'My grace is all you need, for power comes to full maturity in weakness.' So I have come to be glad of my weakness, so that the power of Christ can settle on me.[19]

But this is not the whole truth of mortality. I think that next I need to write you a letter about sparrows.

Reflection

Julian of Norwich wrote, "God showed me two kinds of sickness that we have, of which he wants us to be cured. One is impatience, because we bear our labour and our pain heavily. The other is despair, coming from doubtful fear."[20]

Many people feel oppressed, even panicked, by the slow-gathering crises of our times. Their responses are as varied as their personalities and circumstances—denial, anger, depression, and withdrawal are common enough. Some people are moved to take some action. What are the roots of your fear? How do these roots shape your response? Can you connect with the idea that there may be an opportunity here for you—for you personally?

---

19   2 Cor. 12:7–9.

20   Julian of Norwich, *Showings*. pg 167. E. Colledge, O.S.A and J.Walsh, S.J.. tr. and ed. New York: Paulist Press. 1978.

Meditation: Surprise!

Scene one: afternoon in Michigan. The naturalist is standing on a dock by the lake, observing waterfowl. He notices motion in the water just a stone's throw away: a muskrat swimming by. He records that the muskrat was moving in a leisurely manner. Watching the animal, he notes that the animal also is watching him. Just as he is turning his attention back to the birds, he realizes that the muskrat is swimming in reverse—it hasn't turned around but is actually backing up. It passes the observer and continues backward for a few yards, then changes direction, swimming forward and proceeding on its way and out of sight. He consults local hunters and trappers, but they haven't seen such a thing in years of muskrat encounters. The naturalist communicates with his learned society.[21]

Scene two: the boy has gone out through the snowy woods to a point along the swift river where a bend slows the water, and the ice reaches from bank to bank. A thicket of huckleberry, gnarled apple trees, and bayberry serve as a blind in which the boy can crouch and (mostly ignoring the cold) see what is happening at the ice edge.

---

21 Peterson, Arthur Ward (1950) Backward Swimming of the Muskrat *Journal of Mammalogy*, Volume 31(4):453.

Along the margins, the wintering ducks gather, individuals from several species resting or diving in the chilly water or standing around on the margins of the ice-shelf. The diving is quiet and sudden: a little roll of feathers and—no duck. A few minutes later, silently, in an open patch of water, there is suddenly a duck—first a head, and then all upper decks are bobbing in the cold air.

From time to time, a new member of the club appears. These ducks are high-energy flyers, strong quick wings that whistle as they beat; you often hear them before you see them coming in. New duck arrows down to the water's surface and then lowers its water skis—the little colorful feet extending and spreading so that they hit the water first. The new arrival slides with a tiny swish for a little way, and then the downy body is bobbing amongst the rest.

On this early morning, a male golden-eye comes zinging in, very small and fast. The approach is at a steeper angle than the others have used, but the watcher assumes the duck knows his business. The little feet drop down—the toes catch in the water, and the tripped duck dips headfirst with an ungraceful *plonk!* audible across the winter river. The duck emerges at some distance from the bobbing crowd, as though he has swum downriver a bit to delay his entry into polite society. Ducks, of course, do not blush; but do they not have self-respect?

Letter Four: Sparrows

Dear friend,

Let us consider sparrows.

> Are not two sparrows sold for a farthing? and one of them shall not fall on the ground without your Father (Matthew 10:29).

> Are not sparrows sold five for two farthings? Yet not one is overlooked by God (Luke 12:6).

As an ecologist seeking to cope with the climate crisis, I find myself moved by the first part of Jesus' comparison: the idea of God, the God of the universe, the Law-giver and Shepherd of Israel, being concerned by the life or death of a single sparrow.

What kind of bird is meant by the Greek *strouthion*? Georg Kittel's New Testament word-hoard says that the kind of small bird is not known, but Liddell and Scott's great Greek dictionary unequivocally identifies it with the house or English sparrow (*Passer domesticus*), perhaps the most widely distributed bird species in the world.

So here, Jesus tells us that God attends even to such common and sometimes pesky birdlings, bought cheap in the markets for food or as a pet, in the same way that God attends to humans. This echoes the parables of the mustard seed and the yeast—dirt-common, multitudinous things are somehow like the Kingdom of Heaven.

But there is yet another nuance in Jesus' report about God's attention. God is not interested in sparrows as a concept, a species, but in each particular sparrow—not a single sparrow falls but God observes and accompanies it in the divine cherishing. As Origen wrote, "God does not take care only of the universe as a whole, but in addition to that he takes particular care of every rational being."[22] Here is a thing close to the heart of a naturalist: the life, death, and characteristics of a species are in fact constituted solely by the life, death, and characteristics (personality, even) of the individual members. No one individual sparrow, oak tree, human, trout, or toad is identical to all others of its kind, however closely related.

This is not only a matter of genetics. Every living thing experiences the world as it moves through its life span. Minute by minute, its tissues, its metabolism, and its neural pathways (if it has them) are tuned and retuned to the world. So the uniqueness and preciousness of each individual organism is not only a matter of the eons of evolution that it represents but also of its own inhabitation of the gift of life, of interaction and perception, of learning, suffering, fulfillment, creation or procreation.

Walt Whitman celebrated the preciousness of the particular in his "Song of Myself":

> I believe a leaf of grass is no less than the journey-work of the stars,
> And the pismire is equally perfect, and a grain of sand, and the egg of the wren,
> And the tree-toad is a chef-d'oeuvre for the highest,
> And the running blackberry would adorn the parlors of heaven,
> And the narrowest hinge in my hand puts to scorn all machinery,
> And the cow crunching with depress'd head surpasses any statue,

---

22   in Chadwick 1980 *Contra Celsum* iv:99, pg 263 .

And a mouse is miracle enough to stagger sextillions of infidels.

This, it seems to me, is a necessary practice of compassion, to concentrate our imagination until we can feel the pulse of uniqueness in an individual creature. Once that is our vantage point, we can recognize how often we fall into the trap of generalizing, a technical habit of mind that, notwithstanding its usefulness, is the root of much evil.

Sometimes, of course, it is useful to speak in terms of classified groups of things, but the worshipful mind enables us to understand feelingly how, in speaking of any species—including our own—strictly as a mass phenomenon, we put distance between ourselves and the experience of the individuals that constitute the species.

Our culture has increasingly become identified with our economy, that is, with the creation and distribution of wealth. As I wrote to you before, economics and its handmaidens have largely come to talk of (model[23]) humans as units of production and consumption, as masses and statistical objects to be modelled and controlled or nudged or molded for the greater good, itself an idea that obscures the individuals who are (or are not) experiencing the consequences of controls, nudges, mandates, and so on.

From this point of view, we can blithely justify the negative consequences of a new educational policy or environmental insult or war and then pass on. We become accustomed to the compromises that sin, incomplete knowledge, or imperfect methods may make unavoidable—accustomed and complicit rather than taking it as part of our calling to address prophetically and in compassion.

Our society urges us to speak as the fallen wizard Saruman does in trying to persuade Gandalf to compromise with the Enemy[24]:

> We can bide our time, we can keep our thoughts in our hearts, deploring maybe evils done by the way, but

---

23 "All models are wrong but some are useful." George, E.P. (1979). Robustness in the strategy of scientific model building. In *Robustness in Statistics*. (Launer, RL & Wilkinson, GN, Eds.). New York: Academic Press. p. 202 Much learning both moral and otherwise comes from contemplating wherein a model's "wrongness" lies, alongside its usefulness.

24 JRR Tolkien *The Lord of the Rings: The Fellowship of the Ring* "The council of Elrond."

> approving the high and ultimate purpose: Knowledge,
> Rule, Order; all the things that we have so far striven in
> vain to accomplish.

The sentiment here is related to our modern notion of collateral damage, of sacrificing some people (other people) for the greater good. It is an arrogance that says, "My policy choices will damage you, but I think it's all for the best." This permits us to commit all kinds of crimes against humans and also, of course, against nature. But it is not consonant with the gospel life.

When I wait until I can see and love the particular sparrow that God notices; the one wandering sheep that the shepherd seeks; the one stricken child; the man possessed by the demon, who is healed and made one, whole person—then I know that the Spirit that I feel, when I am dwelling faithful, never can forget the one, the one, the one, in his, her, their, its preciousness.

More than this: the Spirit warns us, when we feel that preciousness, never to pretend to be free of our kinships with the particular creatures in our story-telling about creation and our place in it. This is one of the great insights of Darwin, that there is in the world no type—an ideal of a species—apart from myriad individual lives, sharing in the fundamental unity of life. Is there not in this insight an endless spring of prophetic witness?

We will not be able to inhabit the Anthropocene in harmony with the gospel without the searching, persistent compassion that frees us from the mind that says, "Only some are suffering," "Only some are beautiful," "Only some matter to me." None of us is here by our own power, nor is the world that makes life possible and gives life to our souls anything we deserved, except that all beings begin by deserving the world. A conscious being cannot "take it for granted," but that being can receive it because it has been granted, because it has been given.

Reflection

God says (Isaiah 58:6–8),

> Isn't this the fast I prefer... to free the oppressed, to unlatch
> the yoke, to share bread with the hungry, and bring the
> afflicted and homeless under your care?.. Then light will
> break upon you like the dawn, and you will be promptly
> healed.

How does your worship remove the veil of convenient general-
izations and reawaken your active compassion? Active because "it is
not the hearing of the truth that purifies the soul, but the obedience
of truth which makes the vessel fit for the master's use" (Nayler *Works*
iv:33).

Meditation: How a Day Went

A still cool morning, just before dawn. Up before any of the birds, I remembered how yesterday I awoke fully clear and intent on my agenda.

By the end, though, the day was a bit dishevelled. My initial sense of tranquility and purpose was dissipated and (as I thought) wasted.

Yet here again, a new day is given to me, and after the catbird completes his morning announcements, I hear the tree-swallows chattering as they whiz about in the clear dry air.

On the grass, little cobwebs are spread, silvery with dew. So fragile, they seem a metaphor for my passing tranquilities—but then I think: when they appear to vanish as the sun rises, it's not as though they evaporate. They contribute a modicum of substance, all that they are, to the land, and after all, the creature that spread each of them during the night is down in the grass, going about its work.[25]

So my passing prayers, intents, and hopes perhaps leave some residue to be worked with; and the work of learning and building goes on, often in ways I cannot see or know.

25　These morning webs may be created by spiders or by dollar-spot fungus. Look closely to see if there is a tiny spider there or not.

Letter Five: The Cattle on a Thousand Hills

Dear friend,

Today I am thinking about a paradox. On the one hand, to Arcturus and Everest, the Kennebec River and the citizens of Lagos or Los Angeles, I know—intellectually—that I matter not a whit. On the other hand, I see myself at the center of events and instinctively give all things in the world a value as they relate to me. Much of human culture has the same bias toward self-importance; naturally, in consequence, we feel authorized to exploit the world at large and exploit other people(s) as well for our own comfort. It is just common sense, a most powerful force for social engineering.

> And I am right and you are right, and everything is quite
> correct (*The Mikado*).

This delusion is one that revelation has persistently contradicted—both in the book of nature and in Scripture.

> For every beast of the forest is mine, and the cattle upon
> a thousand hills[26]

In this psalm, God reminds us of the divine sovereignty over the world, its givenness, and puts us humans in our place in the creation. While Genesis 1 speaks of "dominion" and "subduing," by far the

---

26 Psalm 50:10. KJV

weight of the Scriptural message is one of stewardship, responsibility, and dependence, as in Genesis 2:22—

> God took the human that he'd fashioned, and placed him
> in the garden to work it and protect it.

At every point in which human pride or greed come to the fore, God reminds us that, though we are precious in God's sight and created in the divine image and likeness, yet we are creatures with definite, that is finite, scope:

> When I consider thy heavens, the work of thy fingers, the
> moon and the stars, which thou hast ordained, what is
> man, that thou art mindful of him? and the son of man,
> that thou visitest him? (Psalms 8:3–4 KJV)

Over and over, we are taught that we can make right use of the (other) creatures (animal, vegetable, mineral), or we can misuse them, but we rely on them and on the biological and astronomical rhythms of the earth and its inhabitants.

Jesus tells many parables about stewardship and accountability, and very often, the thing being accounted for is a material blessing— money, a vineyard, a fruit tree bearing fruits or requiring cultivation and pruning, works of mercy and healing, and (in the footwashing story) our love and service to others. Seed-time and harvest, rain and sun, the cattle on a thousand hills—all these are there for us but not as our possessions. Our relation to these things is first rooted in reception and gratitude, as it was in Eden, and though we must work and hope to take joy in our work (Ecclesiastes 2:24), it is God that gives the increase and who may require our lives or whatever we have in God's service.

And the creatures are not there only for us but also for their own purposes. The beasts of the forest, the birds of the air, Leviathan, the humble and instructive ant, the owl and dragon, hyraxes and gazelles, ravens and sparrows, the flowering trees and the weedy mustard are all living their lives as they are created to do. Sometimes humans hunt or harvest them or, in building, push them back from our habitations—but they are always there, occupying their stations in the world. The prophets remind us that, when humans misuse their gifts, forget their dependence, abandon the path of gratitude, and reap the judgment—that is, the consequences of their folly or evil—then the wild beasts and the untamed plants come in to fill the deserted spaces with the primordial energy that testifies to the wildness of God. This same God is the One who brought healing through Jesus' mediation, worked the transfiguration, covered the garden of Gethsemane, and (nearer than Jerusalem) works in and through us now for liberation.

Moreover, deep down, at a visceral level, we know that our place is within the creation. While recent scientific research has shown that experiences of nature are calming, healing, and restorative, this is really no new discovery. People in every age and tradition have found for themselves that "the world is charged with the grandeur of God," that the heavens declare God's glory. We have always taken comfort, amidst the woes and uncertainties of life, in the reliability of nature—and this deep participation in the joy of the Creator is woven into our fabric. It is no matter of ideology. Lucretius, no theist, sings:

> Why do we see the rose brought forth in spring, grain in
>   the hot weather,
> grapes coaxed out by the autumn,
> If not because every kind of creature is manifest
> When the specific seeds of things at their proper time
>   have come together
> When the seasons for them come, and the earth
>   abounding in life
> Safely brings tender things out onto the shores of light.[27]

and in similar vein, Hopkins, having registered his soul-sick perception of the condition of the human-managed world[28]:

> Generations have trod, have trod, have trod;
> And all is seared with trade; bleared, smeared with toil;
> And wears man's smudge and shares man's smell: the soil
> Is bare now, nor can foot feel, being shod.

then reaches for comfort to the "nature of things" not human, and that enables him to lift his gaze toward the fountain of renewal:

---

27   *De rerum natura* Book 1, lines 174–179.

28   Gerard Manley Hopkins: "God's Grandeur"

And for all this, nature is never spent;
There lives the dearest freshness deep down things;
And though the last lights off the black West went
Oh, morning, at the brown brink eastward, springs—
Because the Holy Ghost over the bent
World broods with warm breast and with ah! bright wings

When we are famished and parched and know ourselves to be, then it is with gratitude and relief that we can accept the bittersweet truth that our powers are great but not unlimited, that our knowing is only in part. And we are embedded and embodied in a transcendent (beyond the self, beyond the human) web, whose being preceded ours (we late-comers to creation), and whose well-being feeds ours. It is not by human doing that, in the city of God, John the prophet saw:

> In the midst of the street, and on either side of the river, was a tree of life bearing twelve kinds of fruits, yielding its fruit every month; and the leaves of the tree for healing the nations.[29]

Emerson, post-Christian, stoicism-inflected, wrote :

> The world proceeds from the same spirit as the body of man. It is a remoter and inferior incarnation of God, a projection of God in the unconscious. But it differs from the body in one important respect. It is not, like that, now subjected to the human will. Its serene order is inviolable by us. It is, therefore, to us, the present expositor of the divine mind. It is a fixed point whereby we may measure our departure. As we degenerate, the contrast between us and our house is more evident. We are as much strangers in nature, as we are aliens from God. We do not understand the notes of birds. The fox and the deer run away from us; the bear and tiger rend us. We do not know the uses of more than a few plants, as corn and the apple, the potato and the vine. Is not the landscape, every glimpse of which hath a grandeur, a face of him?[30]

29 *The Revelation of John* 22:2
30 *Nature* chapter vii.

These words emerge from reverence, humility, and gratitude. Have we learned, however, that as we have wandered away from a "unity with creation" (to use a phrase of George Fox's), we now can in fact violate the serene order with impunity and to suit our desires? So it might appear, as we mostly live in the first Adam nature, being "of the earth, earthy" (1 Corinthians 15:47). Yet the message and the fact of creation's transcendence and our embeddedness in that larger being suggest otherwise.

Reflection

A man of the Quileute people of the Pacific Northwest once told me, "The salmon, they are our relatives."

Modern science has begun to unpick the myriad ways in which each of us is threaded into the lives of other creatures who were here before us, preparing a place out of which our lives might grow. How does my way of life, my daily choosing, reflect this reality—or not?

Meditation: Lady's Slipper Orchid (1)

It is late May, and the bumblebee queen has been hard at work building her family and their growing home since the air grew warm enough a few weeks ago. Her eye is caught by a new pink blossom nodding above glossy leaves that lie low to the ground—a lady's slipper orchid. The blossom's darker veins point the bee toward an entry, and the faint odor suggests a nectar reward within. She has visited another blooming nearby.

It takes all the queen's strength to push through the vertical slit in the pink veil—the stiffly flexing sheet on either side sliding over her cheeks and glassy faceted eyes. Pulling herself through, hunting sugar or pollen, she finds herself in a room just large enough to hold her. This orchid, like many, is a deceiver: there is no nectar and no pollen to collect and carry home.

The bumblebee decides quickly that her time is wasted here and starts to leave, but there is no returning by the way she entered. The walls of the folded petal pouch do not yield to her pushing, pulling, buzzing; and in any case upward-pointing hairs allow only upward motion. Above, the light is brighter, inviting her attention, and the thin tissues form two little skylights that suggest a possible exit. Upward then, and all the blossom aids her progress now. She ducks under a lintel—and any pollen on her fur is scraped off, harvested by the orchid's stigma. Then another tight squeeze on the way out, and a new pollen packet is stuck to her as she exits. There is nothing in her mental processes to let her generalize from one failure, one failed collecting trip. She will visit another blossom or two before she calculates at last that these flowers offer nothing of substance. The bee loses time, nothing worse, and she carries messages for free from one orchid to the next.

Letter Six: Reap the Whirlwind

Dear friend,

The other day, I remembered the prophet Hosea's comment (Hosea 5:7): "They have sown the wind, they will reap the whirlwind." Now, this was directed to the people of Israel and Judah of the eighth century BCE, but it feels relevant to our time as well. So I have been thinking about consequences and judgment, faithfulness and unfaithfulness.

Although Scripture is full of events or rules that arise solely from God's will—the dietary laws, for example, or the healing miracles of Jesus, the parting of the Red Sea and the sun standing still at Gibeon, or the calling of a prophet—the world is seen to be essentially lawful. Seed time and harvest come in their turn; rain and droughts arise from the normal dynamics of the atmosphere; animals and plants obey their natures and bring forth offspring according to their kinds; you see a red sunrise and know that a storm is approaching. People, too, will enact their natures for good or ill. David sins and repents; lepers healed of their disease are grateful or ungrateful; Peter quails at the tests of the Passion Week; weak old Eli, corrupt and self-indulgent, yet retains enough reverence and insight to give Samuel the guidance he needs as he begins to fall into the hands of the living God.

The biblical prophets, seers, have a strong feeling for the systematic connections of events, motives, creatures, and the land. Much of their ministry consists in pointing out the consequences of human choice—for the great, for the humble, for the innocent and the wicked, for the health of the earth. Often their teaching emphasizes that small things matter and (as Hosea intimated) can have very large consequences. Even while the prophets are announcing the impending fate of nations and the dynamics of international power games, the health and viability of their society are seen in individual choices. Moses tells the children of Israel to choose life, each of them living according to the commandments. The ten that Christians think of as "the" commandments are all individual in their focus—keeping the Sabbath, honoring your father and mother, not telling lies—these are things that you or I do, each of us as a particular actor. The way you treat a stranger, make mindful use of material goods, or indulge in conspicuous consumption, offer a little incense to a local nature god, or stay focused on the One—these, too, are individual choices. If widely enough indulged in, they can set a trend and become a communal or collective norm, a consensus about what is valued.

It is in this way, too, that a whole culture can shift away from faithfulness without any explicit decision that it shall do so—one decision at a time, one person at a time, but all building a "common sense" together. All the while, people can continue to believe that, on the whole, they are being true to a set of values that in fact they have long abandoned. "This people draweth nigh unto me with their mouth, and honoreth me with their lips, but their heart is far from me."[31] In this way, individual choices can be evaluated with reference to the largest of scales, the will of God. In a world where the sacred is recognized, my failings and my healing are oriented toward it, but if it is shared by my culture, at the same time, I am oriented in my society. Thus the Divine, if a living presence, provides coherence and supports the making of meaning.

Now, Hosea is warning Israel about the consequences of such a shift, in this case the adoption of idolatry. He sees, with sight enhanced

---

31   Isaiah 29:13 KJV

by the spirit of God, that the people's consciousness has changed to focus on the local and immediate—they have come to think in the language of little gods of field and forest, wind and air, fertility and the hearth. Before, when they placed their faith in the God of Abraham, their scope of concern could reach beyond today's weather or this year's harvest, bearing in mind that, whatever their diligence and skill, their daily lives are embedded in a larger system, much of which is not under their control.

God, through Hosea (Hosea 4:6), says: "My people are destroyed for lack of knowledge." Because they have turned away from the wisdom they had before, when their allegiance was to the true God, their teacher, he cannot accept the prayers of the priests anymore. They are in no condition to represent God to the people, and they care to connect people only to concerns at the local scale. Abraham Herschel writes:

> Without abandoning the cult of the God of their Fathers [but only going through the motions—bd], the Hebrews worshiped…a god of the land rather than of the Creator of heaven and earth…Who was the Lord of nature everywhere, as well as the Master of history at all times.

Though these chthonic gods are to be propitiated, they are seen to be powers closer to a human scale, and thus they can be manipulated by people for their own purposes. It is natural that they can be represented by images whose absurdity is lampooned by Isaiah (44:16–17 KJV), who derides a man who grows a tree, chops it down, and makes various uses of the wood:

> He burneth part thereof in the fire; with part thereof he eateth flesh; he roasteth roast, and is satisfied: yea, he warmeth himself, and saith, Aha, I am warm, I have seen the fire: And the residue thereof he maketh a god,even his graven image: he falleth down unto it, and worshippeth it, and prayeth unto it, and saith, Deliver me; for thou art my god.

Thus, in a curious fashion, the move from worshipping the Creator to worshipping the creation (even the elemental things of the universe) brings the focus down to our comfort level, to the human world, the world as we have shaped it for our habitat, the world we can most easily comprehend, control, predict, indeed model in every sense. Nature worship becomes a selective worship of the parts of nature that impinge on human health and wealth.

Such a complete preoccupation with the works of our hands, the meanings and activities of people, is far advanced in our own day. It is iconically seen in the reality that the growing majority of the world's population dwells in cities, clambering about in a geography of infrastructure, with the walls of the cocoon paradoxically woven tighter by the webbing of mass communication, suffering from a deficit of nature. In a sense not usually meant, it is thus the case that the world has grown small in our ignorance of the whole, and we are comforted by telling each other smooth things, reassuring things, comfortable things—and rebuking any leader or prophet who speaks uncomfortable truths.

But it is the work of a prophet to climb upon a watchtower and scan the horizon, looking beyond the city's walls, across the verdant or blighted landscape, and give, by God's teaching, some understanding of the web of relationships and dependencies into which we all are woven. Such vision is based the prophet's "If... then." And Hosea also knows that when great forces are incited, the results can be uncontrollable.

It is characteristic of such a web (such as, for example, a food web) that a change may have easily predictable local or immediate consequences—but also may give rise to additional, extensive, less determined impacts throughout much of the system. When a key predator is removed from an ecosystem, when someone tells a lie and breaches trust, when the choice is made to go to war—the damaging results can grow like a living thing.

There are positive examples as well—when a dam is broken so that the river can become again a living system; when forgiveness is given and accepted; when a child is nurtured, or a spiritual gift is used in joy—who knows how far the ripples will spread? It is incalculable.

Hosea's grim pronouncement reminds us that, in an immensely complicated system, the results of our idolatries, our follies, our gestures of fear and anger, can be amplified—incalculably. We may think in our self-confidence that we can stir up the air and keep control—but the world (social, spiritual, or physical) has powers, momentum, gravity of its own. Seeing human self-sufficiency, God warns: "Thou thoughtest I was altogether such an one as thyself!"[32]

How carefully we must listen; must receive; must follow, must repent; must learn, not with the ears alone or the head but heart, soul, strength, and mind! How much we need wisdom.

> Wisdom crieth out: How long, ye simple ones, will ye love simplicity, and the scorners, delight in their scorning, and fools hate knowledge ? Turn ye at my reproof!
>
> I will pour out my spirit unto you, I will make known my words unto you. Because I have called and ye refused, I have stretched out my hand, and no man regarded, but ye have set at nought all my counsels, and would have none of my reproof, I also will laugh at your calamity, and mock when your fear cometh, when your fear cometh as desolation, and your destruction cometh as a whirlwind, when distress and anguish cometh upon you; then shall they call upon me but I will not answer. they shall seek me early but they shall not find me.
>
> But who hearkeneth unto me, shall dwell safely, and shall be quiet from fear of evil.[33]

Reflection.

Pick some choice you've made and trace its probable (or known) consequences over time: for yourself, for your relations and descendents (or their generations), for the earth. Where do your acts end?

---

32   Psalm 50:21 KJV
33   Proverbs 1:21ff KJV

Meditation:
Searching Through Space and Time

Every year, here in the eco-region known as the northern hardwood forest, wildflowers release their seeds abundantly. They move across the landscape, powered by gravity, birds, insects, or furry things. All that survive the trip fall to the ground at last, but that is just the first stage, and the future is still uncertain. Weather matters, and the land must also be receptive: an animal burrow, tree-fall, wind-throw, soil-scrape, a patch of scat—the seed needs some opening where its roots can find a little moisture. Failing this, the seed perhaps can wait through a year or a few—maybe things will improve in time. How likely is it that this seed will fall on such an opportunity? Not one in fifty or a hundred or a thousand will take root and last to another spring. Perennial wildflowers may live as long as trees (there are wildflowers growing in Concord, Massachusets, today, that Thoreau, that surveyer of leaf and bark, noted 150 years ago).

The wildflowers send out their seed epistles year by year, searching for hospitality, hoping for a hurricane or a wildfire or a hard winter—if not this year, maybe next, and on and on. The rich, abundant woods are strangely unwelcoming to the little visitors, the rain of seed-explorers. The woods say: we are busy, the land is fully occupied, but things will change, no doubt of that. A better world for you may yet come.

Letter Seven: Authorities

Dear friend,

This is what I hear the Divine saying to us:

"Creation is one thing, one whole thing. You, Earthling, are within that whole, and so the wholeness is ever beyond your understanding. Remember, you cannot even see or know fully the workings of your own body nor the life in the landscape around you nor even the landscape itself. You wander and study, measure, reflect, depict; delighted or disturbed, you learn some of what is there, some of what there is. Your discoveries nourish and engage you and help you learn still more. Yet your representations, your inferences, your explanations are and must be partial, and your valuable conclusions live within limits, the ever-moving frontiers of ignorance. This is part of what it means to be an individual—mortal and finite."

As with all organisms, our personal survival requires a certain minimum engagement with the truth of things. Our senses bring us news about what the world is like. Our basic needs also persuade us that we should expect to find their satisfaction out there in the world. Indeed, we are containers full of expectations, anticipations, and curiosities, and our experience grows in large part as an account of expectations felt and acted upon, fulfilled or disappointed, thought about and investigated.

No wonder our stories are so often about quests—"There and back again," "Slay the dragon and achieve the prize," "Bring back the lost beloved from the underworld." No wonder we grasp for ways to sort and make sense of the "blooming buzzing confusion"[34] of reality and foresee value and fulfillments to come. We live in a web of stories, and we are nourished by the stories we are told about the world and ourselves in it. But you and I are not stories. We are living and choosing, doing and undergoing, all fresh and for ouselves. Part of our choosing is: What stories shall we listen to as we are living our lives? This is such an old struggle within our culture. Sometimes it is cast as a choice between science and religion; and some others will say, "Away with dead authorities! This is my moment, your moment: touch it and shape it in your time and with your own powers, never-mind what others have said."

But I hear the word of the Lord echoing: "Creation is one, as I am one. You, child of your parents, of your culture, of your clay, feel that you are not yet one; that is your gift and your challenge. Hear me: you can come to know that you are my child, the child of the One, and all creation waits eagerly for you to step forward clothed in that knowing, seamless and shining."

Speaking as a child of my times and as someone trained in science, having taught it most of my life, I have felt the competition of worldviews within myself as well as in society. The gathering dangers that humans have prepared for us make a resolution agonizingly important.

I have to tell you here that I have often been tempted to throw away spiritual things because our ignorance of the world is so great.[35] Feeling that ignorance and the splendid complexity of the world, I want to learn more and teach more, help explain and engage, and invite people to see and think with the sight that ecology and natural

34 William James *Principles of psychology*.

35 Recent studies suggest that we "know" perhaps 20 percent of the species on earth; "know" means "have given names to," and often that is all we know. See E. C. Alberts (2022) and references there. https://news.mongabay.com/2022/04/global-biodiversity-is-in-crisis-but-how-bad-is-it-its-complicated/

history provide. Surely, if people come to see the sheer wonder and beauty of it all and themselves in it, some tenderness will grow, the heart of a steward or a gardener, not for ourselves alone.

But though people may have their minds schooled in facts about the world, their hearts evidently are hungry for something more: "Behold,the days come. saith the Lord God, that I will send a famine in the land, not a famine of bread, nor a thirst for water, but of hearing the words of the Lord" (Amos 8:11 KJV).

Mostly, we settle for food that nourishes deceitfully, whose fruit in its season is tasty enough but whose roots and seeds are poisonous to other living things and whose flesh in time burdens and blights. Within modern, militant Christendom, the book of Scripture is seen as the sovereign remedy in opposition to the book of science, which is our current representation of the book of nature. Yet, no matter which authority we appeal to or reject, our deeds diagnose our condition: we do not withhold our hands from actions and systems that have dealt death and misery and continue to do so. While science is much, it is not enough; and religion is very often idolatrous and self-serving. We know—but we choose not to know—that we live in a world that, in large part, is fictional. As such, we are likely to catch Pygmalion's illness or the fever of Narcissus. No wonder we also seek more, the experience of transcendence—which can also be fake or faked.

Feeling this struggle in myself, I want to tell you that the gospel life, the Christwork in our day, can be a path toward unity. But we have to see and accept that the Christ we are taught to settle for is too small. Of course I am not the first to say this— indeed, it is a discovery that began in the earliest days of the Christ movement. Still, I had to do some seeking and finding for myself first; only in this way have I been able to discover other teachers.

My first intimations of transcendence came to me—so far as I can remember—from the nonhuman world. Watching a swallow swoop chattering by or hearing the wild geese going over in the night or the seasons' or the rivers' ebb and flow: something, a longing awe, opened in me like flowers.

Later, when I had more words, I encountered scriptural stories: Noah, the shepherd king, Ezekiel's visions, the lions' den, and the gospel stories. No one connected my encounters with transcendence with the tales of the culture. The two kinds of knowing and telling began to communicate, sitting as they did side-by-side within the little box of my head; and one curious bridge formed between them early on. For I was struck by the warnings against idolatry, and the Lo here! Lo there! of the pseudo-Christ. I glimpsed the danger of self-delusions, the temptation to construct a god to suit me and then worship that— let it be my justification, my authority for doing and thinking things that I wanted to do or think or that I was told by others to do or think even when conscience twinged.

Idolatry can arise as well among those who claim rational science as the ultimate authority. How often we hear that something is "just human nature" or "in our genes" or "because of evolution," when the evidence is little more than an affirmation of social norms or anti-norms. But science does have tools that are designed to test claims, seek evidence, and remove error—not infallibly but to a great extent. And these tools can be learned and used well by anyone who wants to learn the craft. It is no wonder that science has been embraced by many as the best way to overcome the follies, deceits, and criminalities that are baked into every culture and that are presently directing the course of human history toward catastrophe. Still, science is conducted by encultured individuals, and any scientist is liable to the influence of cultural follies, deceits, and criminalities. This is why wise scientists avoid scientism, an uncritical reverence for the scientific enterprise.

And yet, in a world that is as much process as products (and all of its products or entities are in process themselves), the methods of intelligent inquiry represent the best way to identify and ameliorate or even correct the errors of idolatry.

So I came to see that my reading of scriptural teaching (or church teaching based in Scripture) needed to be confronted by the questioning inquiry of science and *vice versa*. Since the foundation and fundamental constraint of science is the natural world, the dialogue can be described as a debate between the revelations of nature and

Scripture. A modern, post-Enlightenment voice says that science trumps Scripture (indeed, it renders it obsolete). Other worldviews give priority to Scripture.

But why should we not take seriously the view that each of these is a source of information and insight, expressions of the one *Logos*, each saying things about the one world that can only be said in their own way. The revelation of Scripture expresses (hints at) what can be said with words—teaching, story, poetry, prophecy. But the God of meanings has some things to say that can only be expressed in the languages of organisms, of wind and weather, of physical law, and historical, evolutionary, and ecological process. These, it seems to me, are the utterance of the *Logos* about those things, using their native language for their fullest expression.

We can translate the meanings we construct from our inquiry in the natural world into words and numbers, theories and narratives. We can expect that Scripture and nature will echo each other, paraphrase each other, even explain each other sometimes; but there are things that can only be expressed as a bird or a tree, just as there are things that can only be said in Greek or Hebrew or Abenaki or Welsh. Naturally, this is frustrating to us for whom the universe—to an astonishing degree—is intelligible; but there is no reason to think that we can comprehend conveniently all meanings, all secrets, all teachings.

As with Scripture, so with nature: some meanings are directly accessible such that he who runs may read. Most, however, require interpretation, investigation: humble, reflective and also with the rigor that is brought by mental disciplines and the constraints of Christ's love. As we contemplate and interpret the book of nature, our first task is to understand the phenomena, using the tools and methods of natural history and other sciences. For some people, this study is enough for a lifetime, and in this realm, science must be our teacher.

Yet most of us are not scientists in the strict sense however much we may value and attend to the insights scientists achieve: our own callings are focused elsewhere. Reverent living with whatever purpose includes the search for meaning, and this inevitably means meaning in creation because all our ways and works are those of creatures deeply implicated in this natural world. If the world is truth, then we need to shape our thinking and doing to reflect and to meet it. And so we are free to—compelled to—seek in nature as in Scripture for spiritual meanings and connections (allegory), for ethical guidance (tropology), and perhaps most of all for pathways to awe and joy and a connection to that flow of life that we connect with the divine (anagogy), which somehow feels both immanent and transcendent.

Whether this awareness of the "little lower layer"[36] comes on us by surprise or because we search for it, it can make us aware of the root of reverence, which is the *Logos*, the wisdom that is within the world, constituting it and offering us humans, the children of choice, paths that branch toward life and collaboration with it rather than toward the destructive sacrifice of everything else in worshiping the idol *Homo regnans*, the Earthling whose habits of domination have brought about this present age.

Seeing souls have always known that "a person is greatly mistaken who believes that they can succeed in penetrating the true meaning of Scripture without being inspired by the Spirit by which gave it forth."[37] It is, in the end, the Spirit who is the revealer of truth, as it is the giver of life. If, as we find, the *Logos* of creation speaks to us, not only through Scripture and through humans who have become instruments of peace and compassion but also through other ABCs innumerable (atmosphere, bowerbirds, crustal dynamics...), then we must take care to seek our meanings companioned by that Spirit that gave them forth.

So we come to the need for a renewed understanding of the Spirit, which is the Spirit of Christ. Just as our understanding of what is meant by "human" has been too small and too definitive, so also is the common understanding of Christ. It has served our cultural purposes to be satisfied with an idol Earthling and an idol Christ—unbreathing, unhearing, unmoving, and unable to speak in power and peace to our hearts in these times of judgment and desolation. But this Spirit is both revealer of truth and transformer of souls and, like creation, is ever at its work.

---

36   Melville *Moby-Dick*, Ch. 36, "The quarter-deck"
37   Erasmus *Ecclesiastes* 1, lines 227–8.

People in many traditions have reclaimed the ancient practice of *lectio divina*, which moves from an attentive, prayerful observation of a passage in Scripture or other devotional writing to a time of focused but relaxed reflection on some portion or detail and then, perhaps, into contemplation. The early Fathers such as Basil of Caesarea applied this same practice to the contemplation of some aspect of creation. Basil taught that this was a way for us to participate, to get beyond the distanced or superior role of spectator, and feel our unity with creation and, through creation, with the Creator. Thus, meditative practice, which often is seen as taking us away from earthly things to spiritual things, actually brings us into closer embrace of our earthly being, but under the guidance of the Spirit of Christ, we can see incarnation as the opening way to holiness (availability): "In that day shall there be upon the bells of the horses, HOLINESS UNTO THE LORD; and the pots in the LORD'S house shall be like the bowls before the altar."[38]

Reflection

What authorities do you turn to in confronting the troubling, the open question, the unknown? What is your practice for integrating head knowledge with heart knowledge and these in turn with intention and action?

---

38 Zechariah 14:20 KJV

Meditation: A Passing Eel's Regard

I am fifteen years old, paddling upriver in my pirogue (a boat like a miniature dory that my uncle brought north from the Louisiana bayous). The tide's rising and slowing, near its flood, and after I'm whirled past the bridge, the broadening of the stream robs it of the sense of hurry, and I float into the sun, heading upstream with little work, free to daydream.

I look over the port-side gunwale, and out of the corner of my eye, I see a little bright dot—pale greenish in the brown water. As I watch, it grows larger; soon, I make out small dark eyes. As it slants toward the surface, an arm's length away, it becomes three-dimensional. It is a little eel, moving with the current and, like me, not working hard, sliding up through the green-black water, weaving past the sun-shafts reaching downward. There is no breeze, no sound of birds or distant traffic. The eel and I are part of the silent flow.

The little head brushes the water-ceiling; it skims along beside me for a few dozen heartbeats. The head tips away, a little eye meets mine; we move together eye to eye for another moment or two, and then the eel slants easily down and out of sight. I continue up along the fragrant marshy banks, accompanied now by an eel somewhere below, who has sometimes visited me again in dream or revery.

Letter Eight: Wisdom Speaks

Dear friend,

The declarations of God the Creator, the All-Mighty, whether in Job or Genesis, speak of a transcendent, unreachable power, whose ways are not ours, whose intent and works are, in the end, mysterious and awe-full.

> Thus saith the **LORD**, The heaven is my throne, and the earth is my footstool: where is the house that ye build unto me? and where is the place of my rest? For all those things hath mine hand made... (Isaiah 66:1-2 **KJV**).

Yet we have always sought to penetrate the mysteries, whether out of pure curiosity or from a desire to work with the powers that be, to increase the chance that we will flourish—not only by propitiation of an arbitrary and unpredictable Monarch but by the works of our hands and minds, the upbuilding of culture, including the arts and sciences. How intently, ingeniously, and persistently have humans scrutinized the world and its ways, seeking patterns, building understanding, developing an account of how things work.

Moreover, people have ever sought to derive from our understanding of the world some guidance about our own nature and the conduct of our affairs and ethics. Long ago, Epicurus, finding the world enchanting and rich enough without invoking any divinity within the machine, sought to create a system of physics so satisfactory that it would provide the ground for the building of an ethical and fulfilling life. His disciple, Lucretius, describes an atomic theory that famously accounts for free will by subtle, random "ripples" or "swerves" in the motion of the fundamental particles.

But in the Hebrew account of the world, God is not a distant demiurge, unknowable and unapproachable. Rather, God wishes to be known and not only by direct revelation (whether walking in the garden with Adam and Eve or by acts of law-giving or prophecy). The thing is, the good work of the creation is filled with the personality of the Creator, and thus it teaches, it opens to our questions and our wondering. Day unto day uttereth speech, night unto night declareth knowledge. The creation speaks to us through the voice and action of wisdom, personified (using the Greek word) as *Sophia*.

Sophia has been used (for example by great theologians such as Reuther or Johnson[39]) as a way to speak about the feminine principle in God (since the Greek word's gender is feminine, and Wisdom is spoken of as a bride). This then helps them clear away some of the ways that God has been seen to be allied with patriarchy, militarism, and exploitation of humans and of nature.

That is an important viewpoint, but I am now thinking of Sophia as God's active, energetic, creative, loving, yearning presence in creation and its creatures (including us)—God's *eros*.

> When he established the heavens, I was there, when he drew a circle on the face of the deep, when he made firm the skies above, when he established the fountains of the deep, when he assigned to the sea its limit, so that the waters might not transgress his command, when he marked out the foundations of the earth, then I was beside him, like a master workman; and I was daily his delight,

---

39   See for example their essays in Stevens, M., ed. (1993) *Reconstructing the Christ symbol: Essays in feminist Christology.* New York: Paulist Press. R.R. Reuther "Can Christology be liberated from patriarchy?" (pp.7–29), and E.A. Johnson, "Wisdom was made flesh and pitched her tent among us." (pp. 95–117)

rejoicing before him always, rejoicing in his inhabited
world and delighting in the sons of men (Proverbs 8).

As portrayed in the wisdom books (e.g. Proverbs, Wisdom of
Solomon, Sirach), Sophia is to be sought or courted ("I loved her and
sought her zealously from my youth"). As "the breath of the power of
God and a pure influence flowing from the glory of the Almighty,"
Sophia is a revealer, not in words but to the one who observes
open-heartedly and persistently. To this true-hearted seeker, God
through Sophia [40]

> gave me true knowledge of the things that are, to know
> the establishent of the world, and the operation of the
> elements: The beginning, ending, and middle of times:
> the changes that come with the turning of the sun, and
> the succession of seasons: the circle of years, and the posi-
> tions of stars; the natures of living things, and the raging
> of wild beasts: the forces of winds, and people's deliber-
> ations: the diversities of plants and the virtues of roots,
> and whatever things are. hidden or secret I came to know.

This is revelation of a different kind, a knowledge hidden in plain sight
and embedded in the complexity of the world of which we are a part:

> For wisdom, the artificer of all things, taught me: for in
> her is a perceptive spirit holy, unique, manifold, light,
> mobile, clear, unblemished, plain, invulnerable, loving
> the good, quick, which cannot be hindered, ready to do
> good...

And Sophia also sounds the note of joy:

> When he got the heavens ready, I was there with him and
> when he marked out his throne upon the winds, when he
> made ready the clouds above, and founded inviolable the
> the watersprings under heaven, when he made firm the
> foundations of the earth, then I was there in harmony
> with him. I was his delight, rejoicing before him daily
> in every season, when he took joy having completed the
> world and delighting in the children of the human race. [41]

40   Wisdom of Solomon 7:17–21
41   Prov.8:27–31

Moreover, one of Sophia's missions is to help us work, in our measure, as she does:

> by your Wisdom, you prepared people so that they can husband creation, which is from you, and manage the ordered world in holiness and righteousness.[42]

What are some of the lessons of Sophia perceptible in creation that seem important for our present time?

- God's wisdom loves diversity, which is the astonishing, delightful, overwhelming message of life and the universe, while God's unity pervades and is expressed in this diversity. We humans love diversity, texture, novelty– this is the ground of our love of the new and different.
- God's wisdom loves growth and transformation; where there is life, there is process.
- God's wisdom has set us among the creatures, the earth, the seas, and the heavens, and it is in that system that our growth and transformation happen, including our spiritual growth. If we were not in this body, in this system, we could not grow toward the Light.
- Moreover, our bodies are interpenetrated with the world—inside and outside are in constant interchange; these exchanges constitute our life. Like all creatures, we shape our environment even as we are shaped by it.
- God's wisdom loves the little things. Among all the great and astounding and heart-piercing things in this world, there are also as many or more small, simple, transitory creatures, objects, and events. Just as God is present in fulness, no matter how small may seem his manifestation to us, so also the wisdom of God is found in the mean and low as well as the high and impressive. Most of the essential processes of life are rooted in the little, the humdrum, the quickly ending things.
- God's delight is in service and creation, and so Sophia is to be found there; this is the power of the Gardener of Eden, not the Commander of Hosts: "she manages the world sweetly" (Wisdom 8:1).

42 Wisdom 9:1–2

- Transformation may require a loss, a dissolution of beloved forms, and the experience of the crucifixion is part of the experience of transfiguration.
- Finally, Sophia teaches us about the play of creation, the importance of experiment, delight, and desire.

The more I meditate on these things, the more challenging, scary, and exhilarating they seem as I look with intent, delight, and sometimes terror on the world. I exult at the realization that this is really the same message that the prophets taught, that the Light has taught, that the apostles of truth-force and the eightfold path have taught. I can see how the wisdom of God is indeed folly to the world, as humans want to see it. And Christians are called, like Jesus, to be fools in the world's eyes, loving creation, loving diversity, loving the little things, loving service, called to accept messages that so much of human culture is designed to deny and to walk more and more in the perfect freedom of God.

Reflection.

How in your worship do you encounter Sophia as a living power rather than as a possession, a concept, or an accomplishment?

Meditation: Lady's Slipper Orchid (2)

In the middle of the summer, the lady's slipper seed-pod dries out and opens. A dust is released, seeds so light that they can travel miles on the wind. Their lightness results from parsimony—the smallest of embryos is enclosed in the time-and-space capsule. Blown about, a seed may be interrupted by any leaf or twig—but a rain or a shaking wind may help it get to soil at last.

Yet it cannot drink, awaken, swell as other seeds do. Its fate depends upon an encounter with a fungal thread of just the kind that recognizes an orchid seed. If and when the encounter happens, the fungus curls around the tiny orchid grain, and its secretions weaken the seed coat, lets the water in, awakening the sleeper.

In time, a radicle will form and reach to the soil, but the little being is nurtured by its partner still. Eventually, the plant has reached a size and strength that makes a leaf possible, and once the first veiny green strikes the air and sun, the fungus can be repaid as the orchid fulfills its potential in its measure and condition. The fungus then is fed by sugars made from air and water, but the partnership never ends and links the orchid to the vast below-ground web of branching mycelia and roots that began forming half a billion years ago, and that sustains terrestrial life at every moment still.

Letter Nine: Sophia and Logos

Dear friend,

I have never been free of the grief that comes when I admit how much evil is daily done in Christ's name—and has been all through the "Christian Era." It has intensified my spiritual searching, seeking to pierce the veils of history and culture that wrap us round so as sometimes to stand in the presence of the true Christ rather than an anti-Christ, a compliant puppet savior of the status quo, or a lifeless human simulacrum whose worshippers are asleep or dead. How just are the accusations of skeptics in every age, who say that the God that is taught and preached through the generations is something fashioned in our own image and likeness! And in nothing is this clearer than in the general neglect of the world we live in as a matter of reverence.

Despite the recounting of Genesis stories and hymns to the Creator, my religion growing up made little room for the living world—wood, water, fish, bird, river, storm, mosquito, elephant, and, yes, for us hominids. The dominant religion, at least as taught in this country, leaves out the actual majesty, complexity, and strangeness of the world. How rarely did I meet anyone who understood how the contemplation or the study of the nonhuman world in all its diversity could be a gateway into profound reverence!

It is true that human nature is full of enough paradox, wonder, and challenge to keep a seeker busy for many lifetimes. Yet it is evident that we cannot make much progress, even in the understanding of this one species, if we do not remember that it is one of many exhibits in the world cabinet of curiosities, one thread in the fabric of nature, one part of the great always balancing and never-balanced system.

These three persistent questions—the nature of the Christ revelation, the divine givenness of the cosmos, and the longing to understand my nature and that of my fellow humans—have driven much of my spiritual and intellectual seeking through the years. I believe that God is one, and therefore, all revelation trends in a single direction, though I may never live to see the harmony made clear. (Origen says about the mysteries of revelation, "anyone in their right mind, and not plagued with the vice of boasting, will confess in the spirit of true religion that they do not know.") Nor have I been as persistent or acute a seeker as others; so here I can only recount what I have found in my blundering path toward Zion.

A few years ago, I finally decided to read the wisdom books of the Hebrew Scriptures and Apocrypha (Job, Proverbs, Ecclesiastes, Wisdom, and Sirach) all together. In Proverbs, I met Sophia, with which (or whom) I had a glancing acquaintance already. The passages in each of these books that portray wisdom as God's creating, healing, sustaining, comforting, delighting spirit reached deeply this time, and it became clear to me how much Jesus, the Gospel writers, and Paul had been nourished by and spoke from this tradition.

Then I found Thomas Merton's great prose-poem, "Hagia Sophia," which explores with tenderness and prophetic power the wisdom revealed and active in nature (including humans)—and in Christ's life and teachings. I began to see dimly that Sophia and the *Logos*, the Word of which John's gospel sings, are two faces of the Christ. With this realization, I could read Paul and John with new eyes. I also found (of course) that thousands of others had got there before me, from Origen in the third century to twenty-first century voices such as Elizabeth Johnson's.

Sophia and Logos

Sophia, characteristic of God's activity from before the beginning of things and by whom all things were made, radiates light and life from every element of the teeming world. Her lessons are mostly implicit; she reveals herself (gives understanding) to those who seek her earnestly and humbly. Indeed, she welcomes the devoted seeker, and when one decides to follow after her, she prepares her friends, building their capacity to reflect, to inquire, and to be patient in not-knowing.

The prologue of John's Gospel echoes these aspects of wisdom:

> In the beginning was the word, and the word was with God, and God was the word. This was in the beginning with God. Everything came to be through it, and without it nothing that exists came to be. In it was life, and the life was the light of human beings. The light shines in the darkness, and the darkness does not accept it.

In contrast to Sophia, much of whose teaching must be inferred from the nature of things (she is *natura naturans*, nature doing what nature does, as Spinoza has it), *Logos* is a fresh wave of God's self-revealing in terms that are more accessible to us: "The *Logos* became flesh, and dwelt among us." But the wisdom whose teaching is present to the seeker through creation is one with the *Logos*, for which "word" is an inadequate translation.

Logos can be translated as "discourse," "account," or "sermon," the nuance being that of interaction rather than mere utterance. In Plato's *Symposium*, when the friend of Apollodoros presses to hear about the conversation, he demands "Tell me what the *speeches* were!" and the word (in the plural) is *logos*. This word in Greek is of masculine gender—in contrast to *sophia*, which is feminine, or Latin's *verbum*, which is neuter. There is poetry, even wordplay at work here. *Sophia* is personified in the wisdom books as a woman to whom the seeker can pay court and espouse. *Logos* in John gets personified, too—with the added nuance that it is linked to Jesus, a man. Yet Paul speaks of Christ as God's *sophia*. Choose your pronoun!

Now Paul, the first Christian mystic of whom we have any record, says (in Colossians) that Christ is the visible image of the unseen God and thus revelatory of God's intent for us. But more than that, Christ is active, freeing us from the power of darkness and then leading us into the kingdom of the "child of his love." Even though everything from the beginning has come into being in and through this being (the same words are used for both Christ and wisdom), this work is ever-new, an always-fresh initiative; *Logos*/Sophia are both called "only begotten," or uniquely born (*monogenēs*). Their activity strengthens, with joy and insight, those who seek to learn and live in this light and life.[43]

The *Logos*, expressed as a human person, can teach us lessons that may be very hard to learn from the luminous but inarticulate mistress of wisdom, whose lessons are freely available but accessible only through observation, meditation, and inference. As Origen writes (in *On Prayer*):

> The possession of the wisdom by which everything was established was an impossibility for human nature.... Nevertheless this impossibility has become a possibility by the boundless excellence of the grace of God. Who could say that it is possible for human beings to know the mind of the Lord? Nevertheless, even this is given by God through Christ. For he says, "No longer do I call you servants... but I have called you friends for all that I've heard from my Father I have made known to you." He teaches them the will of him who wishes no longer to be Lord, but turns into a friend

Paul saw and felt yet another aspect of God's wisdom, which the *Logos*/Christ makes available when interpreted as a human personality set in a specific culture and time. This is that divine wisdom, which shows such splendor in the heavens and power in the mighty creatures and forces of earth, when brought to expression in a human, living according to the constraints of love, compassion, and truth, is all by itself

---

43 J. Rendell Harris suggested long ago that the prologue to John's Gospel, which has long been understood as a fragment of an early Christian hymn or psalm, can very easily be seen as a re-working of a praise of Sophia. Moreover, he argued that this, in turn, has affinities with pre-Christian veneration of Athena, Greek goddess of wisdom, who herself was termed "only-begotten" or "uniquely born," in reference to her mythical birth from Zeus's head.

a prophetic challenge. Christ's revelation of the wisdom of God for us seems but folly and dangerous folly at that. When it demonstrates its power (even unto the cross), changing lives and freeing folk from the conventional wisdom that upholds the mighty and oppresses the weak, the mourner, and the dispossessed, it can expect to be rejected, scorned, and extinguished.

A person inhabited by and fully committed to this wisdom that permeates the creation and even can be seen in a human form (of which Jesus was the firstborn of many siblings to come), tastes joy where the culture sees none, sees blessing where the culture sees a curse, knows herself to be a friend of the love at the heart of things, and is taught to serve as a good steward of God's household—the *oikoumenē*. Of course, such a person would seem to Mr. Worldly-Wiseman to be disconnected from reality—yet they have simply regained the radical wholeness of vision that is original to and intended for those created in God's image and likeness.

Sophia is God's wisdom to be discovered, *Logos* is God's wisdom experienced within, in terms by which the human heart is understood and embedded in language—the distinctive human faculty, the means of reason and of poetry, the way we build community, maintain memory, render an account of our past, present, and future.

P.S.

As a result of my explorations (so far!) of Sophia, I have understood a little more of what Paul and the Apostles thought Christ was about and why Jesus could have said, with such assurance, "I am with you always, even to the end of the world." The *Logos* renders a human account of wisdom, the matrix of creation, delighting in the multitudinous world and providing us with a framework of reason with which to speak truth and, through the foolishness of preaching, hope that the witness of wisdom will be reached and moved to offer the sacrifice demanded by God of the forest beasts and of the cattle on a thousand hills: mercy, justice, and the fruits of a teachable and contrite heart.

Reflection

How do your worship and your practice relate to this passage from Jeremiah?

> After those days, saith the Lord, I will put my law in their inward parts, and write it in their hearts; and will be their God, and they shall be my people. And they shall teach no more every man his neighbour, and every man his brother, saying, Know the Lord: for they shall all know me, from the least of them unto the greatest of them, saith the Lord: for I will forgive their iniquity, and I will remember their sin no more.
>
> Thus saith the Lord, which giveth the sun for a light by day, and the ordinances of the moon and of the stars for a light by night, which divideth the sea when the waves thereof roar; The Lord of hosts is his name (Jeremiah 31:33-35 KJV).

Meditation: Symbiosis

This morning, I read a passage of Scripture and settled into worship—except that I could not settle. My posture said, "I wait," but my muscles kept saying, "We need to act, we cannot wait, time passes and your burdens need their carrying." I continued in the silent struggle that comes to most who meditate, with tension working secretly in all one's usual places. The sun was rising, stirring up the world's wind as mental breezes set up currents in my inward pool.

But as usual on these summer days in the cool morning twilight, the catbird stole into the lilac below my window and began its intimate morning comments: melodious, quiet, individual, improvised. Since there are no other catbird pairs on our land, the song is for his lady and, incidentally, for me—and perhaps for the singer most of all. Through no plan of his or mine, the catbird's song thread led me through the labyrinth to the quiet of the heart. This morning, my meditation was the catbird's song.

Letter Ten: That Word "Dominion," and Nature in the Fall (and After)

Dear friend,

I have been thinking about how much damage has been done by these few words:

> ...have dominion over the fish of the sea, and the birds of the air, and over every living thing that moveth upon the earth. (Genesis 1:28 KJV)

This line from the first Genesis story of creation broods over any theological discussion of humans' relationship to nature. It has been used often over the centuries to justify unfettered human exploitation of natural resources, and it is often also coupled with a doctrine that all creation fell when Adam and Eve fell. This can conveniently push off any sense of responsibility for stewardship until the millennium comes, and we all will actually live by the Sermon on the Mount. (Surely Jesus didn't mean for us to apply his teachings in our own day!) That's the same future in which the prohibition against violence and retribution (and hence war) will be acceptable to human sensibilities. (But for now, it's just too hard; surely we are not meant to take it seriously.) Until then, on this line of thinking, all creation is unfaithful, too.

Other theologians, from the beginning, have seen nature as one important source of revelation about nature's God (and also from early times) while reasoning and investigation have been seen as appropriate ways to interpret the revelations in the book of nature, just as various exegetical methods are used for interpreting the revelation through Scripture.

One might say that God's wisdom is shown in this, that the revelation must be interpreted and is not a simple list of orders, however frustrating that can be for the seeker. In this way, each person can come to the Teacher with their current need and seek for the guidance appropriate to the moment.

For example, Erasmus, in his colloquy "The Godly Feast," has his character, Timothy, say that people prefer cities because, while nature delights and refreshes us, it has nothing to say and therefore teaches nothing. But the host for the feast, Eusebius, rejoins that "nature is not silent but is everywhere talkative and teaches many things to a contemplative person if she finds them attentive and teachable." Moreover, this comports with Erasmus's understanding of Jesus' pedagogy, which allows for and, indeed, advocates growth in insight with experience, not revealing all truths at once, as exemplified in how he explained the parable of the sower to the apostles in the Synoptic Gospels.[44]

You may not be interested in that kind of theologizing and may not care about Genesis and all that. But the problem remains that our culture (and that means us, too) is still deeply imbued (stained, dyed) with the presumption that all is to be used as we wish, perhaps moderated by some aesthetic or cost/benefit considerations. Doing a little theology is a way to identify and confront assumptions like these.

Moreover, no theology of creation (and hence of earth-care) can be disconnected from our doctrines on human nature and atonement—its reconciliation with God and the role of Christ (the Light) in all that. That, in a way, is one aim behind these letters: I am not

---

44   Drayton 2021 "Functions of nature in the *Colloquies*."

just trying to work out for myself some ideas about spirituality related to climate change—that can too easily keep climate or earthcare theology separated from other spiritual commitments. Rather, I am trying to see how a more complete understanding of the gospel can be found through reflection on the challenges and opportunities of the Anthropocene crises.

Perhaps more directly, the interpretation of "dominion" and similar terms is a way to explore our responsibilities vis-a-vis the creation in these times and to do so in dialogue with other seekers and finders across the centuries. So I will start first with an apparently nontheological story.

In Which I Confront the End of Nature

For my master's thesis in conservation biology, I studied how the species of an urban nature reserve had changed in roughly a hundred years since it was set up. Though subsequent research by others has improved on my work, my basic finding was that this reserve had lost many native species during this time—and that some of these would not return by normal, ecological processes, the reserve having become an island in a sea of roads and buildings. If people wanted the reserve to include the plant species that once had been present, people would have to bring back the lost ones.

Standing out in the woods, I realized that there was probably no place on earth where such restoration might not be needed if human impacts were to be countered. Humans now must take on the role of gardeners of the world (if we are going to be anything besides plunderers of the world, to the impoverishment of our children). This responsibility was not something we'd taken on intentionally, and it came upon us just at a point when science could start describing the depths of our ignorance of this world, which was now (in some ways) at our mercy.

This was in the early 1990s, and the implications of climate change, soil loss, deforestation, and the unfolding mass extinction were already clear to anyone who was paying attention. It was a moment of profound grief. Yet in the grief, the next realization was that the most urgent thing facing us is the curing of soul-sickness, to the point that reverence (or awe) is a living ingredient in our daily lives, a condition of gratitude and humility for the *kosmos* (the ordered world) in which we are given to live out our lives.

Dominion and the Fall

Now, I am going to ask you to indulge some reflections from a Quaker point of view. The first Friends, like other Christians, looked around the world and saw that something is seriously wrong. It seemed clear to them that the root cause must be related to humans' inherent tendency to sin. Because people are beings embodied like other animals, they are almost inevitably drawn to place first priority on physical, sensual, or cultural phenomena, and they build upon this inherent inclination a whole body of habit and rationale whose consequence is to further distract and alienate us from the promptings of love and truth in our hearts as the principal rule and guide of our lives.

This path entails, therefore, a wholesale but often subtle distortion of our understanding. When we privilege human wisdom and a solely human viewpoint, we are less open to being informed and regulated by the Wisdom through which the world came into being and which—despite our alienation and ignorance—continues to sustain the world in every part. Indeed, early Friends said that a key ingredient in the fall, the loss of capacity to live in right relationship, was an eagerness for knowledge without wisdom—in the myth, eating the fruit of the tree of knowledge results in exile from the garden of the tree of life. As a consequence, ignorant by our own choice and inclination, we have abdicated our dominion; we no longer know how to exercise this role as it was given to Adam and Eve.

It's no wonder, then, that instead of regarding ourselves and the whole of creation with reverence and humility, we use (misuse) the creatures to indulge our appetites beyond the due requirements of our bodies, to gain status within society, or otherwise to serve pride, overweening desire, and unjust ends. The focus is thus on self and on the idols we freely create and worship. These all reinforce our alienation from God's wisdom. Yet God's life, flowing through all, seeks always to move us toward reconciliation, and so, by grace, many have been given (or grown into or preserved) some partial access to the continuing divine intent: the *Logos*, which/who is light and life in all.

Now, full reconciliation needed not only to be invited and advised (as it was by law, Scripture, nature) but also modeled and enabled in the revelation of God's Christ in Jesus and by his Spirit. The sign of the incarnation and the many teachings and signs that Jesus gave show that God's continuing commitment to humans exists in harmonious relationship with the rest of creation.

Friends have taught (an old idea that they rediscovered) that our restoration in the light of Christ through the Lamb's slaying of the "man of sin" results in a renewal into Adam's condition before the fall, with the result that we can again see and live by the wisdom of God. In that wisdom, our use of the creatures is appropriate, in accord with the ordering that comes of dwelling in the power of the gospel. Its harmony with the will and design of the Creator is a sign of reverence and an enactment of the ordering light and life.

This becomes possible to the extent that we live the judgment and the reconciliation that happens as Christ is formed within. As we accept the diagnosis and the remedies provided by Doctor *Logos* (to borrow Erasmus's image), we are joined by that healing to the body of Christ, living from the common life under the one Head. Indeed, in our renewal through this process, we can fully regain our role as God's image and likeness, bearing witness to an authority beyond our own, and enacting our nature in accordance with the will of the Lord of Life.[45]

And here we can see how creation theology is inseparable from the rest of the gospel teaching. While it's cheering to think that, in the light, we are enabled to re-establish right relationship with the creation as we become reconciled to God, yet it's too easy to accept the insight, approve it, and then neglect actually to make it real in our heart, soul, strength, and mind. If, indeed, we can come to claim with

---

45 For a searching and helpful examination of resonances of the phrase "image and likeness" in the ancient Near East, see Wilson, G. H. (1990) Restoring the image: Perspectives on a Biblical view of Creation. *Quaker Religious Thought* #74 Vol. 24(4):5–21.

Paul[46] that "we have the mind of Christ," (by which to hear in our measure the *Logos*/Sophia by which all has become and is sustained), we need to see and experience the Light's work as both terror and power—really be transformed by the renewing of our minds, our ways of seeing, knowing, and valuing. We are thereby given the ability to bear the fruits of the Spirit. After all, God asks from us the sacrifice of a contrite heart, a heart so tendered and opened that it can allow the life, the Lamb's blood, to flow in, to refresh and nourish it to awe, to compassion, and to joy. Consequently, as we pray for guidance and witness amidst the challenges of our time, we must confront the call to repentance, the first and most fundamental of Jesus' proclamations: "Repent, for the Kingdom of God is near at hand!" So, now, I have to reflect on the troubling word "repent," starting with the Greek original: *metanoia*.

Reflection

Think of a resource that you use: time, fuel, money, space. Now consider: Do you exercise dominion over the resource more as exploitation or as stewardship? How does your use of this resource affect others' access to or use of it? What are other consequences of the way you exercise dominion in this matter?

Are there some resources that you steward and some you exploit?

Are there ways you should alter your practice of dominion? What hinders your enacting the change you are being led toward?

---

46   1 Corinthians 2:16

Meditation: Cattail Town

Walk down the road to where the cattail prairie spreads out on either side—odorous, green-tan-chocolate brown, tall, rustling. Here the marsh stretches north to the woods; but it also spreads half a mile south to the river; fingers of the river stretch out and bear the tide's pulse almost to the forest's edge; they ramble, divagate, anastomose between mud banks, rich-smelling, slick, and sticky with little juicy sounds suggesting that things are alive and conducting business all around.

There are more sunny sounds, too, as little birds cheep and twitter, hidden in the grasses, and red-winged blackbirds call loudly from the cattail heads. Insects shrill and click, cars whoosh by, gulls yodel overhead, crows roll and wallow in the air.

Step off the road, and the sound drops low, as if a blanket has been thrown over all the singers. The water and mud sounds are close, and the air moves not at all among the tall leaves. You make your way slowly along, eyes peeled wide but often thwarted with the horizon merely feet away—no perspective but the here and near, except when a hummock lifts you up, and you can re-orient yourself toward the up-rising woods.

As you slog and slip on the reeking mud, pushing cattails and mosquitoes aside, you come across little, shallow channels in the mud, perhaps six inches wide, flat-bottomed, clean and smooth, zig-zagging between hummocks. Turning, like Gulliver in Lilliput, to follow a path that opens at your giant feet, you find it joining to another, and by the second juncture, it seems undeniable that you have stumbled upon a highway system. Your passage bends or breaks some of the cattail ranks on either side, where no damage was visible before: the makers of these roads were smaller than you.

Soon the little avenue brings you to a dwelling: a round platform of mud supports a hut made of cattail leaves and mud, shaped like a gum-drop, just over knee-high. A slow circuit of the hut reveals a little entrance, low down at the base of the foundation. Pathways lead away from it, and as you follow them, you find you are in a neighborhood, the little houses a few yards apart, some the size of the one you first came across, some perhaps waist-high and an arm-span across.

When you are eleven years old and on summer vacation, you often have time to spend as you choose. Soon, as it seems, you find the tide is surging toward the land, then up the river, then even up the tendrils extending into the marsh, and as the nearest guzzle fills, it pours some water into the maze of pathways you've been following, and lo! they become canals.

Wait a little longer, till dusk approaches, and you see who makes the ways. Energetic little animals, the size of a small cat but plump, with a back that slopes up to the hips, and then down to the scaly tail. Little face, rounder than a mouse's, not as blunt as a beaver's, small black eyes, a shy smile, little clever hands. They glide from their houses and along the canals, hauling out from time to time to dig in the mud or pull down cattail stalks. Sometimes they munch on the spot. Sometimes they bring the roots or shoots back to the house and climb up onto the roof, which then serves as picnic table. The food is held or rotated in the little hands, while the busy mouth nibbles, pulls, gnaws, chews.

Cattails provide several kinds of snack, but the best are roots and the inner leaves down low. The inner leaves are tightly bundled, like leeks, green where the light has hit them, white below. Nibble from the white bottom, and you get a mild salad. Work higher up, and the leaves become indigestible to people but not yet to muskrats, who grind through the scratchy green.

The muddy root looks most unpromising. The outer rind is tough and leathery, hairy with rootlets. Underneath, however, there is a white, stringy/crunchy rind, not flavorful but perhaps nourishing if chewed long enough. Within that, however, is the pith: starchy and floury, like a nicely baked potato but bitter. I can only eat it if I soak the root in cold water and pound it to release the starch, to be processed like potato flour. The muskrat has no kitchen and makes do quite well with the root in its original state.

Supper over, the 'rat must clean, looking about alertly and combing its whiskers with the little hands and claws. It washes its face completely and wiggles its nose for news. It may sit up, clasping its hands and surveying the scene, or it may rush at a neighbor come too close or watch as a family group passes on its evening constitutional—or, more likely, seeking greener (browner) pastures upstream.

The muskrat mom may have two or four kits, who whiz about on the water from an early age, like little, furry racing cars, dipping under and bobbing up again, scuffling and splattering. Night time is a time for serious eating but also play and sudden naps near mother in heaps. The muskrat kit, when half-grown, might sit nicely in your hand with chestnut-chocolate fur, black-tipped and silky—silky even on the round little ears.

Their coats are desired by those who wear furs, and the muskrat is probably the most abundant, wild, fur-bearing animal in the East, rivalled only by the once-fashionable racoon and the champion, the beaver, which with legendary diligence is multiplying steadily and doing great works.

Once I was caught by the spell of the trapper and loved to think of the long lonely winter work as the Indigenous or the French trappers worked their lines in the big woods. It was the idea of the great, crystalline silence of the northern winters that I loved, the idea of trekking on a slow-motion snowshoe hunt through the white and green great woods, silent and full of hidden life and a hundred ways to die. In my youth, there were not mink or ermine enough to trap in my woods, and besides, I loved the little fierce weasel family, a treasure to admire, not molest.

The muskrats, I reasoned, were like little cows or squirrels, and they were fair game. That is, I could imagine bringing myself to trap them, skin them, cure their hides, and triumphantly sell them, thus participating to the degree that I could in the life of the northern frontier.

So I got some little traps and meditated long on how best to lay out the trapline, where to start, how to space them, how to hide them. I practiced setting them and tripping them until I felt I knew their cold and predatory natures as well as I needed to. Then, on a morning, early, shy to let anyone see me enacting my serious play, I slung the clanking pack over my shoulder and walked the mile and a half to the cattail village. I stood by the road and looked confidently across the waving marshscape, seeing all the little lodges I had come to know. I strode toward the muskrat town, and there, in the early morning, I saw a muskrat, sitting on its lodge, combing its whiskers, and smiling a bit after breakfast (or dinner). The first sun was on it, and it loved the warmth, loved it so much that it sat there, visible to me, to cars, to the sky full perhaps of hawks, and in its silent, rodent way, offered thanksgiving. I watched it with my whole self, and overwhelmed by the privilege of observing what most people don't think to see, I waited until the little animal slipped down to its door. Then I walked home again. I don't know to this day where those traps got to.

Letter Eleven: *Metanoia*

Dear friend,

In the Anthropocene, much depends on whether we Earthlings can learn to look past the reflections of ourselves that we rely upon and worship. In a recent letter, I wrote to you about idolatry and the culture of deceit that it fosters, because this seems to me to be the heart of our present crisis. If we can change the way we see ourselves in the world and then change our way of life to accord more fully with the truth of human nature, it will be possible for future generations to live abundantly and at peace.

I do not mean by this "live with abundant consumer goods in an economic system dedicated to exploitation" but rather that people can live good lives, within the means that the earth provides, exercising their gifts and interests, and taking harmless delight in the works of their hands and minds. To do this will require a thoroughgoing change in values and ambitions so that compassion and reverence play a central role in social life.

This means a spiritual change, to put it bluntly, and that's why, in this letter, I want to speak of *metanoia*, a word that is central to Jesus' preaching. It should be central for us, too, because it is the gateway through which we must pass, individually and as a society, in order to walk free of the un-reverent idolatry whose consequences have led us to the tribulations of the Anthropocene now unfolding.

Metanoia: A Short Word Study

Maybe I should say, from the outset, that I am using the Greek word rather than one of the usual translations, because the English words are full of distracting associations, and also, they tend to over-simplify, turning a journey into a postcard. Indeed, the baggage and the over-simplifications are a symptom of the need to take the *metanoia* journey. Maybe I should start by explaining a bit more about the word.

The noun *metanoia* (or the corresponding verb) occurs several times in the Christian Scriptures, for example in Mark 1, where John preaches the baptism of *metanoia* for the forgiveness of sins. Later in the same chapter (verse 15), Jesus begins to preach, announcing that the time has come for the fruition of God's next intervention: the kingdom of God has come near to us, and people should do *metanoia* and have confidence in the good news.

What does this word mean? Well, the Vulgate used the word *poenitentia* for the noun—"repentance" or "penitence"—and *poenitentiam agere*, "enact repentance." The translation was later used as part of the argument for the sacrament of penance (first promulgated in 1215), though this was not Jerome's intent.

Now, what do you think of when you hear the word "repentance"? I suppose that, very often, people imagine it as an event, a moment of realization that you've done something you shouldn't have. You understand the misdeed or mistake, wish it hadn't happened, if necessary commit to repair the consequences, and intend to avoid it in the future. "Regret" is one nuance.

Erasmus, however, argued that, as used at the time and in Greek, generally, *metanoia* has additional dimensions. The word implied that you were acquiring or re-acquiring a new frame of reference—as when, for example, you were for a long time subject to some deep misconception or disturbance of mind, perhaps taken leave of your senses, and were now recovering. *Metanoia*, therefore, suggests a return from such a distracted or mistaken worldview—to return to your senses, to come to your right mind (*ad mentem redire,* as Erasmus has it).

Thus, John and his cousin, Jesus, were calling for people to see the world so freshly that they could feel the truth, live in the truth of the kingdom whose time had ripened to fruition (so we could bear fruit worthy of *metanoia*). And Erasmus argued that this really was a matter of returning to "your right mind" in a very deep sense, since, if we take the challenge, we return to a way of seeing the world that God intended for us from the beginning and longs for us to re-inhabit. Indeed, in Jesus' proclamation in Mark chapter 1, *metanoia* comes first, and then it will be possible to have confidence in the good news that the kingdom is arriving.

To provide a Latin translation that would lend itself to this understanding, Erasmus chose *resipiscere,* a word related to the stem *sap-* we know in words like "sapient" and "sapiens." Though *resipiscere* might be translated as "reconsider," Erasmus found other nuances in classical literature that made it a good fit with *metanoia.* As its opposite, Erasmus used *desipere,* which means "to be foolish, to be devoid of understanding." So, *resipiscere* means to (begin to) to return to the path of wisdom.[47]

"Path" is an important idea here. Erasmus sees *metanoia* in effect as the beginning of a journey. From earliest days, Christians spoke of their religion as "the Way," even as they knew Jesus as the way. Once we come to our senses, we have much to learn, because every day and every fluctuation in our inward and outward condition may distract or baffle us. We are required, even after our shift of mind—indeed, as a consequence of it—to re-interpret the values we hold and those of our culture, our ambitions, choices, fears, habits, worship—all.

Through grace, "We have the mind of Christ," as Paul said, but Christ is also a teacher who knows us well; we are to learn of him whose yoke is light—if only we preserve our longing to learn and grow in him. As Erasmus writes in the *Handbook of the Christian Soldier* about Divine Wisdom's tutelage,

---

47   Cook, B. (2007) The Uses of *Resipiscere* in the Latin of Erasmus: in the Gospels and Beyond. *Canadian Journal of History XLII(4):397–410.*

That divine spirit has her own language and figures of speech, which you must from the first learn by diligent observation. The divine wisdom talks baby-talk to us, and like an attentive mother accommodates her speech to our infant condition. She provides milk for babes, and herbs for the sick. But you should hasten to grow towards adulthood, and become fit for solid food. Wisdom condescends to your humble station, but you, on the other hand, should rise towards her sublimity.

And here we need to recall another element in how Erasmus (following Paul), understands the gospel, which is that Christ, the Wisdom of God, is foolishness to the world. Indeed, at first, it seems foolishness to ourselves as long as we are "of the worldly mind" (as Marley's ghost described Scrooge). How can the way of the servant, the outcast and upstart who made a triumphal entry into Jerusalem on a lowly beast of burden (not a warhorse or fine palfrey), represent any kind of response to the demands of life?

In coming to our senses as Jesus invites us to do, we have to cut loose our moorings from the conventions of the culture, perhaps of our families, of our ambitions, and our fears. So different is the renewed mind that we may seem to ourselves and to others (surely those in power) as having taken leave of our senses—just as we, learning to live by the love that casts out fear, are convinced that we are returning to our right minds at last.

Metanoia as Journey: **The Progress of the Soul**

A first operation of Doctor *Logos* in its work within us is to show us the truth of our condition: as Erasmus writes in his paraphrase of Mark, "It's a big step to recognize what ails you, a giant step toward the light to come to know your shadows."

What can jolt us into this recognition, disturb our peace so that we begin to long to see and become different? It may be a moment of self-accusation or a need for forgiveness. It may be an experience of beauty, whether in nature or as when Rilke hears the serene, strange bust of Apollo say, "You must change your life." It might be a prophetic challenge or the presence of an undeniable evil. It might be seeing the example of someone else's courage, compassion, or establishment in joy. In each of these cases, we are shown something of ourselves and some hint of how we might be different.

Once we begin the process of self-knowledge, then we are to lift up our hearts in prayer, at first yearning for relief from our afflictions, which now we can name and recognize, though they long plagued and corroded us inwardly. We can begin to hope in the promise that it is God's good pleasure to give us the kingdom. Once passing through *metanoia*, the opening of the way, we are supported along the path to perfection; the process consists in gradually, step by step, dying to sin, seeking earnestly for the best gifts of the Spirit, and living by the new life that is liberated or poured out for our comfort and healing—and through our faithful actions, for the comfort or healing of others. The stutterer will be enabled to testify with power, the mourners will be comforted, the famished or deadened soul nourished and lifted up. It is a life-long task but one which will be suited to each of us. We can come to participate in the victory of the Lamb that was slain, the childlike delight of Sophia, the foolishness of the God whose love for lilies, for sparrows, for lost sheep, and for sinners overturns the world's wisdom.

Metanoia in a Time of Climate Change

Metanoia is a complex process. It's not only that it take time to adjust our lives and habits to harmonize with the truth we have acknowledged—the conversion that follows convincement. There is also a pre-history to such a grand change. Think of the people that came down to the Jordan River to hear John's preaching—and perhaps to accept the rite of cleansing in flowing (living) water as an outward demonstration of a change begun. Those that came and accepted his call came out of a sense of search or need, a longing for rededication that perhaps they could not put into words, at least at first—the Holy Spirit whispering and prompting them to awaken to a renewed consciousness.

Of these, some sought for a yet more radical understanding of themselves, their times, and the requirements of the Holy One of

Israel for them. John himself declared that one greater than he would come with power to effect a deeper transformation than they yet had felt—a baptism of the Holy Spirit and fire. A few listened and received that expectation. Staying in company with John in the fellowship of intense focus along the riverbank, they would speak of discoveries made, and questions yet unanswered. To a few of these, John said, "Behold the Lamb of God." We know of two whose experiment began with the question, "Where do you live?" to which Jesus replied, "Come and see." Their eyes were opened further, and *metanoia* revealed new dimensions in Jesus.

The first motions of the Spirit, whether they feel like judgment on our ways, dissatisfaction with our lives as we are conducting them, alienation from our society, or a simple longing for a feeling of integration or for the open life—these fresh visitations are precious, and vulnerable. We may welcome them with joy yet later find them choked by busyness, parched by trouble or scorn, trampled by opposition (our own or others'). How much care, longing, persistence, and grace are required to bear in mind through all our trials the sweetness and promise of the new life just taking root and unfolding within!

I believe that many people are feeling inward promptings to enlarge their spirits to accept the reality of climate change and the gravity of it, and their openness to these promptings has been long in preparation. Yet this new growth is vulnerable.

How are we to comprehend our responsibility? In Psalm 19, David prays

> Who can understand his errors? Cleanse thou me from secret faults. Keep back thy servant also from presumptuous sins, let them not have dominion over me. Then shall I be upright, and I shall be innocent of the great transgression.

With climate change, we discover that, without knowing it or willing it, we have had a share in the wrong-doing, the misuse of creation, whose results we are now experiencing. When I first realized this, I found it frightening, and discouraging. A natural response is avoidance, denial, or compartmentalization. But the wound, the sense of transgression and a debt owing, gnaws persistently within, even when one pretends it is not there.

Metanoia, Desolation, and Action

I don't have to tell you that as we allow ourselves to understand the problem, a way of expiation or redress seems almost out of our power, the scale is so large, and we have so many co-offenders. How can I know what is my share in the solution? How can my activities, at my scale, make any discernible improvement if so many of my brothers and sisters, co-constructors of the problem, do not share in the work, and the "principalities and powers" actively resist change or drive all the harder in the direction of destruction? As we move deeper into the new understanding that *metanoia* opens to us, where climate change is concerned, I have come to realize that hope itself must be re-examined and rediscovered. A renewed spirit may first require us to enter a landscape of desolation.

I have found myself losing illusions that I realize have been sources of hope or consolation, which cannot be relied upon any longer. They are not grounded in the truth of our situation and condition, and though they are useful in their place, they are tools, and my reliance on them has been like the psalmist's lampooned idolatry: placing all my hope on human constructions, which should be used, instead, in the service of truth and compassion.

Some of my hope has been placed in enforcing social structures, such as government or other political agencies. It is increasingly likely that the major social structures will not respond in time to prevent protracted climate disruption. Some of my hope has been wedded to the idea of progress and reform. God's will is peace and justice, abundance, *agape*, and creation—but I no longer see how this translates to progress as Americans and optimists have usually meant it. Finally, I have placed stock in knowing, being able to comprehend, not only my personal dilemmas but also the trends in which I am embedded. And I must admit that the hope that I have in knowing really reflects my deep desire to have control over my life, for my well-being and that of those I love.

We have not confronted the spiritual challenges of the Anthropocene until we recognize that some of our grounds for hopefulness are false. We are left in a liminal time, a time of choice and action, in which we need, again, to ask where the Holy Spirit and the gospel story (including the chapters in that story in which we are appearing right now) can be found in the midst of all the griefs, changes, and impasses. With a simple heart, standing in the garden we have ravaged, bringing our grief and our need before the living God whose children we are, we must put our heart, soul, strength, and mind at the service of the One.

Many have experienced surprising grace when driven to such an extremity, seeing that many of their props and resources were unreliable. We cannot tell God what to do, but we can know some things about how God moves among us.

Removing False Hopes, Discovering True Hope

It may be that our calling is first to be intentional about descending into the depths as we encounter them and then waiting there for the power to call out in thanksgiving and in a hope that lives without any illusion of control.

True Worship in a Time of Impass and Desolation

In this time of lost assumptions, our yearning for healing and for unity must be met by worship that is searching, direct, and personal: true encounter with the Living One, as creatures of a creation not our own, as stewards not plunderers, servants not masters. Purely conventional worship, constructed by human art (however beautiful) is not enough. The true worshipper must be listening more than speaking, contemplating the books of nature and of Scripture under the tutelage of the Holy Spirit whose imperative is love and who promises freedom, joy, and abundant life; the Spirit to whom we bring our deepest longing, our wounds, and our griefs. Free worship, truthful worship, listening worship is the laboratory in which we discover both what we are and what we are to do.

True Concern

In our distress, we can feel guilty of insufficient faithfulness. The frustration and confusion that accompany this diagnosis suggest that we are not looking in the right places for the way forward and that we may not have gotten clear, each of us in our own hearts, about what the roots of our urge for action may be.

Here I would like to mention the complex, empowering, and risky condition that Quakers call "concern"—a condition in which we come to realize how our response to a particular person, issue, place, or need is for us an essential and unavoidable next stage of our spiritual life. Such a sense of active requirement emerges in the encounter that is worship.

It is a fruit of *metanoia*, and it is nurtured in patient attentiveness to the Guide. We may see that something is cause for alarm or regret or outrage, but it may remain an outward threat only until, by the action of the Spirit, some link of service and necessity is forged. Until that gap is closed, my activism will not reach to my core, nor will it be fed from the divine life. I may be under preparation, but I am not yet sent!

A concern is a spiritual challenge with specific practical consequences, which often unfold as we follow it, and so it is particular or makes particular demands on each of us, even if we feel the concern to be widely shared by others. In fact, for each of us, a shared concern is really unique because it confronts each of us with the limits, uncertainties, and temptations that are ours alone; and however supported by friends, the inward response to the challenge must take the form of inward change in each individual.

This change, this *metanoia*, the return to our senses, can (if we continue to dwell in the new mind and worship in truth) become so thorough that it erupts naturally into acts of service, of proclamation, of solidarity, of imagination, of endurance, and of witness to the source of our constructive, compassionate, hopeful living.

Reflection

In the face of the unfolding crises of the Anthropocene, where does your hope lie? What does "hope" mean to you, and in what ways is your action part of your hope? How does your hope relate to your worship? When has your worship opened you to *metanoia*?

Meditation: Fog and Dolphins

One day in my youth, I went out in my Grand Banks dory—beloved but never named; eighteen feet; white inside and gray without; pushed by just a few coughing, fuming horses; and laden with stinking red-fish and whiting—to pull my lobster traps and then cross over the Sheepscot to sell my week's haul.

I took my usual snaking route, down and up Robinhood Cove and around the Knubble and its bay. I stopped at each trap and, while the boat drifted, pulled it up by hand from the cold depths into the summer warmth, emptied it, refreshed the bait with my home-made bait needle, buttoned up and reset the trap again. Back to the mooring to pick up the lobster cars—floating pine boxes in which a few days' haul were waiting, uncomprehending, for their fates to unfold—and also the crab cars as well, seething with choleric captives not so precious as the lobsters but worth enough to fill my gas tank for the week. Hauling in the cars was absorbing work because wet wood and inmates together made a good heavy weight, and no straight lift was possible if you had no winch or a boat big enough to mount one.

All aboard, I headed out the eastward passage to Sheepscot Bay, past Goose Rock, aiming toward its other side, and the pound along Townsend Gut where I sold my crabs and lobsters.

When I got to the bay, I saw that a fog bank had taken temporary possession of the estuary. I knew the bay by chart and by experience, knew by the set of the tide which way was up or down (or out and in), and had my little binnacle compass screwed to the transom. (Many years later, it now waits to do its job again, sixty miles from any shore, sitting patiently near my work-table; though the course our house has set rarely shifts enough for me to consult it.)

It was not long until I lost sight of the homeward shore, and there was still a mile to cross. The channel was mostly deep with a spatter of islands and swell-washed rocks, beloved of sea-gulls, seals, and terns. I was not at first dismayed, but as I pushed along in the quieter, quieter fog, the soup closed in and in until I could see just past my prow and a bit astern but no more: my boat and I were in a room of dirty cotton white. I soon came to feel that a fathom's worth of sight in each direction was too small for comfort, especially since those fathoms were shifting seaward gently and relentlessly. The foghorn's voice from around Newagon was getting louder, but as long as it stayed to my starboard and I mostly couldn't hear the gong which meant, "Ledges ahead and next stop: the Cuckolds," I was still roughly headed toward Southport Island, at the head of which ran the Gut, rather than out to sea—Damariscove Island, then, or Portugal. I shifted my course, with only a little concern, more diagonally inland, thinking to strike the eastward shore and creep up along it to my landing.

Lightless and hornless, I kept a sharp ear out for larger craft that might come steaming at me unawares. All I heard above my motor's grumble was water and fog sounds until, suddenly, someone sighed loudly not too far away—just over there beyond the fog-wall. I paid attention.

In an instant, my little water circle was crammed with dolphins, blowing and splashing, seeming to spin round and round my boat like a living whirlpool, dipping and rising easily, only occasionally rolling an eye at me, and so much faster and more agile than my boat that it seemed as stable and motionless as a Maypole while they wove and danced around.

Crossing the bay in sunlight or rain, I'd seen these roisterers before, chivvying the mackerel up and down, dodging the sail boats and the stinkpots and having a hell of a time. On the bright days, with the gulls and terns, the ospreys and the fishermen, the cormorants and the day-sailers, the porpoise added a feeling of holiday to the crowded scene. Once in a while, a larger cousin might roll through, just where the Sheepscot widened so far that it could no longer be distinguished from the Gulf of Maine, and then it was as though a baseline was added beneath the birds, the wind, the white-caps, and the dolphins' dance.

I'm saying that, on any day, they were good company, these little whales, zipping and wallowing around me. My boat was a curiosity, a plaything for them, and I myself was of no account. Yet their presence today—sentient, sportive, vivacious—transformed the little spot of black water that my eyes could see and, as the poet says, made "one little room an every where."

The pod stayed with me for I don't know really how long. I started to feel the fog thin out and lift off the water a bit so that I could peek under the curtain to see just where I was. As yet, no ledge had stopped me, and I heard no warning breakers. As I reached at last the skirts of the fog, the dolphins, one by one it seemed, each took a bow and vanished back into the soup. And then I saw the shore ahead.

It was not a rescue or a favor to me. Their visit was a game they played for their own amusement and the unaccountable pleasure in human company that dolphins seem to take. Still, I have never lost the gratitude I felt that day and the wonder—the sea smell, the sound of dolphins breathing hard and flipping up their tails an arm's-length from me, heedless of my propeller or my prow, fearless. Quite impersonally, I was accompanied; it was a grace.

Letter Twelve: In a Forest Clearing, Reflections So Far

Dear friend,

My letters to you sometimes feel like a journey through a little-traveled forest, as I try to express what (in my measure) I **have heard and looked upon with my own eyes and what my hands have handled of the word of life.**

As I write to you this morning, it seems as though I have come to a clearing whose openness offers a time of refreshment and orientation. So, here I will reflect on the path taken and the path ahead.

We are called to freedom, to living with abandon and delight in wholeness. Though this has always been our calling, it is time, in the Anthropocene, to take it seriously as a path of formation and action. This means we must be eager to learn from all the ways of instruction through which the divine Teacher can be encountered and received (in heart, soul, strength, and mind).

Sophia, the wisdom of God, is expressed in the endless torrent of forms that matter takes, beautiful and terrible in all their operations. Much of this wisdom seems alien or ungraspable for us Earthlings, yet we find our own place in it, being ourselves one inextricable effect of that wisdom whose work is generation, transformation, and flow. In contemplation and in wonder, we find the warmth our life and our imaginations need if we are to flourish.

The *Logos*, the speaking of God, is seen in sequences, structures, patterns, and implications, logical or analogical. As participants in this account, we build replicas for ourselves—languages, stories, sciences, traditions, and other tools and domiciles. The *Logos* is a fabric in which we all are woven, the human and nonhuman, the living and the not living (never living, no longer living, not yet living). We cannot help but put our hands and minds to work, conjecturing, expressing, reasoning, telling. It gives clarity amidst the maelstrom of the world and a fervor and a hunger to those who live at the edges of understanding.

The Light of God is a showing and a cleansing power. In it, we can discern our way forward, can see distinctions and shadows, colors and perspectives within us and around us. Standing in the Light, we can reckon up our condition. While it blesses us with vision, it also intensifies around our shackles and our bonds, the wounds and compulsions, distractions and deceits that keep us unfree, illuminating them and heating them until they burn us: adding to our wounding and the iron of our confinement until we accept the Light's offer to dissolve them and remove the burden.

We will not free ourselves from the misconceptions that have resulted in the current environmental crises, that have supplied excuses for our continued destructive behavior, or that have led to the construction of elaborate rationales of denial unless we acknowledge our intricate interweaving with the rest of nature. Christian tradition has had relevant alternatives from the early days, but these have been relegated to the margins (even when praised) in favor of theologies that comfort power, wealth, and security for people as they wander in the wilderness of this world. These marginalized alternatives—in combination with science and many other fields—can serve as resources for the kinds of change that are needed.

The work means recasting our mistaken ideas about individuality, accepting our mortality, and rejecting dominion myths as a source of meaning or as tools for meaning-making. Moreover, it means renewing our attention to the three great modes of revelation: nature, Scripture, and Spirit. From the point of view of humans, these are revelations of a way of reverent participation in the world, which is one, and together are revelations from the Divine, which itself is one and in unity with the world. The hope of sharing that unity is derived from the experience which Paul (and some later Christians, including Friends) have described as "having the mind of Christ."

This path requires of us a recognition that Christ is to be experienced not only as the Jesus of Nazareth but as the *Logos*, Wisdom, and Light of God. Instructed in our measure by this Spirit, we can with faith read in the book of nature and of Scripture. In that reading, we learn how to be servants and prophets in the Anthropocene. None of these modes of encounter is privileged; none is to be dismissed. All must be engaged with honesty and also with a humble recognition that our answers or discoveries will only be more good or less good. Creation is too large, too multiform to fit into any one box.

We are completely participants in creation. *Logos*, wisdom, and light are not external forces; they are in the processes and the materials that, for a time, give us and everything we see a visible, tangible form.

So, do not make the mistake of seeing the meditations that I have sent only as interludes or respites from the letters I have been writing you. They are theology, or (if you don't like that word) they are prophecy, truth-telling. In my letters, however limited, I have been trying to connect you to a living body of ideas and insights that you can investigate in books and in your own thinking and doing, so the meditations are citations (incitements) from that other living body of revelation, direct and unmediated: nature doing what nature does. Indeed, nature and the inward Light are the aboriginal revelations with which all other revelations must come to cohere, being (as we perceive them) different expressions to us of the One for our flourishing.

It follows, I think, that we must do more than read—we must push ourselves to a transformed and renewed mind, a changed vision, transformed by a baptism of fire and the Holy Spirit. I have written to you that *metanoia*, "repentance," for our times is better understood as "coming to our right mind," but this must be a matter of soul, strength, and heart as well as mind. It is not conceptual but a comprehensive challenge to our culture, our identity, and our allegiances, a pushing forward toward wholeness both inward and outward.

How does this pushing happen? First, it requires a vision of alternative ways of living, what in Quaker teaching has been called "gospel order," an approach to social behavior (personal and collective) whose coherences and harmonies are imposed by love, including the love of creation, our substance, and our home. The law of love is as foundational, as constraining, and as mysterious as the law of gravity. Here, also, the self-forgetting experience of wonder is a necessary ingredient and the lens with which we can see and live in gospel order, incarnating that love in our structures and ways of working, as well as in our personal conduct and outlook. I will try to put what I see, suspect, and understand of all this in my next series of letters.

Further, though, it means that the formation of souls is not and cannot be a private matter only. Implicated beings, our spiritual maturity and growing wholeness necessarily require us to embody gospel order in our works and ways and to work for its realization in the world. This unifying practice is known in Quaker tradition as the Lamb's War, a topic on which the final collection of letters will need to concentrate. Its mainspring is worship, in spirit and in truth, of the Spirit of Truth, the divine Prophet who calls us to unity with ourselves, with each other, and with the rest of creation—a unity which is not an accomplishment or finish line but a way of being and acting.

> Be ye doers of the word [*Logos*], and not hearers only, deceiving your own selves. For if any be a hearer of the word, and not a doer, he is like unto a man beholding his natural face in a glass: For he beholdeth himself, and goeth his way, and straightway forgetteth what manner of man he was (James 1:22–24, KJV).

Theology renders service if it weaves together the disparate parts of ourselves into a whole. Theology includes our doing and our action. After all, God's word (narrative, message) is spoken as light, dark, stars, earth, creatures, and the Spirit walking among and within them. Our theology must be clothed in substance, active and alive.

> That person is the true theologian... who by disposition of mind, by the expression of face and eyes, and by life itself expresses [the virtues that Christ loved].., Whoever embodies them in their lives are, in the final analysis, the great teachers, though they be ditch-diggers or weavers. [48]

48 Erasmus *Paraclesis*.

Part Two: Spiritual Formation, Reverence and Gospel Order

Of the challenges that will engage us urgently and seriously in the Anthropocene, the two most important intertwined—climate change and biodiversity loss—are what some have called wicked problems—fast-emerging, multi-causal, indeterminate, cascading.[49] Because we don't know enough about our world, our understanding of these problems is partial at best. We can expect, therefore, to be regularly confronted with disconcerting news, whose meaning and importance will very often add to our confusion and anxiety.

As always, when important matters are at issue, there must be time to reflect, debate, and then make choices—but the unforgiving tempo of changes will give little space for the discussion and negotiation of ideas and practices.

In an age of bewilderment and anxiety, the temptation will be to fall back on what we have known, on our accustomed ways of working, living, and assigning value. But our society's "common sense"

---

49 Dillon, J, R.B. Stevenson, A.E.L. Wals (2016) Introduction to the special section: Moving from citizen to civic science to address wicked conservation problems. *Conservation Biology* 30:450-455. and Rittel, H.W. J. and M. M Webber (1973) Dilemmas in a general theory of planning. *Policy Sciences* 4(155–169)

has brought us to this pass, constructed as it has been to protect the powers and interests whose indispensible purpose has been the concentration and perpetuation of their power and wealth. But common sense is not revelation. It is a social creation.[50] It can be reconstructed, and so it must be now, in accord with the fragile openings that *metanoia* provides.

Jesus tells us (Mark 2:22) that we should put new wine in new wineskins—that the new understanding that the gospel offers can't be contained in practices and ways of thinking appropriate to the the traditional understanding of faithfulness. But here I want to emphasize that the gospel is no static finished product. It is a living thing, and like wine, it develops new flavors, nuance, and depth as it continues to live in its containers. Therefore, it is on us to live, work, and pray that we can come to understand how it tastes, sounds, and means in our times and in our own lives—in our world as it is now and as it is becoming. The Holy Spirit, Jesus taught, works to reveal more of what his teachings mean, as we are prepared to perceive (grow into the capacity to perceive) the new dimensions and implications of his revelation (John 16:12–14). It is in our travails and in our experiments that we can know what he would preach to us today, how he would point us to the ways in which God's message of compassion, reverence, and reconciliation are to be received and given form today, as we seek the healing of the world and of ourselves—which are not two but one.

Thus, our response in our living and thinking to the conditions of today, leavened with Christ's life within us, must be put in vessels that not only contain the new life but also enable it to keep working and gaining in virtue, in active power, continually enriched and clarified by God's wisdom. These are vessels of thought, of collaboration, of priorities or valuation, of hope and intention, of method and of celebration—for individuals connected in a common life, communities in community.

All depends upon the longing, the seeking in the thickets and hedge-rows of our lives, for the fruits in which the new life can be

---

50   See C. Geertz "Common sense as a cultural system." In *Local knowledge: Further essays in interpretive anthropology*, 3rd ed. New York: Basic Books (2000).pp. 73–93.

tasted and gives forth a heart-lifting fragrance. "As the hart panteth for the water brooks, so longeth my soul for Thee!" Gather the fruits that taste of *metanoia* at the right time, and press them out, concentrating them and setting them to work in vessels and with tools that are shaped to hold the gospel wine as a living thing.

That is what this second collection of letters is about.

Meditation:
The Great, Slow Gestures of Trees[51]

Three great white oaks climbed the hill behind my childhood home. The middle reached the greatest height, though the third was rooted nearer to the hillcrest. They were older than the farm, and their gray-brown trunks, which glowed warmly in the sunlight, reached sixty feet or more above me.

Each one had in its long life developed its own personality, but the one nearest the house and lowest on the hill was the one into which I looked from my upstairs bedroom. It was *my* tree. I watched the moon moving through its branches like a bright bird, slowly to the west.

In sunlight or moonshine, it seemed to open its arms to radiance and gathered rain and snow as they came, limbs and trunk streaming and waving in the stir. However gnarled, however wrinkled and venerable, its three-season cloud of leaves spoke vigor and abundance and then became a sere cloak of many shades of brown that whispered through the winter.

One of its greatest limbs grew toward the house, dipping outward over the lilac thicket where children, birds, and Easter eggs were wont

---

51 A phrase from *A wizard of Earthsea*, by Ursula LeGuin.

to hide. The oak had begun to reach toward me decades before I was born, slowly realizing its intent as it added length and girth.

As the gesture continued year by year, the branch gained character of its own, flexible and still unfurling at every tip and branch but hard and strong and durable where it needed to be, back toward the trunk where its long-ago intention had become irrevocable. It did not matter if I climbed on it, tied a swing there, or that my father hung that year's deer, plucked, to dry for a day or two. All this was encompassed in the tree's intention.

Other branches reached out all around, toward other goals, with the roots questing in the soil below. Mistakes or second thoughts were mimed as well. And there were mishaps: branches with evocative twists and turns, limbs stunted or broken, their bark long shed and the exposed dead wood polished bony and gray, now a vantage point for squirrels and a pulpit for the whipporwill's loud assertions.

Letter Thirteen: Calling in Catastrophe

Dear friend,

When last I wrote to you, I spoke of *metanoia*, the transformed understanding of one's self and the world we inhabit. But *metanoia* is a door, not a destination, and if it is truthful, it offers no escape from the times. Indeed, the eye that is opened by a desire for true wholeness is thereby better fitted to understand our own condition and that of the world. We see how the truth can make us free, but in that seeing, we are offered new chains, new invitations to despair or denial to replace or reinforce the bondage we feel loosening in the moment of joy. Our faithfulness, our freedom, our unity must not be an accomplishment but an ever-renewing process.

Since my last letter, there have been more tidings about the warming world and the ways things are trending for humans and for other life, and the picture becomes more ominous day by day. To speak for a moment only of the human costs, more and more people around the world are suffering directly from the physical changes in their landscape and weather—droughts, floods, famines, disease, the destruction of cultures, forced migrations.

Even in communities like mine, whose geography or affluence have shielded people so far from direct harm, there is a measurable increase in anxiety, even despair, especially among the young.

As a consequence, in almost every corner of the world, people are losing their ways of making meaning and the joy that comes of envisioned futures that deepen and enrich the meaning of the present.

Discouragement and alarm are intensified by the abundant evidence that those currently wielding economic and political power are unwilling to see the scale and speed of the threats we face, and many of the people "love to have it so," making a conscious choice to ignore the warnings being sounded all around them.

It is in this world that we must prepare to live adequately as advocates of love. In these times of disruption and overturning, we Christians will either live up to our calling—at last—or abandon it. Our calling is to grow in love of God and neighbor in such a way that we can be transformed to receive Christ's joy and peace ever more fully, living it as embodied, enacted good news (*euangelion*) and as a promise (*epangelion*) of life inexhaustible, ever-refreshed.

It is from the springing of that life that we can taste hope but not a hope focused on solutions, on some victory that absolves us from further engagement. Rather, it is the explorer's or the artist's hope that starts here and seeks the next step forward, working with the often resistant, often mysterious stuff that is the world. It is hope that is understood and realized as we work with the materials of our lives and our world—the hope that is a way of living.

Metanoia opens the door to a new view of the world. How do we grow into the artists, the explorers of this place-time? I'd like to ask you to spend some time with the idea of "calling."

Calling

Calling, I think, actually means several nested processes. A calling can be a task laid on a people or a task laid on an individual within that people (what Quakers call "a concern"), or it can mean the specific thing an individual must do to move forward on their task right now (what Quakers would call a "leading").[52] It is through seeking one's calling and the specific leadings through which it is realized that the path starting from *metanoia* is discovered; motions of the Holy Spirit take material form, and our listening and faithfulness make the world different in some measure.

As I understand the summons of the Holy Spirit, there are three central elements that become compelling as part of our *metanoia* in these times. While part of this refreshed understanding may be visible to any inquiring mind, some may only become accessible to the spiritual pilgrim:

1. In order to take up the calling of the times, we Earthlings (Christian or not) need to take seriously that each individual creature is embedded in a fabric that is continually exchanging the stuff of life. Centuries of scientific research have begun to detail the fantastic complexity of this truth, which some people have always understood intuitively. Now it must be brought into the center of our meditations.

2. In addition to this, Christians in particular need to learn or learn again that their Christ is the active God of creation down to its smallest elements, and the Vine whose life we share nourishes humans (body and soul) as part of the whole cosmos. Origen writes, "God does not take care... only of the universe as a whole, but in addition to that he takes particular care of every rational being."[53] What we name as Christ is (among other things) the spring and current of the ever-flowing creation. Centuries of scholars, prophets, and servants have seen this, known it, and proclaimed it.

Though Christ has been manifested in human form—and in that incarnation taught, prayed, suffered, and died to open a path for our liberation—humans are not Christ's sole focus. Nor are the affairs of our time or even our planet Christ's sole concern. God is one, and the cosmos is one. Consequently, our life is united with the whole creation; our inscape, our *logos*, is one with the *Logos*. Approaching the Holy One, being able to worship in spirit and in truth, requires

---

52 This relation of specific actions which take their meaning from a larger calling is not unlike the distinction made by early Fathers between *skopos* and *telos*.

53 *Contra Celsum* IV§99. H. Chadwick, ed. and trans. 1980 Cambridge U. Press.

us to approach reconciliation with that whole creation. Our personal atonement (at-one-ment) with God will be accomplished fully when our enmity with the cosmos is healed.

3. This is why worship is a crucial matter and, in a way, a reagent with which to test our condition—our intentions and the authenticity of our actions. Worship is the human act in which we learn and respond to what we most deeply value. It is the place in which the divine-human society has its living root in wonder and acknowledgment of the gifts and the limitations that are inherent in our nature.

Worship is not simply to be equated with ritual. Too often, ritual is used to make assertions, to reinforce convention, to utter but not to listen. Invitations for transformation and for the power to live the change come when we cease our performances and our affirmations and formulations. The voice of God comes in the quiet of the garden, in shocking power on Sinai, in whispers to the boy Samuel in the night, in the invitation to Zaccheus, during the night watch in Gethsemane, on the road to Emmaus: not our words and hymns and teachings but the burning in our hearts, the knocking at the door, the word of a friend or stranger, table fellowship, and the Spirit that bloweth where it listeth. In listening, we can find our individual imperatives, whose acceptance and enactment are our path to peace.

For our God is dynamic. The peace that Jesus gave his disciples on the night he was betrayed is "not as the world gives": it was a peace felt and shared in the face of suffering and turmoil, a peace that may be felt at the heart of the earth in all its constant kaleidoscopic change, its dazzle, roil, and wellings up, the hawk's flight and its stooping to the kill, the dissolution of a fallen tree, and the generative ecstacies of spring.

Of all this, Christ is the life and the sustainer, and in the work of reconciliation, he is the elder brother of every one of us who must find our own part of the work. What intimate immensities we lay hold of when we decide to touch the hem of Christ's garment or follow in his footsteps!

It is long past time for each of us to attempt that vision, to make it and live it as our reality. To do this, our calling must begin in listening, an active listening in which we allow ourselves to be reshaped. There is no time left to us but this present.

Reflection

When do you keep vigil, and on what watchtower? When do you let your guard down and truly invite the living God to be present? What are you doing to learn how to listen? Do you listen long enough that love and wonder transform fear or resistance? These are questions I cannot avoid.

Meditation: Incubating the Future

1. Beyond the chill waves breaking on the Atlantic beaches of my youth but still near enough to shore that swimmers sometimes pass above, the moon snail methodically constructs a shapely collar of sand, held together by secretions from the animal's mantle. Broader at the base edge, narrower at the top, the simple vessel sits on the bottom where the water, gentler than at the surface but never really still, moves over and within it. In forming the collar, the snail embeds dozens or hundreds of capsules, each containing one or more embryonic snails, which will emerge in a few weeks and join the planktonic millions until they mature.

2. An earwig mother has hollowed out an oval space in the leaf litter, floored by the soil. Over the course of forty-eight hours, she lays her white eggs, carefully placing them together.

Over the next few weeks, she stays with the nest, sometimes curled around the eggs. Each day, she touches, moves, and cleans each egg, removing detritus or colonizing fungi. She will protect them from potential predators as well, though her only weapons are the "pincers" or cerci at her tail.

The young begin to open up their egg shells from within. The mother watches and sometimes helps them gain access to the outside world, broadening their exits. She watches as they turn to consume their egg shells.

The young stay within the nest as they grow and molt. An earwig passes through five molts to reach maturity. The young remain until after their second molt, when they start to darken in color and their cerci (straight for females, sickle-shaped for males) first emerge.

The mother stays, too, protecting and cleaning the young, and feeding them, regurgitating some of the food she has obtained nearby. At the age of two (molts), the young disperse. The mother is the last to leave the nest.

3. Our guide, a member of the Ehi-Ehowa who live in and cultivate the Amazon forest on either side of the border of Peru and Bolivia, has taken our family out along a trail to see what can be seen. It is winter, so we do not meet the riot of blossom and birdsong that will come a few months ahead. Still, the temperatures are warm, and there are many animals going about their business.

The guide stops and picks up a long, flexible twig, holding up a finger to tell us to wait to see something. He inserts the twig into a small hole in the ground, beneath a tree stump's tangled roots.

There is a burst of activity, as perhaps a dozen small black spiders, stocky and quick, emerge from the hole. The guide continues to stir around in the hole with the stick, and suddenly the mamá comes out, grasping the twig and possibly biting it. The spider is a "hen tarantula," so-called because the spiderlings after birth stay with the mother for some weeks. The mother wards off predators and other curious intruders and may even bring prey back to feed the little ones. Our spidermom retreats into her hole as soon as the twig stops provoking her, and the spiderlings, after scurring around the vicinity, run back to the hole and follow the mother in.

Letter Fourteen: Listening Discipleship

Dear friend,

We are told: "Where your treasure is, there will your heart be also,"[54] and it is from your heart's fruits that your truth, the truth of you, is discernible—including the world you seek to live in and the powers and values you are loyal to.[55] Such bedrock commitments, often unspoken even to ourselves, are the starting place for worship—worthship, acknowledging something as worthy of veneration. What do you really hold sacred, irreplaceable, valuable beyond all else? Such commitments shape all our acts and attitudes—feelings, fears, intentions, how we construe God, the way we use our reason. All these wagons are circled around the central, sacred fire.

I have been using *metanoia* as a handle for the kind of altered orientation of heart, soul, strength, and mind that you need in order to face reality—the reality of your condition and, inextricably, the condition of the world. But, as I wrote you before, *metanoia* is a door, not a destination.

For the journey that opens once you pass the door, there are no maps, only guidance, step by step. The resources you need are

---

54   Matt. 6:21
55   Matt. 12:35

discovered as you go, and the practices, the spirit-craft, are sought and found along the way. Every step is growth, and often, the best evidence of progress is the renewal and enrichment of the new mind.

Yet each step also offers new opportunities to turn aside or turn back. Moreover, at the beginning, the resources we have gathered while in the "old mind" are all the tools we know how to use. Immersed in our culture and in the habits developed as we have made our way through life, the values and methods of the destructive powers of convention and domination come to hand very readily when we are uncertain about what comes next.

The disciples of Jesus first followed him because he touched each of them at some vulnerable spot and offered some hope that they could find the particular health and meaning that they were lacking. Yet it is evident from the gospel record that they did not know what they had found in him, and his full import only gradually came clear to each in their own time. Most especially, they were long in understanding the radical nature of his message. The gospels recount a succession of surprises and unconventionalities that taught lessons about the liberty of God.

After the crucifixion, the disciples experienced resurrection encounters and then passed through the trial of physical separation from their teacher and hope-bringer. By this, they were enabled to know inwardly the abundant life of the Spirit by which their companionship with Jesus was continued and available to others who had not seen Jesus.

Even then, however, they were challenged by the problem, how to live in accord with the Truth that they had encountered, day by day, in today's particularities. Their minds were still woven into the old cloth of habit, custom, belief. As time went on, the stories about Jesus too often became a commemorative monument, as if Jesus (who embodied the free wisdom of God) were a conventional law-giver or ethical teacher, laying down precepts and axioms upon which the mind and will can seize and turn into a set of tools and rules for efficiency and predictability.

The promise and the experience of the Holy Spirit contradicts this. Jesus makes it unmistakably clear that his mission and message is life—lived in and from the Spirit, which is his Spirit and his father's and that is poured out on us as well, if only we open our vessels to receive it. This is the incarnation mystery: that the gift of our being—body, mind, heart, and soul—flows from its source, sacred, not as a finished product but as a process and a possibility. Amidst all the delight, torment, and turmoil of creaturely life, we can recognize and attend to the still, small voice, always sounding, that invites us from dissonance to harmony. One by one, we can each catch the note and tune ourselves to it—and to each other. This attuning (attunement, atonement) has immediate outward effects because we live our lives in a social fabric and cannot become human outside of that web.

Yet, discipleship to the Spirit of Christ brings with it this challenge, that our attunement to that Spirit puts us at odds with the conventions of our lives at every level (personal, economic, political, and more). Jesus in his freedom was accused of being possessed by a devil or being out of his mind (so much so that, at one point, his family comes to take him into custody). The Pentecost stories show that the change wrought in the disciples, the joy and unconstraint released by the gospel Life at work, made no sense to the folk of Jerusalem—Roman, Greek, or Jew—that witnessed them. Maybe these Christians were drunk? Foolishness that reveals divine Wisdom is how Paul understood it.[56]

One of the marks of this wise foolishness, from the beginning, was the formation of a community of the attuned. Of course, because each member is learning, is in apprenticeship to the Spirit, such a community is attended by all the mess of experimental living. Many of the mistakes and misdeeds in Christian history have derived from the way that people turned the process of community into static structures and boundaries that made it hard or impossible for each soul to hear the voice of the Spirit and attune to it. This is the great work by which perfection, spiritual maturity, is approached: Christ is formed in me and you under the guidance of his Spirit so that we can live out

---

56   See 1 Cor 3:18–20

the commandment of love in truth. To be about this work is to be on pilgrimage, not to build a monument. The community, then, is the place where incarnated insight is first nutured and its moral quality examined.

Traditions, practices, and stories are all good servants but bad masters.[57] An order within which we can live the gospel life and incarnate it in community must therefore unfold as the community listens to the guiding Holy Spirit, learning along the way to hear its voice ever more clearly. If the community that forms by the Spirit is the mystical body with Christ as its head and living by and in his Spirit, then its forms and conventions—and its health and growth—will be dynamic ones, just as your own body is maintained by a metabolism that continually builds and rebuilds itself at every level.

The central life-giving act, the source of integration and orientation, is the listening to the Spirit of Christ as the spiritual ear is opened and educated by reverence. In the next few letters, I want to explain why I think reverence is the most important quality for us to cultivate as we live into the Anthropocene, when radical changes will test and terrify and demand new vision, relentless compassion, and the daring that can come from humility.

Reverence is the fundamental ingredient we can bring to the world as it labors, copes, and suffers in the coming decades. One piece of this gift can be as we provide examples of the "ordering of the gospel" or "ordering by the Holy Spirit" by which a people can embody the gospel life and participate in the attuning of life and society to that Spirit.

How can we live this way, in this new age of the world? How do we become capable of living with freedom, endurance, active compassion, courage, and joy? That, as you know, is the question that haunts me and has stimulated me to write to you. But as I try to write as truly as I can, the message is shaped and re-shaped like red iron between

---

57   "Tradition is the living faith of the dead; traditionalism is the dead faith of the living. *Tradition* lives in conversation with the past, while remembering where we are and when we are and that it is we who have to decide. *Traditionalism* supposes that nothing should ever be done for the first time, so all that is needed to solve any problem is to arrive at the supposedly unanimous testimony of this homogenized tradition." Jaroslav Pelikan.

the anvil and the hammer. I am grateful that you are listening, which helps me to keep at the work and near the glowing heart of the forge.

Reflection

Thomas Merton said, "The satisfaction that comes from being in tune with our times is certainly not a charism, still less a sign of supernatural life."[58] Our attunement to the spirit of Christ puts us at odds with the conventions of our lives at every level. When you are in a moment of inward stillness, what is the first discord that you become aware of?

---

58 *Contemplation in a world of action* (1998) Notre Dame, IN: University of Notre Dame Press. pg. 29.

Letter Fifteen: Ears That Can Hear, The Miracle of Attention

Dear friend,

When I wrote to you about listening discipleship, I did not confront the question, "How shall I listen, to what or whom shall I listen?" In what follows, I may weary you by recounting things that will seem obvious but are of the greatest importance if we are to become available to the Spirit's guidance. The listening disciple must contend with the very human tendency to distraction—listening to every voice that speaks to them. The ear has no ear-lid that can block hearing as the eyelid blocks sight.

But it is also true that one can carry on a conversation while attending to birdsong or even following an interior line of thought while receiving a large quantity of other sounds. We naturally attune our reception of our needs or interests as we pay attention to some stimuli and not others.

> Millions of items of the outward order are present to my senses which never properly enter into my experience, Why? Because they have no *interest* for me. *My experience is what I agree to attend to.* [59]

59   William James, *Principles of psychology vol 1.* (1890) pg 402

Every sense has to do some kind of sorting of stimuli so that we find some order and clarity suitable to our purposes, amidst the "blooming, buzzing confusion" that the world presents to us.[60] The ability to pay attention in this way is astonishing, as it is a thing usually accomplished without an act of will. But as we grow from infancy, this "tuning" ability in which desire or intent control the mind's choice of stimuli to bring to the foreground is elaborated as our experience and our purposes are elaborated. The acquisition of attention is as great a mystery as the acquisition of language.

Even in this primal task, however, which is as basic and essential to an organism's life as digestion or respiration, culture plays an important part. Culture, the social world through which we grow and learn and in which we pass our days, gives us strong guidance about what to listen to—what words, sounds, voices, tones of voice are of more importance, command a higher priority for our attention, carry meaning.

As with so much in human life, notions related to power and authority are part of society's pedagogy of attention. Voices that speak to our desires, our fears, our sense of self, and our social standing are compelling. Evidently, this is foundational to the art of consumer persuasion, not to mention the power of rhetoric for political purposes. So, too, are voices that speak to us of well-being and security. For many, these voices will first be learned through our relation with our first nurturers. Parent, caregiver, siblings, friends—what these trusted messengers show us is important, and so we learn to find them.

Thus it happens that, as we come to give higher priority to some voices, some sources of information and orientation, we must give lower priority to other voices and authorities. If we are to be listening disciples of Christ in the Anthropocene—listening to the One whose care is for all the creation, including us—we will need to expand our attention, unlearn some of the lessons we have been taught by our culture about what we should attend to.

This is especially true because highly organized, self-aware institutions in our economy and politics have both emerged from changing

---

60   James, same source, pg 488

social attitudes about what to attend to and have used and accelerated those changes.

Though little of what I have written in this letter is new, I think it's pivotal if we are to understand the task before us, that is, if we are to accept the invitation to wholeness that becomes perceptible in the re-framing that *metanoia* initiates, freeing ourselves from idols and false hopes so that we grow into adequacy to this challenging epoch, this time which we are given.

Reflection

How do you cultivate or protect your attention? In what ways can your stewardship of attention change so as to move you toward the faithfulness you envision for yourself? What are the habits, customs, and circumstances that remove your attention from your soul's keeping?

Letter Sixteen: Gospel Order, Some Axioms

Dear friend,

In the developing challenges of the Anthropocene, the impulses to authoritarian, competitive, rapacious, and retributive response are strong and growing stronger as the crisis deepens and broadens.

Can Christians so worship as to hear the Spirit of Christ leading them to service, to witness, and to endurance in love in a time of turmoil, grief, and fear? Can we get to be that free of the spirit of our times and cultures, the pedagogy of oppression in which we all have been raised? We have fallen short so often! So many people who claim allegiance to Christ are falling short now! Still, it is not yet too late to accept the invitation to testify to the truth of life in harmony with the gospel.

In Quaker spirituality, the word "witness" can mean asserting (in word, deed, or way of living) a truth experienced personally under the influence of the Holy Spirit. Or it can refer to the inward Witness, the light of Christ that, if attended to, identifies where we must change if we are to conform with that light.

Now, "witness" is a translation of the Greek words *martys* (a witness) or *martyrion* (the act of being a witness or the testimony given), and so I need to return to the experience of martyrdom (the state of making a witness) and the kinds of martyrdom described in the early Irish Cambrai Homily: There is *red martydom*, which is suffering physical torment or death on account of the faith; *green martyrdom*, which is severe ascetic practice, especially fasting; and *white martyrdom*, which can take the form of exile for the faith. This state of exile was considered by some to be the most bitter, as it implies a life-long alienation from one's familiar, culturally supportive ways of being and thinking.

I think we are called to a white martyrdom in these times: we are to identify our fundamental commitments and grow to embody them as an act of compassion and of truth—but one result will in effect be an internal exile, a living within society as a sojourner and an alien. You, my friend, may already have tasted this if you have been living out any commitment to peace or justice or environmental protection. As society is increasinly dislocated in the developing crises of the Anthropocene, a person who can be living and acting without desperation and hate will be more at odds with the world and with people who, lacking the resiliency that a culture of reverence can offer, react with the tools of fear and violent control. Jesus told his friends (John 17) that they should be in the world, but not of it. The Anthropocene is a challenge to live this freshly and constructively.

Part of this life in exile must be a renewal of the fellowship of the gospel, a commitment to make real the body of Christ, continuing his ministry of reconciliation: all creation awaits our healing and growth into that stature. Prophecy comes first from an individual in whom the Witness is raised up, who then is convicted and yet plunged into an experience that yields insight about how to move toward faithfulness. If this profound stirring is not to be fruitless, it must be brought to a community and turned into life. This is part of what Quakers mean by "gospel order." A commitment to knowing and living (more and more) in that order has certain consequences:

1. If our allegiance is to be to the heavenly commonwealth, we must expect that our assumptions will be challenged—this is, indeed, the "topsy-turvy kingdom," when weakness is the place where strength is perfected; when the last shall be first, the proud put down from their

seats; where the least of these our brothers and sisters are to be treated as we would treat Christ; where the foolish, the unlearned, and those of no account are chosen as ambassadors for the King of Kings. "My ways are not your ways, neither are my thoughts your thoughts."

Therefore, we must wake up from our self-assured slumber and see the world as the terrifying, beautiful, improbable, abundant, dynamic organism that it is—and see it so freshly, so openly, so freely that we see in it the divine wisdom and the place of peace unto our souls.

2. Where dwells the Spirit of the Lord, the Lord of this turbulent, dizzying world, there is liberty. The comfort of rules is taken away, the structures and strictures that humans use for orientation and for control.

> The wind bloweth where it listeth, and thou hearest the sound thereof, but canst not tell whence it cometh, and whither it goeth: so is every one that is born of the Spirit.

The Lord, the mystery God who calls, invites, and reveals, is Creator and Renewer: "Behold, I am making everything new."[61]

3. Yet there is lawfulness at the heart of this gospel freedom—because the love of Christ, the love Christ preaches and embodies, constrains us. This is the one law at the heart of all—all the abundance of creation, all the work of the Spirit for our perfecting and liberation. All our choices about behavior in community are to be grounded in this love, reflecting our place in the body of Christ and the free flowing of Christ's Spirit. This lawfulness is the lawfulness of convenant, not of legislation.[62]

If we are centered in love, then any acts driven by a disturbance of conscience or new perception of truth can be done in a way that reaches to the life of others, and it must be done so; this is key to living in the covenant. Finding the way to do that can take a long time, often leaving us in perplexity, where we can only voice or pray our un-ease. But we are told that the tender, the poor in spirit, the peacemakers, the ones who long for righteousness, who mourn, who

---

61 *Revelation* 21:5.
62 George Fox wrote (Epistle 131): "Take heed... that with the wisdom of God ye may come to be ordered, and order the creatures by that [Spirit] by which they were made and created that by it (i.e. that Spirit) ye may know yourselves to be governed."

wash their friends' feet—these are the blessed, not those with all the answers. Love is rigorous because we must be prepared to live it, and new occasions require new preparation and a fresh, childlike return to the Center of love.

What is in the Center? It's not just an empty circle, a place of nothingness. There is a Spirit there but not just any spirit. It is the Spirit of the God who sends the sun and rain on the just and the unjust, whose law is summarized in love of God with one's whole being and of one's neighbor as oneself. The Center is also filled with fire, light, and the stream of divine life, which is like a stream of nourishing and cleansing water.

4. Thus, the ordering of ourselves and our community to reflect and liberate the life of the Spirit, the life of God in all, is not a thing made by human hands or cunning: It is discovered. "I myself will teach my people," proclaims the God to whom belong the forests, skies, and thousand hills, with all their beasts upon them. We must have the eyes of children, of Adam and Eve as they walked, astonished and delighted, in the Garden, spiritual eyes; and, accepting our vulnerability and our dependence, seek down the path of Light to the mind of Christ. So we will be able to speak with the tongue of the taught, comfort and blessing for the weary and burdened so that they can take up their own paths and walk into their own freedom as God directs: "Take my yoke upon you, and learn of me, for I am meek and lowly of heart."

5. Our schooling must be in all the tongues of revelation (and we can start our learning from any of them; it's all one fabric): the Scriptures, the teachings and discoveries of our tradition where they are consistent with the Gospel; the wonders and puzzles of creation; but these do not avail without the Spirit that gave them all forth, who guides us in our own path, each according to our measure—and collaborates with us in finding and building up the structures and practices of our common life, for our perfecting as children of the Light.

6. To perceive and dwell in the order (the melody, the shape, the meter, the colors) of the Gospel, we must ourselves be ordered. We must allow ourselves to be shown and shaped, meek and teachable,

followers and proclaimers, feeding on the truth of love as we can best see it, living it in all courage and vulnerability. Is our worship bringing us to a place in which impurities are named and burned away, certainties transformed, and everything dissolved and reassembled by the action of love? If so, then, little by little, we are renewed—a little more free, a little more able to speak to the Life of God in all. If not, we have not yet come to the true worship, the Center of dynamic and turbulent peace.

If we are not finding, in one aspect of life after another, a hint or glimpse of the transcending strangeness, mercy, beauty, and abundance of that love, we are not yet past the threshold of the Gospel. Stepping onward and into that house of many dimensions, reverence is the foundational stance from which all else can be reached. In moments where we occupy our measure of the life thus far received, we can see all as precious, unexpectedly precious.

Reflection

In what ways have you experienced your life being ordered, shaped, or re-oriented by the Holy Spirit to be more in conformity to the mind of Christ? What are some barriers—internal or external—that have prevented your faithfulness?

Meditation: Ant Slippers

The army ant colony, millions strong, has no fixed home. Whether moving or pausing, the ants build their home base, their bivouac—housing their queen and their young—out of ants, layers upon layers, each ant linked to others by the two claws at the end of their legs. The antchains shape themselves into rooms and corridors, chambers and passages. These structures are alive in more than their constituent parts: they change shape and location depending on need and condition.

Antchains form and dissolve for other reasons, too. If the colony comes to a stream that blocks the path, ants quickly join claw-to-claw to build a bridge across the water, and the rest of the colony (including the queen's chambers) passes over the living bridge, which then disassembles so that its members can join the march as it resumes on the other side.

The colony is accompanied—before, behind, above—by predators and scavengers (insect, mammal, reptile, bird) who feast on creatures fleeing from the troop or that are left behind as detritus and fallout from the relentless foraging that keeps the ants moving across the landscape and plays a key role in shaping the communities they pass through.

But there are also dozens, sometimes hundreds, of species, mostly insect or other arthropods, dwelling within the ant-constructed world—beetles, spiders, moths, and more. Many of these live or at least ride on individual ants.

There is a species of mite[63] (a spider relative) that attaches itself to the foot of the middle or hind legs of an army ant in order to sip the ant's haemolymph (blood) from a nearby leg joint. It uses two of its own legs to mimic the ant's twin claws and uses its other legs to cling firmly in place. The ant walks and climbs, using its mite pseudoclaws, and the mite even works like the ant's own claws in the building of ant-based structures such as bridges or bivouacs.

We have no idea of all that is going on in the world, near and far. The work that Adam began of naming the living creatures is not even half complete, and just because a creature has a name does not mean that we know anything else about it. Claiming sovereignty for ourselves, we rule as ignoramuses over a universe of unknown kingdoms.

---

63 Actually, there is more than one species; each species of mite attaches to a particular species of ant.

Letter Seventeen: Reverence as a Practice for the Anthropocene

Dear friend,

I am going to recount a little exploration I was drawn into as the last year ended. It has been a journey of just a few steps.

First Step

As the year came to a close, I was reflecting with some distress on recent environmental developments. There is real positive news about how people are increasingly aware of our many-sided crisis. Most trends, however, are in the wrong direction: more emissions, more heat retention, more disruptions to the biosphere (including human lives), more anomalous weather, and so on. Moreover, decision-making power, the control of key resources, and definition of what is valued in political and economic terms still lies in the hands of those whose principal effort is aimed at the creation and concentration of wealth for themselves and their ilk, rather than toward human welfare supported by an appropriate use of the earth's resources, our common treasury. I confess that, as the year came to an end, I was feeling very low.

Second Step

Then I recalled this passage from George Fox's *Journal*:[64]

> ...I might not eat and drink to make myself wanton, but for health, using the creatures in their service, as servants in their places, to the glory of him who created them: they being in their covenant, and I being brought up into the convenant...wherein is unity with the creation.[65]
>
> People being strangers to the covenant of life with God, they... make themselves wanton with the creatures, wasting them upon their lusts...devouring the creation.

A pivotal word in that passage is "lusts." It is a word used often in Fox's diagnosis of people's spiritual ailments, recalling, among other prophetic passages, the epistle of James (ch.4), who attributes wars and fightings to "lusts" (literally "pleasures" in Greek). This word in the past (as in the 1600s) had a broader meaning than it has in modern usage, and it can be paraphrased as "an unhealthy and acquisitive desire" for anything. (For those who read Tolkien, recall Gollum's insatiable lust for the Great Ring). Fox sees that the covenant that God has made with creation includes a proper role for humans as consumers and (by their right use) stewards of the commons (see Genesis 2:15) but that people, unconscious of the covenant of life, let their desires for enjoyment drown out their discernment of their place so that they are not in unity with the creation.

Third Step

It happened that, in the lectionary I am using right now, the morning psalm for December 31 is Psalm 147. From the King James Version, some verses:

> ...it is good to sing praises unto our God... He healeth the broken in heart, and bindeth up their wounds.
>
> He telleth the number of the stars; he calleth them all by their names.

---

64 George Fox (1624–1691) a central figure in the origin of Quakerism. His writings include a *Journal* and more than four hundred letters or epistles.

65 Cf. *Genesis* 8:22 and 9:8

The LORD lifteth up the meek: he casteth the wicked down to the ground..covereth the heaven with clouds, who prepareth rain for the earth, who maketh grass to grow upon the mountains.

He giveth to the beast his food, and to the young ravens which cry.

....He maketh peace in thy borders, and filleth thee with the finest of the wheat.

He sendeth forth his commandment upon earth: his word runneth very swiftly. He giveth snow like wool: he scattereth the hoarfrost like ashes. He casteth forth his ice like morsels: who can stand before his cold? He sendeth out his word, and melteth them: he causeth his wind to blow, and the waters flow.

In my mood of need, I drank this in, and it was ringing inside me as I watched the dawn come. The awe, the re-centering that the psalm gave me brought a time of healing: for that moment, "all creation gave forth a new smell," and I tasted peace.

But I knew that this peace could be taken from me—or I could banish it—when some test in the hustle of the everyday broke the mood, shook me, or led me out of my centered condition. So, too, it happens when we go on a retreat and are given spiritual gifts among our friends for healing and refreshment—and then we go home, and the blessings are dissolved in the flux of affairs. Our inner weather fluctuates from moment to moment.[66]

Fourth Step

But later, I returned to the following passage in the *Hexaemeron*, homilies by Basil of Caesarea on the six days of creation:[67]

> The invisible things [of the Spirit] are brought to mind by the things made from the creation of the world (cosmos), and his eternal power and deity, so that in the earth,

---

66   Ch. 4 of the *Cloud of Unknowing* says, "Even so many willings or desirings—no more and no fewer—are in one hour in thy will, as are atoms in one hour." One manuscript divides an hour into 23,560 atoms.

67   From his *Hexaemeron*, a series of sermons on the six days of creation.

and in the air, and in heaven, and in the water, and in the night, and in the day and in everything we can see, we plainly see reminders of the Crafter. For we will neither give any opportunity to sins, nor make any place in our hearts for the enemy, because we are keeping God at home within, through unremitting awareness.

Basil here is recommending a practice, an exercise that can increase and maintain capacity. (Elsewhere, he compares a spiritual practice to the workouts of an athlete.) He is saying that the wonder that is aroused by the contemplation (reflective observation) of nature is a delight, but it is not enough. If we are going to integrate these moments, which can come unbidden and beyond our control, into the reality and substance of our lives, we need to bring our wills to bear with some intentionality, some linking of ends and means. The exhortations that often appear in popular media to "seek out moments of awe" do no more than encourage us to repeat the moments of uplift or transcendence. This is no bad thing, but it can remain quite separate from the work of spiritual growth, the building of substance and ability. Daily attentive practice is not the same as mere repetition because practice has an aim in mind.

Fifth Step

Now, it is my conviction that our ultimate aim (our *telos,* to use a term from early Christian practice) is holiness or, as I would say it, complete availability to the motion of the spirit of Christ. As James Nayler[68] writes, this Spirit is recognized at work by its effects:

> it is the like of gentleness, meekness, patience, and all other virtues which are of a springing and spreading nature, where they are not quenched, but suffered to come forth to His praise in His will and time, who is the Begetter thereof, and to the comfort of His own Seed, and cross to the world.

---

68   James Nayler (1618–1660) an important if controversial early Quaker leader. From *How Sin is strengthened, and how it is overcome*

Note that Nayler says these effects are known "where they are not quenched." The resistance, the quenching, can take many forms, but one important one in these times and days is best summed up in the fierce old word "idolatry." Humans have rushed into concentrated, urban living, building up and up, out and out, fed by supply-chain tentacles, sending our waste somewhere away (to the outskirts of town, to the countryside, to other countries who accept our waste as a source of income, to the far oceans—away). Rainforests are protected because it's good for us; open spaces are preserved because green is good for our mental health or for cleaning the air to prevent our illness—you know the line of reasoning. And I do not say for a moment that these benefits are not desirable and just.

However, where this point of view is supreme, and human use is the only measure of value, then we are liable to all kinds of excess. We permit ourselves to ignore destructive consequences (ecological, aesthetic, and all the rest) and permit ourselves to mistake short-term satisfactions for long-term goods. Moreover, some humans are seen to be more worthy of respect than others, owing to their mastery of the rules of our society's games, wresting their success by coercion sometimes, by free acquiescence at other times. As a result, we have built for ourselves a prison whose structure and infrastructure are rapidly deteriorating.

Sixth Step

How can we escape this idolatry of the human so as to live in unity with the creation? As the early monastic writers saw it, your *telos* (holiness, the kingdom of heaven, or availability) is not achieved all in one go but by a succession of intermediate aims (each being a *skopos*, scopus), each arrived at by a practice appropriate to the soul's formation for that aim.

Thus, as John Cassian writes, our realization as citizens of the kingdom of heaven is not possible without purity of heart. ("Happy are the pure in heart, for they will see God."). So there arose many disciplines or practices to help one arrive at purity of heart.

It seems evident, then, that, in these times, we must overthrow the idol *Homo sapiens* as the measure of all things, when it prevents the Holy Spirit from working its transformative cultivation on us. This is an important step toward removing a resistance to the Spirit so that it can "come forth to His praise in His will and time, who is the Begetter thereof, and to the comfort of His own Seed."

I suggest that, for this aim, the necessary practice is reverence—taking a spontaneous experience in which we feel ourselves and our kind removed from the center of importance and transforming it by intentional exercise with the aim of freeing the Holy Spirit's access to us.

Seventh Step

It seems to me that reverence has at least three important elements, which can serve as guides for contemplation: (i) givenness, (ii) humility, and (iii) love. I think I will break off now and write again soon with some suggestions for how to shape a practice of reverence.

Reflection

Everyone has experiences with reverence to draw upon. When have you experienced reverence? What were the circumstances that reached you? What was the most surprising episode of reverence in your life? How does reverence feel to you? What changes in you when you feel it? What residue lingers?

Meditation: Reverence for Falling Water

A ribbon of water, perhaps six feet wide, leaps down a fathom or so and collects itself briefly in a rocky pool before dashing onward to a further pool, where, its momentum finally restrained, it travels onward, lively but wild no more, into the forest that presses in all around. The sounds of water, flowing and falling within its rocky constraints fill your ears with a multitudinous, soothing clash.

A robust chimpanzee approaches the stream on his road somewhere. As his eyes regard the waterfall, and his ears fill with the sounds of it, he stops and stands, grasping a nearby vine. He begins to sway from side to side and then swings and runs hither and yon with uninhibited strength. At first tethered by his grasp on the liana, he then turns himself loose, twirling and dashing through the streamside, but his eyes and ears are still anchored to the falling waters. Though his kind usually avoids entering the water, now he dashes down the bank to the mid-fall pool, splashing about and hefting rocks he finds there. He rolls and hurls the stones over the brink as if adding heft and power to the cataract, joining with the process.

Up on the bank again, he churns down alongside the stream to the lower pool, where the stream emerges more mannerly. Catching here the water's quieter mood, he wades the shallows to a gravel bar amidst the moving water. After his ten minutes' ecstasy, seen only by the hidden camera, he sits down on a stone, water passing around him, motionless himself, and gazes at, contemplates, the waterfall above. His celebration concluded, he departs in silence.

Letter Eighteen:
Notes for a Practice of Reverence

Dear friend,

I worry that I may not have made clear enough in my last letter: our times demand that we move beyond an idea of reverence as a spontaneous response to an event, a place, a person, or an object that we find deeply moving. These are precious, but the kind of reverence that will nourish health in the Anthropocene soul is a conscious practice in which we come to see and apprehend, without possessiveness or rejection, the being and meaning of the things, people, and places that we encounter.

To better explain what I mean, I am going to be so bold as to suggest an exercise that can build one's capacity for reverence. I say I am being bold because you are likely to think it too simple. I do not claim to be a master of meditation. Yet this practice has value because it is not elaborate, it cuts to the quick, and it can be extended indefinitely as one gains experience with it. Moreover, one result of this practice is that it builds relationship, which is a central ingredient of meaning.

You might say that the method of this exercise is to increase our surprise at the nature of the world in which we take part, to diminish our thoughtlessness in our relations with all the other created things, and to practice stepping into the awareness of the givenness of the world that sustains us in all our activities.

You are invited to a contemplation of some specific phenomenon until you can feel wonder and delight. This is perhaps hardest with something that you are familiar with and need first to make unfamiliar in order to see it as if for the first time.

Getting Ready

Choose a natural object[69] (animal, vegetable, or mineral). I suggest at first something toward which you already have some feeling, some attraction or aversion. Position yourself and your object in such a way that you can pay relaxed attention for a sustained period of time. A good photograph will work for squirmy or fragile living things or things not in season that attract you, but at some point, you will want a live encounter with a real object or organism.

This will be an exercise in which feeling and the senses lead the way. The aim is reception, not mastery. Thinking is fine but will need to be firmly reined in so as not to drown out the testimony of the physical and spiritual senses. This is why starting with an object in which you have some investment is useful. The feeling connection that you already have with it can open your perceptions. This is also why actual presence with the object will be more powerful than photographs or other representations. Personality (whether of the intricate variations in color on a stone or leaf or the bright eyes of a living creature) comes through when we are with something in person.

How Long?

Set aside a solid block of time. Twenty minutes or so is good. It should be a bit demanding so that your mind wanders and then needs to be brought back. But several shorter observations are better than one over-long marathon.

---

69 A human being could serve as a focus of such a meditation but not at first, and do not contemplate a human artifact until you've practiced quite a bit on naturally occurring objects.

Now:

First, pay attention. Do not worry about naming, dissecting, or doing any other intervention, except perhaps to move yourself or the object of your attention for a different angle or a better light. Take time to experience your object with as many senses as possible: drink in whatever sight, sound, odor, or texture is available.[70] Be alert to aspects of the object that you were not aware of before—subtle differences of color on its surface, perhaps, or the actual shape of some part and the relation of one part to another. Hope to discover. If drawing or writing help you focus and remember, OK, but do not let these become your focus—you can workthings up later. This is not a drawing or a writing project. The aim is presence, not representation.

After at least one session of simple attention, you can open toward the three moments of reverence: givenness, humility, and love. You may wish sometimes to dedicate one visit with your object to each of these. In any case, be sure to take time to look intentionally with each lens.

For each of these, I offer a starting place from which you will shape your own reflection. Only bear in mind—each of these, good in itself, is not the end; it is a path, and the three paths converge on one destination, where they become one again, like three streams falling into a single pool.

(i) Givenness

Fix your attention on your subject, and wait until you can realize feelingly that you did not bring it into being, nor could you. It exists owing to causes not of your devising, and it is healthy, renewable, continuingly existent on the basis of laws (dependencies, relationships, resources) not fully understood. It has its own fragilities, its own

---

70 Louis Agassiz, the great Swiss-American naturalist, was famous for the "fish lessons" he required for advanced or graduate students: no matter whether they were hoping to study insects or geology or botany, each was provided with a fish (usually one that had been collected and preserved in alcohol or formaldehyde solution). The assignment was simple: look at the fish intently. Drawing was permitted but no dissection or other operation on the body. This lesson might go on for days before another fish was laid beside the first. Samuel Scudder's firsthand account is good fun.

strengths. Time passes differently for it than for you. In these and other ways, no one can possess it, and it has dimensions of existence you do not know.

(ii) Humility

While continuing your attentive observation, reflect on some ways that your understanding of it is limited. Wait until you can see these limits as sources of delight; honor them first by accepting them. Stop to reflect that, like yourself, any natural object is the present form of age-long processes still at work in the world (and in our own bodies and artifacts as well). If it is a living creature, then spend some time reflecting on the aspects of its life (daily, monthly, life-span) that you do not know about. Consider how human activity may be an intervention, perturbation, or interruption in these processes of creating and sustaining.

(iii) Love

Love has many varieties. Here, I mean a sympathetic participation, an intentional suspension of self-reference. This is a thing that is not manufactured but must grow. Wait until you start to feel how there is value in the object of regard that is not owing to its use or service but just because it exists. Wait until you can feel warmth toward it and its welfare and integrity and toward the world that contains such things: the world and the object of your contemplation both unique in the universe. Here, gratitude is a close ally.

*   *   *   *   *

When you have been through this exercise with a familiar object to which you have paid enough attention in the past to have positive or negative feelings, repeat with new objects. If at first you chose an object that you like, now choose one that you are uncomfortable with. For the third repetition, choose an object you have never looked at closely before. As you get more comfortable with the practice, try doing a brief version with things you encounter by chance during your day.

After you have practiced on animals, plants, and mineral objects for a while, perhaps including such things as stars, moon, clouds, bodies of water, then start over again with humans: positive, negative, unknown. How do givenness, humility, and love feel different in each relationship that you build?

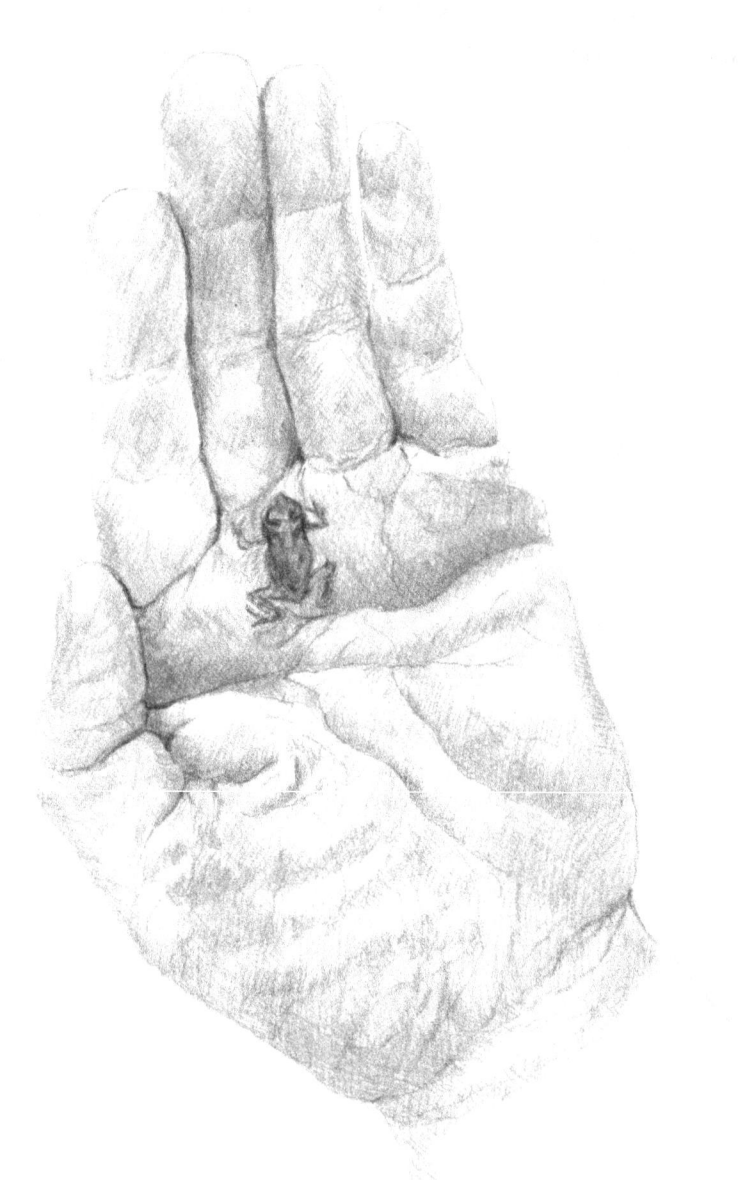

Meditation: Toadlet

A tiny dark creature struggles through the grass near my bare toes in late spring. At first, I take it to be an immature cricket. When I look closer, however, I see that it has only four legs, moving it jerkily along in the undergrowth: a toadlet. It could fit on my fingernail, yet it is a complete, working toad, lighter than a raisin of about the same size.

I scoop it carefully into a little glass so it can't get away, and then I sit down and peer at it so that it becomes the center of my regard. What happens? First, I see its perfection: four little fingers on each "hand," slightly askew from each other in the toadly way, and five little toes on the rear feet. Already, the skin is speckled with dark dots where warts will be. Slightly moist in the slanting light of the morning, it is a dusky and tan jewel.

The eyes are little dark spots as well but mobile and attentive, not yet visibly encircled by the patterned, colored rims that adults have. A little swelling behind each eye hints at where the poison-gland will develop, but right now, the toadlet is defenseless; it makes a simple mouthful for a gartersnake or pecking bird.

Toads are not sociable except at mating time, but now that my eye is tuned, I see that the grass around me is crawling with toadlets. Toads have a safety-in-numbers strategy for ensuring a next generation, like codfish or masting oaks: perhaps 2 percent of the toadlets survive to the end of their first year. That seems to be enough, since we always have toads around. It is true that our land is not crammed with toads, which means that we share the place with toad predators, mostly unseen. When they are tadpoles, dragonfly larvae and other water predators consume them. Once their legs appear and their tails vanish, snakes take over.

It is easier to imagine what eats toadlets than to imagine what toadlets eat. When they were in the water as tadpoles, they were vegetarian, eating algae and other water plants. Once on land, however, their mouths change shape as their diet changes to tiny invertebrates. What masses of miniature worms, centipedes, new-hatched crickets, and all the rest must be alive and at work with the toadlets striding among them, hunting and gulping! I have never been so aware of their presence, yet still unseen by me, as now, as I hold the toadlet within its glassy pen and look at its obsidian eye. Holding it, I sense that I am once again plucking at the fabric of nature, and if I were to follow the threads that my toadlet knows, I would travel through astonishing labyrinths that know me not at all nor even suspect my interest.

Letter Nineteen: Standing by the Pool

Dear friend,

I am standing by a pool into which several streams are pouring. Each brings its own burden of sediment and debris down from the mountain; waters of different colors mix in the pool before me and unite. I had followed a line of toadlets down to the brink, and now, while they clamber away up the hill, making noises too small for me to hear, I am given the everyday gift of water, woods, birdsong, wind, and moving leaves. The longer I stand, the more kinds of lives I recognize; the myriad unseen links among them tug at me, real if infinitesimal, like the gravitational pull of Jupiter or Cochab. None of this needs me.

The contemplation of this situation—the land where I am located, its long existence before my time, and after; my little understanding of what is happening here even at my feet; the opening of heart and mind to the birdsong and the active pool— re-centers me, decenters me. Accepting how little I matter, the limited ways in which I belong, gives me the gift of an office, a role: an anointing as a steward, a shepherd of trees, mayflies, chickadees, and fragrant, fragile dogbane.

It is the gift of the Light of Christ to show us what we are and where we stand. Only so can we begin to guess how we, too, take our place among the miracles of the creation, each of us. But this unitive experience—the most common and lovely mystical experience that rejoices and disconcerts the human heart—is not enough until it is the place from which we operate and not just a place we are graced to visit on occasion. "Give us this day our necessary bread." And what is more necessary for a living creature than that it know its place, know in its bones where it belongs and that it is welcome?

Once we know that, we sapient Earthlings, then we can begin to know the world, the whole creation in its terror and its beauty supporting us but not us alone. The Word is spoken livingly, actively in every thing that is now present or lingers in memory and lore in molecules circulating through the biosphere and every track and trace in hill and rock, glacier and ocean bed.

If we let our presumptions of lordship go, the world is given back, whole, for our cherishing. The practice of reverence is a way to know and remember the frameshift. Basil of Caesarea teaches that the person who contemplates reverently is not only an onlooker but a participant, just as spectators at a race are participants in the athletes' gift as they give it. This I know to be true in my own experience. An intimacy is available in such contemplation that makes gratitude most piercing and persistent.

Reverence, as far as it is incorporated into a newly whole personal awareness, is a central method and nourishment for our travails in the Anthropocene as we choose how we use resources, how we relate to our neighbors, how we decide about policies and technologies and other collective practices and rituatls. The element of givenness teaches us to consume, to build, to travel, and to cultivate in such a way as not to destroy the world's ability to recover, to maintain the power of growth. The element of humility teaches us about our own preciousness and fragility and the limits of our understanding of consequences and connections so that (as Ged[71] said) we learn to do only what we must do and no more. The element of love teaches us the heart of the Creator in whose image and likeness we are made, who holds all the worlds and yet does not possess or exploit, seeks for each

---

71 in LeGuin›s *Wizard of Earthsea*

the good according to its kind, and whose gift is reconciliation and healing, abundance, truth, and joy.

If our contemplation is participatory, in heart, soul, strength, and mind, givenness, humility, and love become indistinguishable as they flow and nurture our life, building our endurance and the constancy of our faithfulness in service and in gratitude.

With all this, it must be said that reverence is a hard practice, hard to be consistent in. It can come to any of us spontaneously for a brief time, often in childhood, and when we feel it as adults, it may connect our now with our then, bringing a momentary feeling of wholeness. Yet it does not persist for most of us: it is reached and lost again, over and over. As with many kinds of wholeness, our culture plays an important part in setting a contrary, even hostile attitude, and more than once, I have seen ostentatiously religious people to whom reverence seems unfamiliar.

I have tried to understand what it is in our culture that alienates us from reverence. Some people talk about disenchantment and re-enchantment, and I have come to think that some insight might be found here. I'd like to return to that in another letter.

Reflection

How are reverence and love related in your experience? In what ways are they related to action? More specifically, in what ways does reverence move you to action?

Meditation: Tadpoles of Death

It is a spring day at a woodland pond in the Northern Hardwoods. Later in the season, the pool will vanish because the spring rains will fail to replenish the pool begun by the snowmelt. Now, though, in the cool shallows, the tadpole larvae of the tiger salamander swim and forage, shredding plant matter and filtering the water for algae and other edible chunks in the pond. By midsummer, they will have shed their gills and begun the land phase of their lives. Their survival depends, in part, on whether the short-lived pools last long enough that the nutrient-rich medium allows them to complete their metamorphosis. The little crowds of tadpoles browse energetically.

At another vernal pool not far away in the same woods, other salamander young are facing more of a challenge. So many eggs have hatched in their pool that resources are under much greater pressure. Algae is scraped off the twigs and leaves as fast as it grows; as the water evaporates, the salamander larvae are packed tighter and tighter. The food and space resources available to those tadpoles are heavily overused.

Over the course of a few days, some tadpoles undergo a transformation: their heads broaden, their teeth lengthen, and their digestive abilities change. They solve the problem of an overexploited food

172

supply by switching their prey. No longer do they eat algae and sludge. Instead, they eat what is available in abundance—other salamander tadpoles. The cannibals grow faster than the vegetarians and make the change to dry land sooner; the vegetarians must contend with the losing equation of less food to feed ever larger tadpoles. There is starvation, as well as cannibalism.

Not only have the cannibals changed in a way that allows them to exploit a plentiful food source: the food itself provides more, and more accessible, nourishment. The flesh of the salamander tadpoles has more calories and a higher percentage of protein than does the available plant material, so the cannibals get more nitrogen and other nutrients per bite than do the vegetarians. Moreover, the calories in the protein and fat in the tadpoles are absorbed with less waste by the carnivorous individuals.

The flesh of their fellow tadpoles is a higher-quality food than the algae. Such higher-quality food enables faster growth rates, so the carnivores can change their lifestyle and escape the deteriorating conditions of the pond.

In many species, as young mature, they change their food habits. Baby birds, for instance, switch from being fed insects by their parents to an adult diet that is often vegetarian or seed eating. Our tadpoles, who switch over under pressure of starvation and maybe crowding, foreshadow their adult role as predators on invertebrates of the forest floor. Yet not all the tadpoles in a vernal pool, under the same pressure, will react in the same way. There is much that is not simple about a tadpole's life and work in the world.

Letter Twenty: Disenchantment

Dear friend,

I have a tide clock on the wall in my study. When its single hand is pointing straight up, the tide is high in Georgetown, Maine, where I grew up. When the hand's pointing down, the tide's out. Most days, I cast it a glance, and though I am landlocked here in the Monadnock hills of New Hampshire, the tide clock brings to mind long hours in my youth on the rivers and salt marshes along the Maine coast.

Now, when the tide's coming in, and you're not right on the shore (being upriver, say), there's little noise—no waves curling into the beach or dashing against the rocks. Instead, there is a slow filling up, a silent increase, and an insinuation of water in and through the vegetation and the mudbanks. Tethered boats swing on their moorings and point out to sea, but someone fishing, dreaming in the sun along the bank, may find their feet wet suddenly—as it seems—though the water will have been rising for a long time before.

The secular age has been a rising tide in Western culture for the past few centuries, and it has quietly seeped into all sectors of life. Few places or people are untouched by it—including most people who think of themselves as religious or spiritual. They may not be aware of this influence, of the ways in which their worldview is founded on quite materialist assumptions, which make them more closely allied than they might think to the irreligious or unspiritual people and institutions that dominate our society.[72] Though they may deploy religious or spiritual words (often stridently), they can seem to be robbed of reverence.[73] One face of this centuries-long development has been called "disenchantment"; because reverence is a necessary grounding for a faithful way of living in the Anthropocene, I think it's important to reflect upon how it is diminished.

The term "disenchantment" first appears in this sense, I think, in a lecture by the sociologist Max Weber.[74] He said that we moderns live under the assumption that, however ignorant we might be about how our technologies work, we feel we could in fact learn how it all works if we only wanted to:

> In principal all things can be brought under control by calculation…No longer are there for us, as for primitives, powers that we must use magical means to command, or petition spirits to direct.

Weber goes on to say that, as we have moved into a world in which we need only consult our own wills, using our science and technology to effect our desires, we have lost traditional ways to make meaning in our lives.

How does that work? It seems to me that, as we have assumed a kind of sovereignty, rooted in the dream that humans can achieve complete knowledge and complete control, we have thereby chosen a kind of exile, performed a radical amputation of context. Over the centuries, humans have gradually sought to draw all the world into the grasp of our hands as the instruments of our own intent.[75] You will

---

72 The picture is made more complex by the evidence that pseudo-sciences of many kinds are still flourishing among us; and most of them have taken on a scientistic veneer to keep up with the times. See Josephson-Storm 2017. Yet they often express a longing for mystery or awe.

73 "This people draweth nigh unto me with their mouth, and honoureth me with their lips; but their heart is far from me." Isaiah 29:13 KJV.

74 "Science as a vocation" ("Gewissenschaft als Beruf"). delivered at Munich University in 1922

75 So a proposal like E.O Wilson's to preserve half of the earth unexploited can seem nonsensical upon first hearing. *Half-Earth: Our planet's fight for life.* (2016) New York: Liveright Publishing Company

recall how Jesus said, "What good does it do someone if they possess the whole world but lose their own soul?" It appears now that, by claiming mastery, we have lost something essential to soul health, and in turn, by losing our own soul, we are losing our world.

Charles Tayler, in his book, *A Secular Age*, explores how this process of disenchantment changes our relationship to the world. He summarizes his thoughts this way (page 61):

> I have been drawing a portrait of the world we have lost, in which spiritual forces impinged on porous agents, in which the social was grounded in the sacred and secular time in higher times; a society moreover in which the pay of structure and anti-structure was held in equilibrium; and this human drama unfolded within a cosmos. All this has been dismantled and replaced by something quite different in the transformation we often roughly call *disenchantment.*

Taylor traces three key developments through the centuries, from the middle ages through to modern times. These relate both to our spirituality and to our relationship with the earth and challenge us to examine the way we understand our experience. I will try to unpack his conclusions as a way to explore why it is that reverence is so elusive and why, as a consequence, it is so hard in our culture to be a listening disciple.

The first trend is the change in our view of time. In the past, Taylor argues, people occupied two kinds of time. One has been termed *chronos* or ordinary linear time—one thing after another. With this, Taylor contrasts *kairos* or "sacred time," which is not linear. It relates to natural cycles and human participation in them: the stages of human life from birth to death, for example, or the seasons and their associated festivals and values. Indeed, *kairos* can simply mean "the right time to undertake a task that needs to reach a certain readiness," such as harvest-time.

From the point of view of *chronos*, one hour is like another—just a quantity of duration, nowadays regulated by the marking of a certain number of atomic vibrations in a reference element.[76] In *kairos*, the units of time—days, hours, minutes—are also often units of meaning, embedded in stories and episodes in development. Thus, *kairos* is the time-space in which social, psychological, and spiritual events take place—life-stages, miracles, the formation of bonds, the re-enactment of key events in the story of your people. To paraphrase a point Taylor (among many others) makes: in important ways, Easter in the year 2020 was closer to the first Easter than it was to July 4th, 2020. Our view of time is related to our understanding of priorities, of urgencies, the difference between progress and improvement—and all these relate to our ideas about who matters, whose experience matters, and whom we are responsible to and for. (There is an echo here of the way attention is tuned to our needs and interests, as I wrote in an earlier letter.)

The second development is the emergence of what Taylor calls the "buffered self." The buffered self has firm boundaries. It is, in a sense, an atomic unit, free agent, and locus of control (I am the master of my ship) whose relationships to other human atoms and external factors take place as carefully managed transactions across the barrier separating self from other. The buffered self is a self-contained unit that can be computed and modelled with, just as the uniform time-units of *chronos* are.

Taylor contrasts the buffered self with the permeable self. The permeable self also has boundaries and free will but is felt as an inter-dependent, interactive element connected with many others—human and nonhuman, material and spiritual, natural and supernatural or mysterious. Its boundaries are porous so that separateness is not complete, and they are only partly amenable to our control.

This permeable self lives in *kairos* because its community includes others participating in sacred time, in a time saturated with meanings. It is a deeply ecological way of understanding our participation in the dance of time and the elements.

---

76 According to the SI, the International Standards for measurement, a second is defined as "the duration of 9,192,631,770 periods of the radiation corresponding to the transition between the two hyperfine levels of the ground state of the caesium-133 atom" (at a temperature of of 0°Klv at mean sea level."

The way I think about my self-ness shapes where and when I seek for help; how I value (evaluate) the events that come to me; how I view the consequences of my actions for myself, for others, and for my world—the world I live in, depend upon, and care about.

Finally, Taylor names a third change, from *cosmos* to *universe*. By *cosmos* is meant an ordered and meaningful world in which humans and everything else have their proper places, functions, limits, glories, and detriments. Once again, it is a way of seeing the space (of time and extent) in which we pass our lives as having meaning.

It is worth stopping here to remember that "meaning" and "well-being" are not really separate feelings. They both relate to a sense of coherence, of participating in a world of which we can make sense. When we feel well-being, we understand what the song, "Simple Gifts," calls "a place just right," a moment in which desire, purpose, need, or fear are not external motive forces pushing us hither or yon. We know who and what we are and what we stand upon.

Max Weber, who was speaking to a meeting of technical students about the challenges of disenchantment, stresses that, in the modern, technical world, it is the problem of meaning that is most poignant and urgent. He is sympathetic to some young people who, in the chaos of modernity, turned toward spirituality of various kinds because the challenge to the human spirit when it exists in a homogeneous, mean- ingless space and time is so heavy and can be so corrosive to our sense of well-being. Weber, in a way, takes a technical approach to this or- ganic problem—modernity needs some debugging—and he calls the audience to the great challenge of making meanings for ourselves— in terms that clearly reflect his assumption that the buffered self, the atomic self, is from henceforth our native condition.

This isn't to deny that scientists and others have certainly been able to derive a sense of wonder and nourishment from the contem- plation of the heavens—or rather, the universe as we understand it in an ever-expanding time-space continuum of down-flowing energy and cycling matter. Ecologists and those who think like them have found beauty and power and a sense of unity with all life, from their unfolding understanding of the web of life. Darwin's famous passage still speaks eloquently for this experience:

It is interesting to contemplate a tangled bank, clothed with many plants of many kinds, with birds singing on the bushes, with various insects flitting about, and with worms crawling through the damp earth, and to reflect that these elaborately constructed forms, so different from each other, and dependent upon each other in so complex a manner, have all been produced by laws acting around us... There is grandeur in this view of life, with its several powers, having been originally breathed by the Creator into a few forms or into one; and that, whilst this planet has gone circling on according to the fixed law of gravity, from so simple a beginning endless forms most beautiful and most wonderful have been, and are being evolved.[77]

Moreover, "this view of life" can be generative of fresh perspectives on ethics—think Henry David Thoreau or Arne Naess's "deep ecology" or Aldo Leopold's "Land ethic," which influenced such different radicals as Rachel Carson and Wendell Berry.[78]

Now, these valuable, moving philosophies do not have much to say about the progress of the soul, about how the pilgrim self can grow into freedom, compassion, and truth. They argue powerfully that a right understanding of nature is necessary for such growth; they may even tell us about how they have been changed by their encounters with a newly understood experience of humans as part of the natural world. But they don't offer process, method, or guidance for the spiritual traveller—they rely, indeed, very much on the power of reason and correct understanding to somehow bring it about, as if to say, "To know and feel the right thing is to do it."

---

77 These are the concluding words of *On the origin of species by means of natural selection* (1859)

78 John Woolman, an anti-slavery and right-living advocate, understood (like contemplatives before and since) that a true dwelling in reverence would bring a recognition of our unity with creation. As Woolman writes in his journal,

> While I silently ponder on that change wrought in me, I find no language equal to it nor any means to convey to another a clear idea of it. I looked upon the works of God in this visible creation and an awefulness covered me; my heart was tender and often contrite, and a universal love to my fellow creatures increased in me. This will be understood by such who have trodden in the same path.

Yet you and I both know, from our own experience, that this equation is too simple. How many "right things" do we know that we do not act on! How many things do we profess to value but do not possess in the truth of our actions and attitudes! There is much work to do—to translate one kind of knowing, whether intellectual and emotional, into the integrated self.[79] Once again, I return to what is for me a pedagogical touchstone: "Thou shalt love the Lord thy God with all thy heart, and with all thy soul, and with all thy mind, and with all thy strength...[and] thy neighbor as thyself" (Mark 12:30–31, KJV).

One way of putting the essence of my argument in this series of letters is this: the gospel as understood in some streams of Christianity (including my own, Quakerism) is a coherent spiritual path, whose account of divine-human relationship and its meanings (rooted in reverence) for social behavior intrinsically also accounts for and helps us engage with, the relation of humans to the world and its many forces and inhabitants. It must accept and reckon with the scientific understandings of the natural world but insists on adding to it the experience, the feeling, of participation. It is a process of growth in coherence.

This coherence derives particularly from an understanding of the nature and work of Christ across all ages and cultures as the divine power tirelessly at work creating, sustaining, reconciling, and healing. As we choose freely, with intention, to accept our place in the body of Christ (that is, being active participants and collaborators with *sophia*, integrated in and by the divine creating story/rationale, *logos* which we know in our innermost self), we are drawn into our share of the work—perhaps as tentative learners or as servants under command but finally as friends and collaborators in grief and delight.

As a consequence, for a Christian, authentic worship should be an ecological act with all the world (the meaningful world, the cosmos saturated with meaning) present with us as we worship; and our work on behalf of justice or earth care or any other service can (when rightly understood) be seen as acts of prayer and expressions of worship. We have a very rich gospel to preach, in our lives even more than

---

79 This may be a good time to stop and reflect on Jesus' explanation of the "Parable of the sower" Mark 4:13–20

our words. But we must reach to see the whole and acknowledge when we have fixed our allegience upon an image or an idol rather than a living reality that does not exist only to let us defend our illusions.

Reflection

Consider: How many right things do you know that you do not act on—that you profess to value but do not possess in the truth of your actions and attitudes?

Meditation: Raven Plays on the Wind

I had climbed almost to the top of Dun Í, the highest point on the island of Iona. Before finishing the modest trek, I stooped to look at a brightly colored caterpillar working its way through the wiry grass and heather stems. The ocean was to my right and before me and behind, but my eyes were downward, the horizon for the moment just beyond my feet. The brisk offshore wind—offshore from the Scottish mainland and across the island of Mull—had a bite to it, but the little hollow where I paused was sun warmed. Curiously, on this windswept island, there was no scent of the sea.

The hill crested not many yards ahead, and beyond it fell abruptly, almost cliff, against which the wind threw itself; thwarted, it flowed up and over. I straightened up to finish my climb when I heard a fall of four or five quick hollow notes, as if from a little xylophone. When it repeated a few minutes later, I was able to focus my listening toward the brow of the hill. Repeat, repeat. Not wanting to disturb the maker, in hopes of seeing what it was, I crept, in the intervals of silence, gradually higher among the rocks. As I froze in position on a ledge, the breeze freshened; on the brisker updraft, black feathers showed, and then the xylophone was played again, and the feathers vanished. With a still stronger gust, a whole raven appeared, facing into the wind and riding it upward. Perhaps a dozen feet above the rim, the wings folded, and the bird coasted gently down the windslope, giving its little hollow call. Over and over, all alone, the raven played with the wind and gave out its quiet chortles for no one but itself (and one hidden watcher).

Letter Twenty-one:
Time, Tempo, Temptation

Dear friend,

I know that I left more threads dangling in my last letter than I should have. They all are anchored, in my mind, by the core challenge that got me writing to you in the first place, which is "How shall we live the gospel in the Anthropocene? How shall we grow to be adequate to the opportunities and trials of these times?"

In order to respond to that challenge, we need to act with intention to reclaim and reinhabit what the wisdom of the One tells us is our calling and that the *Logos* of the One teaches us about methods and the unfolding paths that the Shepherd leads us on. Only then are we able to receive the growth and endurance that the bread of heaven nourishes in us.

The more I think in concrete terms about our spiritual formation for adequacy in our living in the Anthropocene, the more I think that the first key must be how we inhabit our time. I am going to try explaining what I mean first by sharing with you a meditation on a passage from Scripture.

Lectio, the Story

Chapter 9 of John's Gospel is devoted to an extended story about a healing. (In what follows, I paraphrase the text instead of quoting directly.) A man, blind from birth, asks Jesus to heal him. Jesus does so: he first applies to the man's eyes a poultice of clay, which he makes of spittle and soil, and then tells him to go wash in the pool of Siloam. The man sees for the first time in his life. Amidst his rejoicing, he has to contend with people's skepticism—is this really the guy whom we've seen around here all these years, begging for alms? His parents are surprised by events but acknowledge without hesitation, "Yes, this is our son, born blind, but now he can see."

The authorities want to know how it happened and pester the man and his parents for more details. "Don't ask us; ask our son. He's of age!" The man himself says, "I dunno who this Jesus is. You say he's a sinner, but all I know is this: I was blind all my life, but now I can see. Facts are facts."

Jesus, in explaining himself to the patient and the onlookers says, "My mission in the world is a sort of test or encounter in which the unseeing might see, and the "seeing" ones by contrast are shown to be unseeing." The authorities say, "You're not saying we're blind, are you?" Jesus says, "If you were blind, you'd have no sin; but as of now you claim, 'We can see', so your sin persists."

Meditatio

The story continues,[80] and Jesus speaks more generally:

> I tell you truly, someone who doesn't enter through the door into the sheepfold but clambers in some other way— that person's a thief and a robber. The one that comes through the gate is the shepherd of those sheep—the doorkeeper opens for him; the sheep hear his voice, he calls them each by name, and he can lead them out to pasture.

---

80 Recall that the evangelists did not compose in chapters; the divisions were added later. The break between the end of chapter 9 and the beginning of chapter 10 tends to feel to the English reader as though there should be some transition of thought. Sometimes there is. In this case, I think not.

I think this relates directly to the prior passage. The claim that you see (know) truly and therefore have authority to lead or guide ("Feed my sheep!" he said to Peter) can only be established by one who has taken the path everyone has taken, going through the proper gate of experience to join God's flock. Experience is what brings authority. If you occupy some position of responsibility without insight, uncritically, owing that power to tradition or privilege, you can't be blamed for your ignorance and your unquestioned assumptions.

But once you make a claim to know what you're doing, you are obligated to examine the grounds for your claim, the truth of your condition. Are you standing amongst the sheep, having followed their path and being so much of their community that you know them each by name? When you are this self-aware, then you are bound to claim only what you actually possess and can clothe in your actions and no more. If you go beyond this, Jesus says, then your sin persists. This, therefore, means setting aside your advantages, the power that comes from social standing or privilege, so as to follow the path of obedience and transformation.

Jesus did this himself, growing up as the child of parents who disciplined and guided him; he had to "grow in grace and stature" through his youth, as we all do. Then he needed to acknowledge and respond to a calling (a yearning or need) to witness and to serve. In responding to that calling, that yearning, he experienced inwardly what the baptism of John advocated, the baptism and challenge of *metanoia*; and Jesus, in so doing, went beyond the baptism of water, being baptized with the Holy Spirit and then the fires of temptation. In that time of openness and humility, he was vulnerable to the wind of the Spirit, which, filling him, drove him into the desert. There, he watched and searched in fasting and prayer for forty days, at the end of which period of intense focus and clarity, he was tempted, even as we all are.

I am not surprised that Jesus was vulnerable then, when he must have felt God-soaked and consecrated. The clarity and commitment achieved during a time apart is always tested when one prepares to return, full of resolution and good intentions, from "retreat." The desert, the cloister, sometimes the vacation are similar in this way to the closet of private prayer. They are designed to give full scope to a particular portion of life and make space for big questions of meaning and purpose. But they offer their gifts by the suspension of daily demands and trade-offs. What seems clear and feasible in such a laboratory setting is battered and obscured by the demands and surprises of our everyday multiplex activities. Blending the rhythm of retreat with the rhythm of return is a challenge that confronts us also when we return from worship or a time of retreat—or even from sleep, as we awaken to our world in its fullness.

This transition tests the reality or the depth of the change or healing that we experience when we have stepped aside for refreshment or perspective. It doesn't mean—though it's tempting to feel it so sometimes—that these changes are not real or not the truth. Rather, it means that even an authentic transformation is at first tender and untried. Think of the fate of the seeds that the sower cast—how some sprang up with joy but withered in the drought that came before their little roots had struck deep enough. Indeed, it is in the growing, the responding to the changing conditions of life, that we build the structures and resources (let the roots go deeper) that can support durable change—change that lasts—and in its turn prepares for (even enables) future endurance and growth.

I hear experience in Jesus' story (in Matthew) about what can happen when a demon is cast out. The poor thing, evicted from its host, wanders in dry places and longs for someplace to call home. It thinks, "I'll go back to the old place and see how things are. Wow! Everything's swept and tidy!" Our demon moves right back in and invites some friends, too, who are even more devilish. So the afflicted soul, healed from its distraction for a while, is worse off than ever. Since the soul has not brought new ways of life into the space, the vacuum can be filled by whatever spirit passes by.

All this applies to me, without a doubt. Have I not many, many times experienced it? A time of concentration or focus is experienced and enjoyed. Whether it is a time of study or of retreat or worship or work—I feel new tendrils of growth emerging and a sense of renewed health. But at transition, it is tested, and I lose the gift of that peace as I am interrupted or turn to the next task or jump into any other rhythm of relationship or work. The old rhythms and habits re-assert themselves. Even if I regulate my outward response, yet I am inwardly disturbed, perhaps even lacerated—and then can be discouraged.

But all time is not the same. The inward tempos, the weather of our moods and attitudes, can fluctuate at an astonishing rate. As great teachers such as the author of the *Cloud of Unknowing* know well, distractions can come from moment to moment—and so also can contemplative focus, which (he writes) is not necessarily time consuming. As the Quaker minister, William Taber, used to say, it can take just a nanosecond to drop into the Stream of Life that is always flowing just within reach. That stream, the abundant life of God's Spirit, is ardent and swift—and yet is inexhaustible and timeless. The time of our lives, our daily affairs, our activities as organisms (and social ones at that), move at other reverberations and beats and seem hardly to relate at all to the serene and inward time of the Spirit.

Yet at the heart of the turbulent world is God's stillness, the peace that is not the world's and yet is there as our gift from God. The transition is itself a journey (short by the clock but so long in other ways). It can be walked in the Light and felt like a modulation, as in music, from one key to another. It's not a path I ever walk with ease or un-mindfully. How shall I feel and live the shift in tempos? What shall I bring with me so that the timed and the timeless worlds need no longer to alternate or cancel each other out when my attention shifts or foreground and background shift? How do you do it?

Reflection

Where in the gospel story above or the meditation on it was your attention arrested, whether at a paradox, a point of wonder, or a feeling of conviction? Return to it, and use it as the door into contemplation, a time of savoring the presence of God.

Meditation: Talipot Palm

The trunks, light brown, stand like temple columns thirty, fifty, and even ninety feet tall. Leaf stalks open from the growing edge atop the tree into huge fans that, unless a human trims them off, gradually bend down under their own weight, making a rustling fringe.

Nowhere now does the talipot[81] grow in the wild, though cultivated, it is widespread across south Asia: its leaves can be used for thatching or for paper on which many sacred books are written; the sap and pith are made into drinks and food; the fruits, inedible by humans but not by other creatures, are used by some fisherfolk to stun fish and bring them within reach.

The trees may live for ninety years. Once in its life, the talipot flowers. A branching stalk grows from the tree's crown, stretching up for nearly thirty feet and just as broad from side to side. Like a slow-motion firework, the massive inflorescence opens millions of blossoms.

The floral display, visited by myriad pollinating insects, yields thousands and thousands of round fruits. Ripening, they hang like a storm cloud overhead, darkening and growing heavier until the big drops fall, thumping and rolling onto the ground. Just a few will fill your hand.

---

81 *Corypha umbraculifera*

Once the fruits have fallen, the tree dies, dropping leaves, drying out, and falling or being felled by human neighbors. Rodents, wild boar, and other animals eat the fruits and seeds. Excreted or just released as the fruits decay, the seeds will germinate at various times over the next decade.

Letter Twenty-two:
Time and the Practice of Reverence

Dear friend,

"Time is of the essence," we say, and usually, we just mean, "We've got to hurry!" But in a way, time is the essential means, the raw material, and the workbench, too, by which we live and act and shape the gift of life that we have been given.

As I sit here writing to you this morning, time's gravity weighs heavy on my heart. Every action we take right now to mitigate the emission of greenhouse gasses into the atmosphere can slow down or diminish in some degree the oncoming disruptions and catatrophes. In this way, it is a real act of mercy for creatures now alive, including humans, as well as those to come. The human world is full of people who, out of realistic compassion or grief or rational panic, are doing their best in this work. I am moved by their service and commitment.

All this heartfelt labor, however, is still far from enough to avert intensifying crises, as well as wholesale impoverishment and turmoil in the biosphere. Moreover, there are people who are intentionally and knowingly adding to the momentum of destruction, faithful to their loyalty to and worship of power (in its various forms, for themselves and their ilk). The willing destroyers are able advocates for their idol, and they are supported by those who see only their own near-term benefits. These "guides" are further enabled by widely shared habits of consumption and loyalty that are hard to change. The daily pressure of real or artificial needs prevents the majority from recognizing and rejecting their further complicity.

> The prophets prophesy falsely, and the priests bear rule
> by their means; and my people love to have it so: and
> what will you do about the consequences?[82]

To act radically, one must see one's condition and one's power, and the workshop of time is where we can see the shape of things as well as the things we can shape. In a previous letter, I suggested that the disenchantment of time represents (among other things) a barrier to our ability to engage spiritually with climate change. This morning, writing in the hour before dawn, I am clear that we need to attend to time through two lenses. One is ecological time, and the other is Christ. In what follows, after some introductory reflections, I will start with ecological time; I will try to explore time in the light of Christ as God's wisdom and reconciliation in another letter.

> Oh as I was young and easy in the mercy of his means,
> Time held me green and dying
> Though I sang in my chains like the sea.[83]

First, a note about the seduction of the measurable. Secular understandings of valuation have resulted in a cast of mind in which the common currency for talking about value is money. It is striking how usual, how everyday it is in our society to use the language of the marketplace for matters of value, choice, or exchange. It is rivalled in its pervasiveness in our talk only by metaphors drawn from warfare. It seems curious that the market has become as sacred an entity in our civil religion as the nation itself. Its anointed interpreters (economists and very rich capitalists) are listened to with gravity on all kinds of subjects not within their areas of expertise. For example, smart people with benign intentions can calculate the value of a human life or of an undergraduate science degree in college. Cost-benefit analyses have

---

82 Jer. 5:31
83 Dylan Thomas, "Fern Hill"

led to monetary valuations for species, for ecosystem services, and just about anything else. The language of investment, productivity, and product shapes much educational and health policy.[84]

Dollars or related quantities are modular, atomic items that are easy to count; you can make models using them that abstract away from the messy complexities of daily life as actually lived by individuals with names, histories, and aspirations for their lives. This abstraction is so convenient and useful for thinking and imagining complex systems that it can be mistaken for truth. It is a good fit for a world inhabited by simulated people, suitably abstracted to serve as elements in models.

The rhythms of that world are most conveniently measured in uniform units of time—minutes, say (also easily converted to dollars). As we think about it nowadays, one minute is identical to another. We have tied our measurement of time officially to natural constants (oscillations of a cesium atom at a standard temperature), and part of the disenchantment process lies precisely in this standardization of time, the loss (or ignoring) of the difference between ordinary time and sacred time.

Yet we all know that time as actually experienced is a lot more various and textured than a succession of identical units. If we want to talk or think about time as it is experienced, we need other terms. More particularly, if we are going to come to grips with climate change, we have to think in terms of ecological time. This requires science but other kinds of imagination as well.

Ecological time is a pleasantly messy thing. I invite you to consider some chunk of landscape with which you are familiar. Living where I do in rural New Hampshire, I naturally think of the forest outside my door, but your front lawn will do or a nearby median strip or neighborhood vacant lot.

---

84 Cost-benefit analyses have led to monetary valuations for species, for ecosystem services, etc. For example, one estimate from 2008 for the value of a human life: $50,000. The language of investment, productivity, and product shapes much educational and health policy. Of course, this approach is most used in management and policy discussions, and there are plenty of secularists who resist the pressure to use monetary language to evaluate everything—though the tendency is strong across many fields (see Michael Sandel's *What Money Can't Buy* for a useful reflection on this trend.)

Now, think about time as experienced there. Neither the soil nor the organisms are identical from one day to the next. The soil is changing physically and chemically—in interaction with the weather and the uncountable organisms on and in it. Then there are the plants and animals whose lives are regulated by the weather that affects the soil as well and by their internal clocks and by interactions with each other. Among all the components of a place, living and nonliving, relations are always in dynamic adjustment.

Further, each organism's experience is framed by its generation time, which is related to both its reproductive timing and its species' life-span.[85] A lifetime for a lucky mouse is (in human terms) a couple of years, but it is many more reproductive cycles. For an annual plant, like the velvet-leaf mallow, time is framed within one growing season and one flowering/seeding event. For one of the oaks outside my window, time includes many tens or even hundreds of seasons, and almost as many reproductive events.

In my youth, I learned from Psalm 90 that I might expect a life span of three-score years and ten. Now that I am arrived at that milestone, I can see that if I reach four-score years—whether by reason of strength, good health, or other factors—I will experience labor and sorrow brought by those years before I am cut off and fly away. My experience of my lifespan reveals yet another strand in the time-tapestry: developmental time. How a mouse (or a clam) experiences youth, adulthood, and seniority, I don't know, but since I am only metaphorically like the flowers of the field that are gathered after a season in the sun and cast into the furnace, much of my life's experience remains as part of my present self (somewhat like the wood in the trunk of a tree) providing support and recording the shape of my years while the leaves and living bark get on with this days' living). Finally, at each moment in ecological time, evolution is happening—the complex processes of reproduction, selection, and change.

There is grandeur in this view of life. Many an ecologist and naturalist has come to see and feel it viscerally (or their feeling for it has led

---

85　There is some research that suggests that mammals' lifespan is correlated with their heart rate. Very roughly, mammals seem to get about one billion heartbeats per life, though humans seem to average about twice that.

them to the sciences of nature). It entails wonder, beauty, complexity, the unknown, and a recognition of the interactions of macro and micro. This kind of time is not an accumulation of identical minutes but of patterns and processes in which every measure of time is relevant and operative, from nanoseconds to eons.

It is just here that climate change in its many aspects intervenes and disrupts, altering and transforming the robust and fragile web of natural systems. It changes the patterns and tempo of things, from atmospheric chemistry to the processes of growth and reproduction. All this comes at a time when we have been able to see how human land use and population and culture are affecting these same processes—and when we know as never before how much is yet to be understood. The anguish of living in Aldo Leopold's "world of wounds" is very real and costly; very late in the game, in some ways too late, this anguish is being shared by more and more people. Over our acidifying oceans, our burning forests, our expanding deserts, fewer and fewer birds fly and sing on the changing winds. This is the time in which we exist, and minutes do not measure it—it is measured in relationship, in growth stages, in generation. The disenchanted view of time as a sequence of homogeneous units is nowhere near adequate.

Our need to feel and think in ecological time is an urgent spiritual problem because our unity with nature is not an act of human condescension or choice. It is intrinsic. If our spirituality does not help us—require us—to see and to feel it, to acknowledge it with assent, then it is in that degree not truthful. And if you think that Christ has nothing to do with this, then I would suggest that your Christ is too small.

Reflection

"Is not prayer a study of truth, a sally of the soul into the unfound infinite? No man ever prayed heartily without learning something."[86] In what ways does your practice of prayer reflect this view? What may be missing from it? What is the role of wonder or surprise in worship?

---

86 R.W. Emerson *Nature*.

Meditation: *Symbion pandora*

In the chill North Atlantic, on ground deep enough to avoid the turbulence of all but the greatest storms but still within reach of traps and nets, lobsters go about their work. In feeding, the appendages before the mouth chew or shred the lobster's food and gradually pass fragments into the mouth. Messy eater! There are particles and shredlets everywhere.

Fixed on or near the bristle of the mouth parts are little, whiteish things that might be grains of rice (really little: less than half a millimeter). Up close, though, they are more complex: organisms, anchored at one end to the lobster, with the body flaring urn-shaped then narrowing upward to a tiny neck, topped with a little bulb whose top opens with a frill of waving cilia. Dainty lobster leftovers are swept into the U-shaped digestive tract, whose exit is outside the circle of cilia. Over the course of the creature's life, the digestive tract is resorbed and rebuilt several times (nothing is known about why or when).

From time to time, the feeding creature buds off a duplicate that finds its own nearby station and takes up the same life. As the population grows and space gets scarce, feeders bud differently. Some of the buds contain a single egg; some contain one to three tiny, dwarf males. The sex-specific buds settle down, too, but do no feeding: they have no guts. The dwarf males, a mere two hundred cells each, emerge (their "father" dies), and each is taken into a female. Maturing, the dwarf male loses three-quarters of its cells and fertilizes the female egg (who knows how?). The new individual develops within its mother-host and then buds as an oval, near-transparent swimming larva (the mother dies). The larva may land nearby, but if the end of the world comes—because the lobster has fed well and grown enough to shed its shell—it will be the only scion of its family to disperse to a new world, perhaps an arm's length away.

Letter Twenty-three:
Living in That Which Is Eternal

Dear friend,

I fear that my reflections may have obscured the urgent motivation that has compelled me to try saying what I see. Think about the fruits of the Spirit that Paul lists in his letter to the Galatians: love, joy, peace, patience kindness, goodness, faithfulness, gentleness, and self-control. If we are to inhabit the Anthropocene while bearing such fruits of the gospel life, we must recognize that we are called to a movement opposed to the values enshrined in the current systems of production and control (economic and political), values celebrated in many aspects of our culture. It is a central concern of spiritual formation to see the nature of the challenge and allow ourselves to be transformed to meet it. In the end, this is a very practical matter of the way we apportion our time and, through it, our energies, skills, gifts, opportunities, and curiosities.

So, as I have written, it was common in the past for human society to live in many kinds of time. We marked both everyday time and sacred time. Everyday time is the primary locus of work and home-making tasks as well as political and legal activities. Everyday time is framed and sometimes interrupted or invaded by sacred time. In sacred time, a different set of values is pre-eminent. In ritual and story, the limitations of human powers are acknowledged, the fleeing nature of individual lives is looked at directly. In sacred festivals of misrule, social structures of power and status are subject to critique, ridicule, or at least playful testing. For the duration of the festival or ceremony, a mixture of reverence, revelry, and reminders of injustice replace prudence, diligence, and even normal kinds of dignity.

The rituals and customs of sacred time offer bridges between the works-and-days world and the world of the spirit, such as the changes in the seasons and the great milestones of our lifetimes—birth, the passage into adulthood, marriage, death—these are everyday matters of human activity, yet also, even now have other kinds of meaning.

With the gradual disenchantment of our worldview, however, the time that is measured by hours, minutes, work schedules, and political rhythms has become the dominant one. Time consists of identical units, time-atoms—one after another. Sabbaths (Jewish, Christian, etc.) are now for most people un-sabbatical, and all days are good days for commerce. The power of sacred time to reset our framing, to remind us that the sequence of identical units is not the only way that life flows and that there are other values in addition to those that predominate in everyday time—that power is lost. Of course, individual people may find a way to seek beyond the life-world of homogenized time, but fewer and fewer experience this as a communal experience; and if it is primarily an individual, lifestyle choice, it loses legitimacy as a place from which to critique or refresh our world. Thus, the momentum of large institutions and of the market determines our present and our futures.

Against this reality, of course, prophetic voices do speak ever and again, and we repeat the cycles of breakthrough vision, movement building, and disillusionment or centroversion. Jesus proclaimed the present kingdom. His followers, thinking they understood him, proclaimed a world-ending cataclysm (what else could overturn Caesar and other powers of custom and control, after all? But end-times stretched on to become mean-times, and kingdom values of mercy, forgiveness, love, and peace were dismissed as incompatible with now—they must be for the future. We look back with kindly, wistful forbearance for the prophetic enthusiasm of the past, and we get on with real life, not forgetting to invoke the heroic rhetoric from time to time, which can be so bracing and re-assuring. Some other residues may remain, but mostly their power lies dormant.

My faith community, the Friends (Quakers), has lived a version of this story. We sometimes ask ourselves why our now is not powerful like it was then: we see in the first days of the Quaker movement an apocalyptic vision, an encounter with the truth beyond convention (and often against it) that Christ is present and active even in our own day.

This truth naturally had to be modified as it was translated into cultural and institutional terms. As a result, the tang and urgency of revelation, the turmoil of transformation, often goes missing. Struggling against the constraints of culture or subculture, seekers after a more open, dynamic experience of the sacred re-engage with apocalypse. We remind ourselves that:

> Apokalypsis means "revelation," a tearing away of the veil. Apocalyptic langugae at its best is language that unmasks the apparently self-evident reality of our mundane existence and makes clear the underlying mythic dimension. Through apocalyptic consciousness, God's presence and activity, the "kingdom" or realm of God are laid bare in ordinary circumstances.[87]

Yes, we feel. This is where I want to live! And in this awareness, sacred time is rediscovered. We recall that we need no special place or implements or ceremonial events or designated personages to enter sacred time, the time that turns things upside down, demonstrating that all life is sacred, and everything is sacramental. Worship as encounter can be such an experience, which feeds and is fed by private prayer or contemplation. Yet the note of individualism continues to echo through all our practice, and nowadays, also our faith. Mostly,

---

87 Gwyn, D. in Dandelion et al. *Heaven and Earth: Quakers and the second coming*, pg. 9

our time is as homogeneous as everyone else's. With our time chained, so is our imagination and what we dare to long for.

This seems to me a weak foundation for articulating or enacting a shared witness in a time of climate change. Moreover, end-times language tends to connote some future steady state, where all questions are settled, and all our current confusions are clarified. And finally, they keep the focus primarily on people, on *Homo sapiens*, and on our times and conveniences. Where do we learn the lessons that can make real a reconciliation with the truth of our life as Earthlings and incarnated souls?

Now, the great Quaker leader, George Fox, was a prophet both "heavenly minded," as Penn called him, and shrewd. He could call us to look beyond normal time with words still resonant and inviting:

> Friends , wait to gather and know one another in that which is eternal, which was before the world was. For knowing one another only in the letter and flesh differs you little from the beasts of the field, for what they know they know naturally. But all knowing one another in the light which was before the world was, this differs you from the beasts in the field, and from the world's knowledge, and brings you to know one another in the elect seed, which was before the world was (Epistle 149).

He urged us to recall that our time is short and its duration not under our control, writing to his parents,

> Look not back, nor be too forward, further than ye have attained; for ye have no time, but this present time; therefore, prize your time for your souls' sake (Epistle 5).

But though he calls us into a durable condition, it is not a static one, nor is it one in which all answers are found.

> Would that all the Lord's people were prophets, said Moses, in his time... when some found fault; but the last time is the Christian's time, who enjoys the substance, Christ Jesus (Epistle 125).

And here I find the path by which to come to a reconciliation in the times of our lives. For it is an opportunity to remember, to re-experience, that we live, not only in human time—the life of a generation—but also in ecological time, in which our environing conditions are created, dwelt in, and shaped into the future. Our coming into this world as individuals, our existing in it for a time, are made possible by the lives and events experienced by the people—but also by the earth and all its inhabitants at every scale. And when we die, we have shaped the world for the future. It is in the rhythms of ecological time—interlocking, overlapping, fast, and slow—that we can experience the functions of sacred time that put our individual and social lives in context, under judgment, as gifts and as responsibility.

What does this have to do with Christ? I want to tell you about an idea that I learned from Erasmus[88] that I have found moving and clarifying: Christ as the unique or only *scopus* for the awakened Christian. *Scopus* is from a Greek word (*skopos*) that often means, "goal or aim." John Cassian (in his first Conference) puts the word in a practical setting: imagine a farmer whose ultimate goal [*telos*] is "a secure and comfortable life, thanks to his fruitful lands." To that end, he identifies tasks he has to accomplish if his land is to bear abundantly. Such a task is a *skopos*, a milestone along the road to his destination.

Other early teachers spoke of the *skopos* as the watchtower from which one can see one's goal and the landscape surrounding it—and indeed, the word comes from one of the Greek words for observing (as in "tele*scope*"). Christ as *scopus* is thus both a destination and a method, as well as the Teacher whose guidance will lead us in the travail (in both senses of "work" and "travel").

For our present times, we have to get used to the understanding that Christ includes not only the incarnation in Jesus but also *Logos*, the active creating story or narrative or rationale in which we are embedded with all the rest of creation and Sophia, the divine wisdom, taking delight in the created world whose origin is in God's love, imagination, and delight in conversation and in growing things.

This is the One of whom Paul said, "We have the mind of Christ," that searches out the deepest truth of God's intent and being and enables us, in our yielding and our faithfulness, to seek, to value, to long

---

88   in a letter to Paul Volz

for, and to find, reconciliation (in Christ, God is reconciling the world to Godself). Jesus prayed[89] "that all may be one," and that is the work of Christ before and since. We, therefore, are invited to seek and be searched by this Spirit, for whom all times are sacred and in whom we can wait to feel the meaning of the times in which we live—the times of our lives, the ecological time in which we have our being. God loves the world, says John's account of the Gospel. In seeking for Christ in Christ's fullness, we can wait to know one another in God's time.

Reflection

Cassian, in talking about a farmer's *scopus,* writes: "He pursues his *skopos* by clearing his field of all the briars and emptying it of every unfruitful weed, and he does not believe that he will achieve his end of peaceful affluence in any other way than as it were by first possessing by toil and hope what he desires to have the actual use of." What are your ends, the goals at which you are aiming? What will be a fulfillment of your self? How (if at all) do the activities of your day, this day, relate to that *telos*, that complete maturity? How (if at all) does your *telos* govern your choices today?

---

89 John 17:21

Meditation:
The Essential Trickle, Photosynthesis

A photon, an almost massless packet of light with a wavelength of 400–700 nanometers, cuts down through the atmosphere. It passes into plant tissue and arrives in a chloroplast, the organelle in which photosynthesis takes place. The photon strikes a molecular antenna; the energy of this collision frees an electron from a chlorophyll molecule, and this sets off a chain of events that power the fixation of carbon gleaned from the atmosphere (in the form of carbon dioxide, CO_2), creating carbohydrate molecules, sugar to power cells. In the process, water is split to replace the electron that split from the chlorophyll molecule, and as a side effect, oxygen is released.

Most of life on earth depends directly or indirectly on this steady, tiny trickle of electrons going on in trillions of leaves, driven by the tons of photons pouring onto the earth's surface every day.

Temperature limits this trickle: Below about 40°F (4°C) the process slows dramatically; above 104°F (40°C), key proteins in the system "denature" or lose their shape so that they do not function. Clouds or other particulates in the atmosphere capture some of the photons or reflect them back into space, reducing what arrives at the earth's surface. Lack of water slows down the rate at which the system can operate; lack of nutrients can inhibit the renewal of the system, too. The process is robust because it is carried on at such a vast scale, yet it is also vulnerable because it depends on good working conditions for all the leaves on earth.

Letter Twenty-four: Re-enchantment, (Re)Birth, and the Buffered Self

Dear friend,

I have been trying in these letters to describe and invite you to three intertwined inquiries: [i] to work out some of the layers of spiritual challenge presented by the current climate crisis (and related catastrophes); [ii] to see how the gospel is intrinsically related to these challenges and to our response; [iii] to articulate some ways that the faith and practice of one tiny portion of the Christian tradition—Quakerism—both sheds light on the subject and, at the same time, can contribute to a strategy for enduring and acting with hope as children of the Light in increasingly trying times. I hope that one collateral benefit of this analysis is that it may provide a way for some people (including some Quakers) to grow into a re-engagement with the gospel message as a source of inward and outward unity and power. So, this is to warn you that I am going to start drawing more and more on Quaker ideas and writings in what follows.

My project has now brought me to ask how we understand ourselves in relation to the universe (or cosmos, depending). I enter on this topic with some trepidation, since so many great minds have addressed the question, but sometimes it's better to take your own look at the sky.[90]

This is not an abstract or purely mental matter for me (and no doubt for others). Since childhood, I have felt the land around me as if it were in fact "the back of my hand," some strange extension of my own skin, bringing me news of its condition, which is also my own. The terrible crystalline beauty and assault of winter cold, the explosive release of growth when the winter is pushed back by spring's extravagant delight, the crushing hush and tense waiting of a drought that presses the landscape down and leaves it gasping, the fruitful and turbulent time of autumn change as we fall toward the dark days again—these and myriad other, smaller rhythms and associations are being jarred and disrupted. My balance is thrown off, and my anxiety rises as if my body feels a wound that I have not yet acknowledged.

Reports come in from around the world that others are feeling something similar, and connecting it with the findings of science and reports of disruptions in field, mountain, forest, and sea. Young people especially are experiencing a rising tide of dread and doubt and passionate resentment of their elders who have squandered their opportunity to take a different path. The work is hard, grievous—but how can we turn away from it?

Porous and Buffered

Charles Taylor argues that one of the major shifts in the modern mind has been a change from seeing the self as porous to one that is buffered. The modern, buffered self clearly distinguishes self from not-self—there is a (mostly) firm boundary between inside and outside.

---

90   As Walt Whitman told us in "When I heard the learn'd astronomer":
When I heard the learn'd astronomer,
When the proofs, the figures, were ranged in columns before me,
When I was shown the charts and diagrams, to add, divide, and measure them,
When I sitting heard the astronomer where he lectured with much applause in the lecture-room,
How soon unaccountable I became tired and sick,
Till rising and gliding out I wander'd off by myself,
In the mystical moist night-air, and from time to time,
Look'd up in perfect silence at the stars.

Inside a self is where psychology happens, where decisions and feelings and thoughts happen, where values are chosen and put into practice. Outside is non-personal, unintentional, value-free—natural forces, forces of chaos, or of order imposed (or emerging) from natural processes. We all know very well the ways that our culture relates to these and shields the self that lives inside the shell. Also, we are all aware of the difficulties that arise from being part of a society of buffered selves.

The porous self, on the other hand, as understood by our ancestors, was deeply open to influences of all kinds—for example, from the stars, from the elementals, from demons, and from good spirits. Though much of what we are linked to and moved by is natural (like the weather or disease), many of the forces that impinge on us are beings with their own purposes and selves. Consequently, in such a world and as such a self, a person would need to negotiate, placate, or contend with these external beings. As Taylor writes:

> the porous self is vulnerable: to spirits, demons, cosmic forces. And along with this go certain fears that can grip it in certain circumstances. The buffered self has been taken out of the world of this kind of fear....an important part of the treatment [of the world by the buffered self] is designed to make disengagement possible....the buffered self can form the ambition of disengaging from whatever is beyond the boundary, and of giving its own autonomous order to its life. The absence of fear can be not just enjoyed, but becomes an opportunity for self-control or self-direction.

Certainly, the buffered self, independent for good or ill, decider, chooser, consumer, is very convenient for modeling, marketing, and manipulation—in the world in which humans are seen first and foremost as (f)actors in a market.

But even if you grant that Taylor has captured something compelling and true about our culture, it's important to remember that no person starts out that way. The world and the culture is created anew with every birth, at least for the newborn. Quakers, whose vision focused on two major ideas—the fact and work of Christ in you and the progress of the soul walking in the Light—understood this simple, most basic fact of human experience—that we come fresh into the world—had profound theological consequences.

About Arrivals and First Encounters

Please first read consideringly the following extracts (and I urge you to find the whole of Whitman's "There was a child went forth"):

> THERE was a child went forth every day,
> And the first object he look'd upon, that object he became,
> And that object became part of him for the day or a certain part
> of the day,
> Or for many years or stretching cycles of years.
> The early lilacs became part of this child,
> And grass and white and red morning-glories, and white and red
> clover, and the song of the phoebe-bird,
> And the Third-month lambs and the sow's pink-faint litter, and
> the mare's foal and the cow's calf,
> And the noisy brood of the barnyard or by the mire of the pond-
> side,
> And the fish suspending themselves so curiously below there, and
> the beautiful curious liquid...
> His own parents, he that had father'd him and she that had conceiv'd him in her womb and birth'd him,
> They gave this child more of themselves than that,
> They gave him afterward every day, they became part of him.
> The mother at home quietly placing the dishes on the supper-table,
> The mother with mild words, clean her cap and gown, a whole-

some odor falling off her person and clothes as she walks
by,
The father, strong, self-sufficient, manly, mean, anger'd,
unjust,
The blow, the quick loud word, the tight bargain, the
crafty lure,
The family usages, the language, the company, the
furniture, the
yearning and swelling heart...,
These became part of that child who went forth every
day, and
who now goes, and will always go forth every day

Arrivals, First Encounters and the Ecological Self

I was such a child—and so were you. We are given the gift of innocence, as every person has been from birth. This includes the first
layers of development of our ecological self, our ideas about how we
fit in with the cosmos.

Here also is the beginning of our re-enactment of the myth of the
fall and all that follows. We accept the world we are given and draw
from it nourishment, instruction, community, delight. As we grow
(and this starts early), we begin to use—not intentionally, it's part of
the gift—our burgeoning powers of speech, of memory, and of reason.
We learn to name things, as we are told Adam did in the Garden. We
question boundaries—because we have learned to ask questions—and
we learn from others who are more advanced in understanding and
experience than we. We develop a will of our own—and often our willing is in advance of our understanding of cause and effect. While still
we have little perspective (how could we within so short a span and
narrow a compass of experiences?), we begin to make choices and to
evaluate good and bad—first in stark primary colors, then with more
shading as we learn of mixed goods and mixed ills. In the growth
of knowledge, we lose some kinds of clarity, and our developing self
gains in power as a center of decision, as a fortress, as a treasure to be
protected.

The early intimations of immortality may wholly be forgotten or retained as shreds of memory—but have left their residue in some longings for safety, serenity, and connection despite our separateness. We can come to see ourselves as a house divided against itself; or to echo in our heart of hearts the cry of the Preacher: Emptiness of emptinesses! All is emptiness!

Our longing for clarity and inward repose is nurtured by hints and guidance from those who have gone before and by suggestions of remedies for our sense of dividedness. Tender or longing to be so, we may go seeking: Lo, here is your deliverer! Lo, there!

Sometimes the search for healing—not just for this wound or that weakness but something more lasting and reliable—is conscious and enacted as an outward pilgrimage; sometimes it is mostly inward and secret. Discovery may come at a dead end or a crisis or as a flower opening. George Fox's moment is a paradigm:

> As I had forsaken all the priests, so I left the separate preachers also, and those called the most experienced people; for I saw there was none among them all that could speak to my condition. And when all my hopes in them and in all men were gone, so that I had nothing outwardly to help me, nor could tell what to do, then, oh then, I heard a voice which said, "There is one, even Christ Jesus, that can speak to thy condition," and when I heard it my heart did leap for joy.

'All Things Gave Forth a New Smell' and What the First Birth Cannot Do, Reconnection in the Light of Christ

At the time of life when we have been fully engaged in the business of living, the first (re)appearance of the Christ is small, however strenuous the triggering experience that opened our eyes to it. It is like the first opening of the seed, when a tendril reaches out to find stability and a first sip of water, and then a tender shoot moves toward the light. But if we pay close attention to what is given, we can feel in some way a sense of fresh nourishment and the possibility of freedom.

Taking that in and "not being more than God would have you," more growth is possible, and we grow fiber and rootedness enough to encounter new challenges—and the drought, wind, distractions, losses, and setbacks are likely enough to come.

Or it is like that babe in Bethlehem—the first appearance has few words and little understanding; its safest way forward is by keeping close to the loving Guide and any who serve that Guide. A few words, the beginnings of motion—but this time, we can remember as we gain some sense of power and ability that "freedom" does not mean implementing our will, but in each step and word, we check with the Guide for permission, invitation, or command. James Nayler wrote (in the *Lamb's War*)

> his kingdom in this world, in which he chiefly delights
> to walk and make himself known, is in the hearts of such
> as have believed in him...And such he rejoices and takes
> delight in... He leads them by the gently movings of his
> Spirit out of all their own ways and wills...and guides
> them into the will of the father, by which they become
> more clean and holy. Deeply he lets them know his cove-
> nant, and how far they may go and be false, he gives them
> his laws and his statutes, contrary in all things to the god
> of this world, that they may be known to be his before all
> his enemies.

Now, because we have arrived at this place of renewal as the result of our first experiences of loss and disorientation, we can understand (being "wise as serpents" in some ways of the world) that renovation is not done by wanting it so but by doing it: stepwise attention and rebuilding. We are to test and probe the spirits by which we are motivated in our choices and hold fast to the good. So we move ahead, even until we can understand and join in the experiences of Gethsemane and Golgotha, the empty tomb, the encounter on the road to Emmaus, the breathing in of the Holy Spirit in the little room where we and our companions wait, constrained and anxious, until we feel in that Spirit's coming that we are released and sent forward. The power is given to be bold in love: "The Light says, Love your neighbor as your self; this, the first birth cannot do," but the second birth is into that love.

In this renewal, we are, if we wait to see, given the gift of gratitude and joy, as if in our childhood again (if we become as children indeed), and as Fox, that countryman found, all creation is opened to us. We see the gift it is and how it is rooted in the same Spirit that is re-creating us. We learn the need to make right use of the creatures, who are children of the same Parent, but we learn also that the world is not ours, and we learn it from the Word of wisdom that was working with delight daily in its birthing and diversity, a faithful craftsman. The will of the Parent is in the inscape of every thing on earth (its *logos*) and in the Spirit of Christ (the *logos* in which all are unified) by which we are led. We are taught to see it and commanded to steward it.

Refusing the Buffered Self

In this new vision of connection and dependence, we are given to see that we are also part of one Body, whose parts are diverse and mutually dependent. And we must be humble enough to see that, not only can the "eye not say unto the hand, I have no need of thee," but the eye cannot know or imagine how the hand works and vice versa. Each must act and serve according to its structure and function within the whole and trust the others to work accordingly. No wonder we feel betrayed when some organ or limb fails us! In this way, our ecological self is renewed, as is every other part of our self—and not to ourselves for our own purposes, alone.

We have been taught by our culture and its demands for mutually interchangeable atoms, that each of us is "an island, entire of itself," but it is certainly not so. The buffered self is an idol that cannot see or speak, smell or touch. Science contradicts it; psychology contradicts it; common sense contradicts it. Only whole selves can see, taste, grasp, and grow. When we come into the Light, and our sight and even our instincts are little by little transformed, we feel and see how always we are interpenetrated, woven into a fabric—human and non-human, animate and inanimate, past, present, and future. The love of God is expressed in cells and molecules, leaves, flowers, and the mating rituals of birds and beasts, reproduction, growth, competition, death—it is all us and thus ours, and we belong to it just as wholly.

> For I am persuaded that neither death, nor life, nor angels, nor principalities, nor powers, nor things present, nor things to come, nor height, nor depth, nor any other creature, shall be able to separate us from the love of God, which is in Christ Jesus our Lord.

Reflection

How can we not drop everything and run to help when the earth, our self and our home, is in distress?

Meditation:
Honeycombs and Murmurations

When a honeybee worker first reaches maturity, her first weeks of life are spent constructing and tending beeswax combs, for storing honey and pollen and for housing their young. It is an enormously costly process: A bee consumes about eight pounds of honey (the product of thousands of foraging trips and nectar deliveries) to produce about a pound of wax.

When a worker is in her wax-making stage, glands that develop in her abdomen emit little flakes of wax that harden upon contact with air. The worker picks flakes off her abdomen and chews them until they are flexible. She then places the little drop of flexible wax onto the growing comb, pushing and shaping it with feet and head.

Though the cell starts out roughly cylindrical in shape, as the cells are packed together and refined by the workers, they take on the familiar hexagonal shape without any planning by the bees. The comb fills its space with a maximum of efficiency and durability.

*   *   *   *   *

The cloud of starlings, thousands together, move up and around and down, flowing like thick black smoke on a wind, never dispersed: they stay close together as they climb and wheel. You can hear the whisper of the many small wings, and if you are close when they swoop low, you can catch their odor, the smell of a flock of birds.

There is no choreography—there is no grand plan or intention or design. The flow of order and dissolution, of shapes and shapelessness is a compound of local decisions—each starling matching direction and speed with its seven or eight nearest neighbors.

Letter Twenty-five:
On Love and Emerging Order

Dear friend,

Remember, we are called to perfection even now. In the face of this astonishing demand, some have always said that the call to faithfulness cannot be taken seriously. It can't be true that our greatness must come from service, that our strength is perfected in weakness, that the wisdom by which we are to live must strike so deeply at the roots of things that it seems folly to the world, that we cannot love our neighbor as ourselves, that we cannot only fight with spiritual weapons, turn the other cheek, worship God in the beauty of holiness.

In part, we plead excuses and accept half-measures because the challenge is understood as an arrival, an accomplishment, something finished. Yet this cannot be the case. We know that the work of creation is a continued unfolding. The command, "Let there be..." is still being uttered. The fulfilling of the commandments—to love God with our heart and soul and strength and mind and to love our neighbour—on which hang all the law and the prophets are not things that can be finished. There can be no rest in the Spirit that is procured by a single act. Life is process, growth, learning, and renewal. When we are in a place of reverence, we are able to acknowledge this.

Jesus told us in many ways that we must seek first the Kingdom of God and his righteousness, sweep and order our households till we find the lost coin, strive to compass the pearl of great price. It is focus, faithfulness in the journey, singleness of eye that is at the root of the process of perfection, which Jesus sent his comforter to help us enact. What we need to overcome is the divided mind and heart. The house divided against itself cannot stand. We cannot serve two masters with equal fidelity. Purity of heart is to will one thing, as the philosopher said. We are promised abundance and joy, power, fruitfulness, and suffering. When Jesus called Peter and Andrew, James and John, he was calling them to travel with him, not to sit beside him in a palace adorned with self-congratulation.

Now, the journey to wholeness of mind, heart, strength, and soul is not a search for self-realization or self-assertion, though through it we can come to rejoice in the gift of our selves realized more fully.

Nor is the journey a random walk directed by chance or the whim of a moment. Although each person must follow their own path, because each path originates in that person's condition when they begin the journey and accept the call, there is an iron constraint, as inarguable as magnetic north is to the compass needle.

No, if you and I are traveling toward the heart of gospel love that the *Logos*, the divine Wisdom, has been speaking in the human heart forever, planting and watering its fragile and powerful roots, the only way toward that goal is under the constraint of that love itself and under the guidance of its Holy Spirit. In the heart of the gospel life, where there is freedom, there is also a lawfulness that is as exacting as it is liberating—but not as the world knows either freedom or law.

That Spirit is fearless, and in it, we can become fearless in seeing the truth in ourselves, its lights and shadows. Creator and sustainer that it is, no truth is taught, no judgment is rendered that does not offer the materials and methods for healing and refreshment. In that Spirit, recognition of our shortcomings and misdoings can open the way to joy, as a naturalist rejoices discovering a new species blooming in famliar woodland, or a poet delights when the right image blooms in her listening mind. So love and judgment can walk hand in hand.

Its compassion is boundless, so as it works in us and we in it, we become more alert to its presence in others. As we become more aware of what makes for life or hinders it in us, we can come to recognize sometimes the symptoms of distraction, oppression, falseness, and self-worship in others and in the institutions and cultures that are shaped in part to serve our illusions, our fears, and our insatiabilities. We see more truly when we see with love, but the love of God makes no excuses and seeks to overcome whatever is of a nature contrary to itself by means of a transformation toward wholeness, a re-creation, a refreshment of life.

And there is no way to understand and follow the guidance toward that love except by listening to the Spirit and shaping all our actions so that we can keep listening. I have come to understand this difficult idea as the invitation and, perhaps, imperative to live wholly available to and at the disposal of the divine Life whose being is both truth and love. Though that is the central goal, it is not always clear how next to move toward it or reorient to it after a time of wandering and distraction. To allow that Life to shape any particular situation very often requires growth and change—which is frustrating to wait for and joyous to experience when at last it comes.

Humans are tool-using creatures. Sometimes we create new tools to solve problems we hadn't recognized before, so institutions and systems proliferate. Spiritually speaking, the problem with this aspect of human nature is that we are always falling, often unwittingly, into idolatry—into giving more reverence to the tools without which we cannot operate in the world than to the Life in, through, and from which we are striving to act and grow. We can idolize our people, our favorite stories, a particular practice and forget that the tools of our devising, however precious they seem, are not the goal. When we are in a place of reverence, we are able to remember.

> All friends, take heed of running on in a form, lest ye do lose the power; but keep in the power and seed of God, in which ye will live in the substance.[91]

It is truthful to recognize this, but it requires love as well as truth (both in their active forms) to free ourselves from too great a

91   George Fox, Epistle #173.

dependence on our forms and structures. So then, the task for me is to inhabit my spiritual family so as to forward everyone's growth toward holiness in availability to the Holy Spirit. This means putting everything to the test of love as well as truth, the love that says, "Inasmuch as you do anything to the least of these my brothers or sisters, you do it to me."[92] In the Anthropocene, you and I need to remember that our family ties extend beyond people or nation, yes, and also beyond species, even beyond the times in which we walk and work visible upon the earth.

My friend, it seems to me that if we are centered in love, then any acts driven by a disturbance of conscience or new perception of truth can be done in a way that is aware of and reaches to the life of God in all, and this is how it must be done. Love is rigorous because we must be prepared to live it, and new occasions require new preparation, new experimentation, new learning.

Do you see? *Logos* means dialogue, conversation, not arbitrary edict. If we are to keep consistently rooted in life, both our life as earthlings and as spirits, the order—systems, culture, habits —we construct to house and shape our shared lives must emerge from that dialogue. Finding the way to do that can take a long time, often leaving us in perplexity, where we can only voice or pray our un-ease. But we are told that the tender, the poor in spirit, the peacemakers, those who long for righteousness, who mourn, who wash their friends' feet—these are the blessed—not those with all the answers.

Reflection

> Dear Hearts, you make your own troubles, by being unwilling and disobedient to that which would lead you. I see there is no way but to go hand in hand with him in all things, running after him without fear or considering, leaving the whole work only to him. If he seem to smile, follow him in fear and love; and if he seem to frown, follow him, and fall into his will, and you shall see he is yours still.[93]

92 Paraphrasing Matt. 25:40
93 James Nayler, Letter to George Fox and Margaret Fell (1653) *Works* 2:573

Meditation: False Tongue

In the warm waters of the Caribbean, an isopod,[94] a shrimp-like crustacean, approaches the clownfish's side. The fish, bright in the sunny coral-reef water, is many times larger than the isopod, who approaches carefully, aiming toward the pumping gills.

It lands near the opening and creeps into the living chamber, bright with the red-velvet fringes of the gills and the light transmitted through the fish's skin. The isopod takes up residence there and soon is joined by others. Eventually, one becomes a female and moves into the fish's mouth—the others consequently mature as males[95].

The female anchors her hindlegs at the root of the fish's tongue and deprives the tongue of its blood supply. The tongue eventually atrophies and falls off, whereupon the isopod takes up the role of tongue. The fish lives normally, more or less—no further damage is done aside from inconvenience, as when the female mates with a male resident in the fish's gills and then reproduces. On the reef or at the fish market, one may see the dark-eyed isopod peering forward from the fish's open mouth.

---

94 *Cymothoa exigua*
95 Sex is not fixed at birth. If two *Cymothoa* in the same host happen to mature as males, one will change to female.

Letter Twenty-six: Formation in Action, Gospel Order Emerging

Dear friend,

I have been writing these letters out of a conviction. Climate change and the other markers of the Anthropocene that affect every aspect of the world system (that means humans, too) give us an opportunity, indeed a mandate, to get into the gospel in a fresh way. And that is the power of God for salvation (liberation and reconciliation). What I've written so far has been concerned with foundations and orientations, but these are not attitudinal alone, for we are called to live in such a way as to prophesy, to bring the consequences of our encounters with God's truth into our doing and that of our society.

The gospel is not about humans alone because the Spirit of Christ, by which we are led (in the Quaker understanding of life in the gospel), is about the whole world. Christ, however denominated, permeates the world as *logos*, as the wisdom of God. This wisdom speaks human languages and the language of prophetic signs, both of which are exemplified in the life and mission of Jesus. But it also speaks the languages of volcanos, nutrient cycling, the water cycle, the rhythms of seasons and of life and death, the wild diversity of living creatures—all of it, from Alpha to Omega.

Humans and human works have a special character, which requires moral reasoning not demanded of maelstroms and mice. This is because we have the power of sub-creation (to use Tolkien's term)—to take the materials given us by the cosmos and fashion or refashion them according to our own designs and perceived needs (and fashion narratives to rationalize what we're doing, in every sense of the word). Once, the non-human world was the dominant force in our consciousness; however, as human population and human culture have accumulated to the modern scale, our sub-creating now puts much of the world's surface—atmosphere, biosphere, seas, and soils—under significant human impact and has given us the illusion of control.

These great systems, obeying their own laws, which we only imperfectly understand, respond to our influence in ways sometimes foreseeable and sometimes not. In any case, we are now riding an avalanche we have prepared and triggered. Our self-satisfaction and our self-worship is now in conflict with a renewal of penetrating doubt and of fear in the face of changes and implications that, to an unknown extent, are now beyond our control. This is so massive a change in our relation to the world as to constitute a new spiritual climate set in an era of a new physical climate.

My contention in this series of letters and meditations is that the gospel provides us with language and ways of being (and acting) that are well-matched to our times—well-matched in the sense that they can support active, compassionate, durable life and witness in these times and those that are coming toward us. Language and ways of being that can enable us to live increasingly available, joyful, and fearless lives in a time of dislocation, distraction, fear, and despair. In this way, climate change and the Anthropocene offer us a spiritual opportunity.

This is because we are facing something that is not a problem that can be solved by information and reasoning alone. It is that, without question! I am, after all, an ecologist, and science is of intrinsic importance in our spiritual engagement with our times. But science is not the only essential ingredient because we are also spiritual beings (as well as time-bound beings of music, imagination, emotion, and more).

We Are Formed in Forming

We act and shape our relationships and our environment (home, community, world) in our acting. Our acting often includes unintentional elements: when we vote, we are supporting some of the political conventions of our country. When we drive to work, we support the way that our society has organized work, transport, and indeed much of our economy as it creates and distributes wealth.

And this forming in turn forms us. It teaches us what we can expect, shapes our anxieties, what we can and should be satisfied with, and what is "normal" and therefore unthreatening to others or undemanding of them.

What we form or what form we uphold also shapes what we worship, what we revere. Paul, in his letter to the Romans, urges them (12:2) to what some translate as "reasonable worship" and others as "spiritual worship." The word used, *logikē*, implies "consistent with the story or account of reality that you accept and choose to live by"— again, that word *logos*.

Our formed society and the conventions by which it operates have for centuries formed us to uphold an order which teaches us to subordinate the commandment of love to political-economic systems that, in return, promise stability and a version of an adequate life. An obvious example is the assumed identity of religious and civil authority,[96] which in turn supports the replication of civil power structures in the organization of religious communities. We have produced forms of worship and definitions of spiritual health and faithfulness that are consistent (*logike*) with that model of the world (*logos*): "Getting and spending, we lay waste our powers.... We have given away our hearts, a sordid boon."[97]

But the bargain is breaking. It is not only that we are feeling the convulsions of climate and weather. More and more of us recognize

---

96   Hans Urs von Balthasar called this "the tragedy..of religious and political integralism" whose implications have shaped much of the history of our civilization. (von Balthasar 1988 *The Glory of the Lord: A theological aesthetics. V: The realm of metaphysics in the modern age.* San Francisco: Ignatius Press. pg. 31).

97   William Wordsworth, "The world is too much with us."

that the exploitive system that has brought us to this place has consumed (continues to consume) not just the substance of earth but also human lives, the physical, cultural, spiritual well-being of countless individuals. It is part of the justice that is being worked upon us that this very system of inequality and consumption is preventing us from acting together to redress our wrongs, to chart a different course. Though many of us (poor and rich, powerless and powerful) feel the imperatives of compassion and biophilia, the system itself is merciless. The merciless system predicating control and predictability on a model of humans as consumers (in which humans are among the natural resources to be consumed) can no longer pretend to deliver on its promises. We are entering a time of wandering and disorder.

Therefore, we need to intentionally walk in paths and act in ways that imagine and implement other kinds of order than what we have relied upon. Many will offer their own model for these emerging or alternative orders. We can offer one based in the gospel imperatives of truth, compassion, and unity with creation, but to envision it and live in it in a way that is as free as possible from the formation our civilization has given us, we must recognize that a new spiritual formation is a matter of urgency. We will be formed in our forming: our knowing, our reasoning, and our action and witness to the world must be rooted in reverence. This whole series of letters, as I have been led to and through it, is about putting that feeling into words in the hope that it can be helpful as others do their work.[98]

Up until now, I have been careful to use language and draw upon wisdom available to anyone who wishes to seek in the Christian tradition. I also have drawn from natural history for orientations and foundations that can help us live and act in the Anthropocene in a way that is consistent with the gospel, whose root and ground is love, the love of the Creator who sends the rain and sun to just and unjust alike. That love is demanding and indeed rigorous, so much so that

---

98 *Thou shalt love the Lord thy God with all thy* **heart**, *and with all thy* **soul**, *and with all thy* **mind**, *and with all thy* **strength**... All must be engaged: emotion, spirit, the life of the mind, and the will in action.

Also, I remember that natural selection does not operate on "genes," but on whole organisms. When it kills my chickens, the hawk isn't hunting for genes.

most people who hear about it abandon it, refusing the invitation to live it and embody it, replacing it with something more comfortable. We have constructed many elaborate arguments to disguise or justify our choice.

In the letters that follow, I want to tell you some things that I think my faith tradition, the Religious Society of Friends, can offer to the wider Christian community and perhaps beyond. Though we are a tiny thread in a vast great fabric, we have tried to shape our society and our prophetic witness in a process that acknowledges the dialogic nature of the gospel-as-incarnated. We have loved and sometimes taken seriously the idea of Christ as present teacher, risen and at work today.

We Quakers have done this haltingly, on a small scale, and not always successfully. We have many times failed in love and in truthfulness and have descended into quarrels, followed theological fashions, been too much "of the world." But year in and year out for nearly four centuries, we have returned chastened and grateful to the Teacher's feet and listened again to understand our errors and hear again our calling. We have learned something about listening worship, learning and action as members of the body of Christ, and the possibility of a social order that can emerge from that listening—and continue it rather than subverting or replacing it.

Reflection

How does listening happen in your spiritual practice? To whom or what are you listening? Does your spiritual community listen together as well? When does this bring unity, and when not? How does the listening relate to action?

Meditation: Call Me by Name

The common raven has remarkable vocal abilities, with vocalizations ranging from the deep croaking that is their most recognizable call to quiet musical songs often sung between mates. Gong-like noises, rattles, howls, and yells—one researcher wrote that if you're in the north woods, and you hear a sound you don't recognize, it probably is a raven.

Given ravens' high, flexible intelligence and complex social structures, it is no wonder that evidence is piling up that ravens have names—calls that are unique to each individual. These are not only used by the name-holder to announce their arrival or location ("Number six present and correct!"). Other ravens, who recognize individuals by a range of physical characteristics, also learn and use these names to address each other.

Bottlenose dolphins, belugas, sperm whales, and elephants also seem to know and to name each other and themselves. No doubt, other social animals do something similar: identity plays an important role in belonging, just as mortality is entailed by our individuality. But identity is experienced even by creatures that have no voice. We are surrounded by persons who are striving to live according to their kind. In the story of Eden, Adam is not creating scientific classifications—that comes later. He was naming individuals, seeing their being as blessed and distinct from his and yet akin.

Letter Twenty-seven: Re-enchantment and Gospel Order, on Being Ordered

Dear friend,

I argued in my last latter that, because we are facing a time of disruption and the loss of many certainties (or conventional wisdom about the way the world works), we have the opportunity to find our way into a way of living that can carry us into the future that is unfolding. And we can preserve the loving participation in creation that is, in itself, the hope that we need in a time of desolation—a time of grief and fear.

Introduction

Friends in their first emergence in the 1650s were convinced (like other spiritual innovators before and since) that they were feeling God's renewed intervention in their day: God, the prime mover, was once again moving amongst God's children in many parts of the world, among Christians and (they assumed) non-Christians alike. Christendom had for 1400 years strayed from and sometimes traduced the original message that Jesus was sent with and had replaced it with structures and doctrines that were entirely conceived of human imaginings. These structures and doctrines were designed more to satisfy human requirements than to reflect a covenant in which humans enjoyed a close relationship with God in return for living as God required as was required by God's nature. They freely admitted that there had been and were godly and faithful persons in all the various traditions of Christianity, but this was despite their participation in the apostate version of the church.

The first Friends brought this understanding to their encounters with non-Christians, including Native Americans, and their first response was intrinsically related to the Quaker understanding of the church as those called by Christ, responding in simplicity to that call within their contexts. The first Friends assumed that God was at work in all, and therefore, the first duty was to seek where this was perceptible, acknowledging these seeds of unity in the Spirit. George Fox, that great traveler and trumpet for "Primitive Christianity Revived," did not see it as his calling to convert any of these peoples but to proclaim the gospel, and "to answer that of God in every one." This meant trying to speak, to listen, and to live in a way that heightened the awareness of God's presence and power in our lives; Friends assumed that God would take care of the rest if only a person were in a "tender" state—convincement/conviction would follow. Thereafter, everyone was to "mind their call, that's all in all."

They also assumed that, if God had placed people in these various conditions, he had his own purposes in mind and would not leave them without guidance of a kind they of which they could understand and to which they could respond. After all, Paul preaches in the book of Acts that God, who allowed all nations to walk according to their own paths, "nevertheless…left not himself without witness" (through the works of Creation). One person's ministry might plant, another's might water, but it is God that gives the increase.[99]

Moreover, they saw or felt inwardly convinced that, if they were faithful to Christ the Teacher, they would be prepared and empowered

---

99   For the honor of Truth, I must note here that in later years as Friends were allowed to move to the North American colonies, they in many cases fell back from this vision, and their dealings with the First Nations, and enslaved people, reflected the invaders' values to a degree that is shaming to acknowledge.

to take part in Christ's work of reconciliation—between humans, between humans and God, and between humans and creation,

Gospel Order a Consequence of God's Nature: The Lawfulness at the Heart of Gospel Freedom

The central Quaker experience in those days of discovery was that "God has come to teach his people himself" (echoing the words of Isaiah 54 and Jeremiah 31).

Further, our God is not a god of confusion (or disorder); God holds truth and is truth, path, and life. The Quaker experience was that both individuals and groups could be guided by the same Spirit from which the prophets, Jesus, and the apostles spoke: "You will say, Christ saith this and Paul saith that. But what canst thou say?" Fox emphasizes that there is a difference between profession and possession and that merely saying is of no value; he quotes James, "Be ye doers of the word, and not hearers only."

Furthermore, Friends assumed that, as God had repeatedly called people to "perfection," that is, complete faithfulness, God must intend it to be possible and must be counted on to provide the help necessary for us to overcome the limitations of vision, strength, and endurance attendant upon the human condition. Therefore, God does not demand things that are beyond human capacity, any more than a parent could reproach a child for not being able to fly. They saw this perfection as a state that was dynamic: you didn't achieve it once and then remain immune from future error. It was a condition of faithfulness and freedom from sin that one could both live in and abandon, yet in God's power, one could become capable of returning to it.

But what is faithfulness, the godly life? How can you tell it when you see it? With all the overlays of culture and history since gospel times, it has had to be rediscovered, in part, by assiduous study of the biblical record but primarily by a close listening to God, who had not ever stopped teaching his people, though they may have largely ignored him. Although the gospel narratives were definitive, they were not complete, as Jesus said himself (John 16:12), and God's Spirit would continue to teach and guide people into fuller understanding and unity with the divine will. So there was a lot of undoing and a lot of discovering to be done, and as in the desert or in the Babylonian exile, God was an active participant in this as well.

Now, it was during a decade of intense persecutions that Fox began to think about how order and lawfulness should be evidencing itself if these people, his Friends, were really following God's teaching. In the early days, the strongest emphasis was on individual clarification of thought, so to speak, the individual evaluating their lives and what they worshipped and realizing that the path of Friends was what they were seeking. Thus, the individual soul was the sensor that detected God's requiring, always within a biblical framework.

Even during the earliest, most inchoate times, there were significant indications that Friends were not all following individual paths that only coincided accidentally but that the whole people were being drawn together and taught a way to live.

These early indications of righteousness discovered and realized in the light, Fox realized, must include some important elements of group life:[100]

- worship is an encounter with the living God, under the direction of the Spirit of Christ;
- decision-making can be undertaken as an act of worship and encounter in which the people seek, under Christ's direction, to shape their actions in accord with the Spirit;
- marriage is renewed as a covenant between the partners and not solemnized by any human authority;
- war with outward weapons and preparation for war are contrary to the Spirit of Christ;
- faithfulness results in a pattern of church leadership, not defined in terms of human qualifications such as formal education or state or hierarchical sanction but in the demonstration of power and the Spirit;
- gospel order should result in a lifestyle (speech, dress, business practices, use of resources, and so on) that is rooted in a daily, even hourly, watchfulness to the Spirit—a foundation

---

100   If some of these had been or would be discovered by others, this was only to be expected as consequence of guidance by the same Teacher.

for just conduct and the foundation for restorative action in the world;

- differences and disputes within the community can be and must be resolved in accordance with the guidance Jesus gives in Matthew 18.

I think it's clear that these are theology and also prophecy. Fox believed that, as God taught us and we received the teaching, such things would come clearer and clearer, and he coined the phrase Gospel Order to describe this system of public and private lawfulness, which was not to be developed by humans but that was revealed to the faithful and implemented as well as possible, as well as they could see. Fox knew that there might well be false trails and mistakes, but he was supremely confident that God wills our close and covenantal relationship with him, so one could rely on the Shepherd of Israel.

Gospel Order, Creation, and Re-creation

The early Quaker vision was of an order that, in the first instance, has to do with arrangements for decision-making and other aspects of human behavior consistent with the experience of the Light. However, this is part of a larger conception, a view of the right ordering of all things, which is an implication of God's action among us. Gospel Order in this cosmic sense is there to be discovered as we are led to it by the Light. Indications of its comprehensiveness can be drawn from the complex and thorough descriptions of the Sinai code. The different nature of order under the gospel has always been related to the passage in Matthew 18 in which the primary task, the removal of grievance, is laid first on the parties involved, then on a confidential support group, but finally on the whole community. This has been the pattern for the solving of disputes in many traditions, but Friends saw it as more than a technique, being instead part of the overall pattern of righteousness of God's design and revelation-in-the-moment.

Finding a Form in Which Hoping Can Continue

This comprehensive view of order flowing from the free Spirit, the way things come to work when all is in harmony with God's will, is related to a vision of the restoration of creation. Despite the successive covenants through which God has guided people over the centuries, the full restoration of unity between God and humanity is only possible through what Quakers call the inward work of Christ in which the restoration of creation is inseparable from our inward reconciliation. As that work proceeds, we can recognize God's longing to heal the beloved world and shape our actions to accord with that work.

Reflection

Perhaps there are ways that inward conflicts or still-healing wounds affect or hinder your faithful action in relationships, work, or social action. How does your prayer life or other discipline address these areas of disconnection? How might resolving one of these have a liberating effect?

Meditation: Minds in the Grass

A wolf spider—tiny, hairy, eight-eyed—moves with quick, short gestures, many-footed along the ground. Its bright eyes catch a glimpse of something moving, something just the right size—a fly landing on a nectar-bearing blossom. The spider freezes; then, slowly and deliberately, it finds a path upward, toward the now invisible prey. Its chosen path takes it to a leaf adjacent to the blossom and a little above. There's the fly head down, wings mostly still, lapping up the sweetness. The spider tenses to jump, but the fly moves around in the flower's center. The spider freezes, watches, plots a course to a new vantage point where it crouches and then leaps on to its supper.

In one experiment, a hunting spider is placed upon a little tower from which it can see two prey items. To reach them, the spider must climb down and cross a little pathway floating in a vessel of water. Then climbing up and over a low barrier from which again it can see and finally stalk its prey, it makes the whole journey with some persistent memory that supper is over there.

If you give the spider two possible bridges, one longer or less direct than the other, it pauses and then chooses the most direct path. If, while the spider is en route, you stealthily substitute the original prey with a different number of items, the spider upon getting within visual range again freezes and hesitates longer before making its final approach—surprised by the new situation, which is contrary to its expectation.

In some way, the spider is thinking. It sees and makes decisions and, to an extent, is no more automatic in its responses to its world than you or I.

As observers look further and further, closer and closer, there are minds discovered everywhere. It's only our lack of imagination, our not looking where we should have looked that made them invisible. Unseen is not the same as nonexistent; out of sight is out of mind but not out of world.

Letter Twenty-eight: Re-enchantment and Gospel Order, Kinds of Knowing

Dear friend,

Suppose we want to live with the truth of this time of climate catastrophe, feel the dangers and bear the pain, feel and face the fear, recognize our culpability, and yet respond to these truths in love, courage, and hope. I have been arguing that our spiritual challenge requires us to see with reverence and to liberate our seeing from the cultural boundaries between "human" and "nature," to see the living skin of the earth as your own, to feel that

> The force that through the green fuse drives the flower
> Drives my green age; that blasts the roots of trees
> Is my destroyer[101]

Then the energy of love to nurture and protect what is beloved and necessary can be tapped and freed for action.

I am arguing for or reminding you of a way to frame knowing and doing. As the "doors of perception" are opened wider,[102] there

---

101 "The force that through the green fuse drives the flower" in Dylan Thomas *Collected Poems* 1957. New York: New Directions. pg. 10.

102 "If the doors of perception were cleansed every thing would appear to man as it is, Infinite. For man has closed himself up, till he sees all things thro' narrow chinks of his cavern." William Blake, *The Marriage of Heaven and Hell.*

come new understandings of my need for spiritual liberation and of the pathways that invite and empower me toward that freedom in the Spirit. Thus, now is our chance to understand that our organic being as participants in nature, our longing and action to protect the living world (and ourselves), and our growth in joy and freedom in the perfection Christ invites us to—all these are facets of the same jewel, ingredients in the same life.

I often recall—with humility—Paul's declaration from 1 Corinthians that "we have the mind of Christ" (1Cor 2:16). It comes as the final element of a brief discussion of kinds of knowledge in relation to the new framing of reality offered by the gospel. In chapter 1, Paul has pointed out that the narrative of the crucified savior, in his experience, represents God's confounding of the usual ways of knowing as seen in the two cultures that Paul and his readers inhabit—that of Greece and that of Judaism.

The Greeks, in Paul's view, seek for wisdom, that is the wisdom of philosophy, which rests (for all its cultural limitations) on disciplined intellectual inquiry. Naturally, they see the gospel as simple folly. Paul's tradition, Judaism, seeks for signs. This translation of the Greek word *sēmeia*—"tokens, signs"—is usually taken to mean "prophetic signs" such as Jesus' miracles, which are seen as evidences of his supernatural powers (whether divine or demonic). As such, there has come to be an implication of irrationality or superstition (for example, in contrast with our enlightened condition or even that of the rational Greeks) that is, I think, wholly unwarranted.[103] I take it that, here, "signs" for Paul means "evidence of revelation," knowledge made available in prophecy seen to be true. For the Greeks, therefore, the gospel is foolishness, and for the Jews, its claim to be revelation is outrageous, a non-starter.

Paul, however, brings in a further consideration, which actually is in harmony with his understanding of the need for revelation (God's

---

103 On at least three counts. First, Paul accepted the fundamentals of Jewish faith and law, including the Torah as revelation of truth. Second, the Greeks were by no means exclusively "rational" (whatever that means)—as discussed long ago by E.R. Dodds in *The Greeks and the irrational*. Third, already by Paul's time the great Jewish tradition of dialectic reasoning was developing, that would in the next century begin to form the Talmud.

need and ours). We are talking, he says, about spiritual knowledge, knowledge that enables our faithfulness to God's commandments.[104] In his discussions about how we come to know the things worth knowing, Paul makes use of a theory about what a human is made of, and though it is not my model, I find it useful as a means of considering ways of knowing. It goes something like this:

You consist in several layers.

First, you have a body. This clearly has close affinity with the earth and, like the earth itself, is full of mystery. It is a source of kinship with the animal kingdom and a boundless source of sensation. It has no morals of its own, and its language is inarticulate and yet intense, a language of urges, reflexes, appetites, and impulses.

You also have a spirit. The spirit is un-earthly, immaterial, rational, and most accessible to the Divine. It works with concepts, ideas, logic, and inspiration. It comes to know by revelation, by reason, and by imagination. It plays a role in the exercise of the will, but the power of the will lives really in the soul.

The soul is somewhere in between the spirit and the body. The soul's language is articulated emotion and cause and effect. It is the strongest locus of personality and of the will because it is closely tied to the body but, like the spirit, is immaterial. It requires training and can either assimilate to the body or to the spirit so that one's soul and, therefore, one's personality can become more and more gross and earthy or more and more spiritual and heavenly, depending on how you make your choices and what spiritual goals you meditate upon.

The point is that each of these levels of being has its appropriate kinds of perception, of information, and of understanding. How do we balance them, and which takes precedence when we get competing messages? We know that the understanding that we get based on sense perception is often misleading; is spiritual perception any more trustworthy because it is less corporeal? But there is a bridge between the human knower and the revelations by the Spirit of Christ. With his dwelling in those who walk as children of his Light, we have his

---

104   The next few paragraphs are adapted from from *Treasure in Earthen Vessels: Letters to Corinthians and New Englanders on Christian Unity*. Worcester, MA: Mosher Book and Tract Fund of New England Yearly Meeting of Friends.

mind: it is shared with us, and we can know by it. When we are spirit people (*pneumatikoi*), we can know not only heavenly things but also the spiritual side of everyday life. We are given, as Rufus Jones had it, "new eyes for invisibles." This is the root of gospel freedom for all the members of the body of Christ, sharing the common life.

Paul clearly teaches that we need to "work out our salvation" in our life here (however near we are to the end-times), and so he often talks about different kinds of faithfulness, of the need for mutual support and nurture within the fellowship of the church, and for compassion for others whose faithfulness may require more accommodation than is required of others—the rule being that everyone should be fully persuaded in their own minds that the discipline they undertake (at this stage in their development) is the one that aligns them best with God's will.

Thus, our bodies and personalities not only do shape our discipleship but they must, and "everything works together for good" for those whom God loves, who are sincerely seeking to know God, to be transformed by the life of Christ taking shape within, and who do not judge each other but seek to build each other up.

Erasmus (following the early Fathers) suggests that it is precisely our embodiment that enables us to strive for perfection. As Sylvia Fitzpatrick (2012) argues, Erasmus sees a particular blessing from our incarnation in the divine pedagogy that comes with the limitations and temptations—the concrete realities—of our physical life in which we are formed to take delight in the other things of creation amongst which we are placed and grow inwardly with Christ's help (light and life) to understand and live past the temptations that come with our condition. As Erasmus writes in the *Enchiridion*,

> if the storms of temptation descend upon you more frequently and more violently, do not immediately begin to be dissatisfied with yourself as if you were not dear to your God or pleasing in his sight, or as if you were lacking in piety or any less perfect. On the contrary give thanks that he is training you as a future heir, chastising you as a dear son, putting you to the test as a friend. It is the greatest

proof that a man has been rejected by divine mercy when he is assailed by no temptations.

Isaac Penington comments, speaking from much experience with community disagreements:

> It is not an easy matter, in all cases, clearly and understandingly to discern the voice of the Shepherd, the motions of God's Spirit, and certainly to distinguish the measure of life from all other voices, motions, and appearances whatsoever. Through much growth in the truth, through much waiting on the Lord, through much fear and trembling, through much sobriety and meekness, through much exercise of the senses, this is at length given and obtained.

But the coming into a condition where we know the mind of Christ has additional implications for our engagement with the creation (bearing always in mind that Christ is known to be the Wisdom of God that permeates all creation), and here, George Fox and other early Friends have much to say about the renewing or the hallowing of knowledge.

Dwelling in the Spirit of Christ gives direct insight (inward sight) into the nature of creation. This insight, which is not propositional knowledge, gives a glimpse, at least, of the meaning of nature—its holiness and its shape and value. (Gerard Manley Hopkins and Thomas Merton after him spoke about a thing's "inscape," and Merton connected this truth-of-the-thing with the work and vision of Sophia, using Spinoza's *natura naturans*, nature naturing.) This perception is part of the "knowledge from above" because it is a gift of the Spirit.

Knowing Unity with the Creation

Getting inside creation is not an academic exercise, merely a way of knowing for its own sake, however delightful and important that learning can be. Our attitude and treatment of creation is essential to the realization of righteousness—right action must be of a piece with right understanding.

George Fox writes, early in his *Journal*, about the relation between humans and the rest of creation in terms of covenant. He finds himself standing in a covenant—and in that place, he realizes that the creatures who are necessary for our life and health are themselves in their own covenant with the Creator. It is through these covenantal relationships with the Creator that we have unity with the creation:

> I might not eat and drink to make myself wanton but for health, using the creatures in their service, as servants in their places, to the glory of him that created them; they being in their covenant [Gen. 9:9] and I being brought up into the covenant as sanctified by the Word which was in the beginning, by which all things are upheld; wherein is unity with the creation. But people being strangers to the covenant of life with God, they eat and drink to make themselves wanton with the creatures, devouring them upon their own lusts, and living in all filthiness, loving foul ways and devouring the creation; and all this is in the world, in the pollutions thereof, without God; and therefore I was to shun all such.[105]

Fox wrote a famous passage about the knowledge that became available after his *metanoia*. It can help us see how knowing is in the service of being, and our being, our inward condition, enables (necessarily) our truthful acting: faith without works is dead.

> Now was I come up in spirit through the flaming sword into the paradise of God. All things were new, and all the creation gave another smell unto me than before, beyond what words can utter.
>
> I knew nothing but pureness, and innocency, and righteousness, being renewed up into the image of God by Christ Jesus, so that I saw I was come up to the state of Adam which he was in before he fell.
>
> The creation was opened to me, and it was showed me how all things had their names given to them according to their nature and virtue. And I was at a stand in my

---

105 *Journal* pg. 2.

mind whether I should practice physic for the good of mankind, seeing the nature and virtues of the creatures were so opened to me by the Lord. But I was immediately taken up in spirit, to see into another or more steadfast state than Adam's in innocency, even into a state in Christ Jesus, that should never fall.... as people come into subjection to the spirit of God, and grow up in the image and power of the Almighty, they may receive the Word of wisdom, that opens all things, and come to know the hidden unity in the Eternal Being.[106]

Finally, the teaching of the Light that all creation is in covenantal relationship with its Creator (a modern conservation ethic would speak of species' intrinsic value as opposed to their use-value for humans) opens the door to the exploration of gospel order as a unified web that connects our individual conditions and life with that of our community and with the whole cosmos. The "bounded self" is re-connected—becomes more porous—as we are brought into the condition that our first parents were before the Fall—stronger than they could have been because of the unity in that Spirit of teaching and healing. And so we come to walk as Children in the Light, amidst all our kin—human and non-human.

People tend to think of the Christian gospel as human business, disconnected from the rest of earth—consonant with destructive views of human dominion over nature. But an understanding of the gospel—by which "God was in Christ reconciling the world to himself"—shows us a world drenched in the sacred, in whose diversity we are to take our place, rejoicing in it and accepting it as a gift from the Source, not only to us but to each element of creation. Each is in its own covenant with the Light and receives the gifts of life for its own thriving. Thus, our use of the creatures can again be saturated with sacramental understanding, and all the ways of knowing and being (heart, soul, mind, strength) can be harmonized to see, acknowledge, and incorporate

---

this understanding. This is part of our salvation, our liberation, our reconciliation (at-one-ment). This is a good gospel to preach!

Like many children, I dwelt for long in this understanding but never had anyone to put it into words (and thus share) except when a parent or friend would stop just to enjoy or remark upon a sight or sound, a creature or a place, the gulls playing on the wind. But then, at age eleven, I read this in the *Lord of the Rings*; it came as a gift and often still will bring tears:

> Haldir had gone on and was now climbing to the high flet. As Frodo prepared to follow him, he laid his hand upon the tree beside the ladder: never before had he been so suddenly and so keenly aware of the feel and texture of a tree's skin and of the life within it. He felt a delight in wood and the touch of it, neither as forester nor as carpenter; it was the delight of the living tree itself.

Reflection

Which kinds of knowing do you privilege or give most authority to in your use of time and other resources, in your relationship life and your social life? Which kinds of knowing are you unpracticed in or perhaps rely too much upon, and what makes you think so? How does your knowing relate to your acting?

Meditation: My Spring

There is a spring that, as a child, I found in the woods beyond the stone fence at the foot of our south field. I had never been so far before—right out of sight of the house. I ventured past the sentinel appletree, which I remember being huge and knarled, tatooed all over by decades of sapsucker excavations in neat rows whose regularity reminded me of the pips on dominos.

There was a gap in the wall a fathom wide where, somehow, the dewberry briars and poison ivy that curtained the stones took a break, too, and the eves of the wood hung down the way a thatched roof overhangs a Cotswold cottage door (an image that came to me from children's books about children or talking animals far away or long ago).

Behind the leafy curtain, there was an open space, walled and roofed by trees and brush and with the carpet of leaves so old and thick that it silenced footsteps and made the whole room quiet.

Right in the center was a circle of water an arm's length wide. I crept to the brink and saw that someone long ago had sunk there a wooden barrel with no top or bottom so that its top rim was level with the ground, and the bottom was paved in white sand, specked with fragments of leaf and bark. Up through the sand, water welled up quietly, keeping the barrel always full, the surplus trickling away where one or another stave had crumbled or been broken off to let the water out. The water was like moving, smoky glass, but the shifting shapes that formed and disappeared on the surface were minute and unhurried.

The silent, unhurried, ever-replenished spring had no doubt been used in years past to fill a few buckets for watering plants or horses, and sometimes I would come and draw some water out for places in our vegetable patch that the garden hose could not reach.

But I fell into the habit of slipping down the hill to sit on the stones I'd placed in the welling-hall, knowing what it would be like in the company of my spring; peace would come over me like twilight as I passed the guardian tree and stepped through the opening in the stone wall. The spring and its attendant trees surrounded me like a cloak with warmth and the freedom of reverie and of gratitude.

When contemplation is hard to come by, alone or in the silence of a meeting for worship, I still in spirit walk down that hill and pass the tree and sit beside my holy well, received and receptive again.

Letter Twenty-nine:
Becoming Adequate to Our Times

Dear friend,

As I write, May is halfway gone; the violets and lilacs are in full spate, and the yellow of early cresses and the white of wild cherries are seen all around. In my garden yesterday, I had to replace some annual flowers killed by a late freeze. As I worked, I wondered: What does a flower mean?

I know what a flower is and what a flower does, and I know, too, something about what flowers can mean when they are gathered for gifts or displays. But when I see the flowers opening, each in its season and its place, at some wordless level, they speak to me of wholeness and the rhythms of health and renewal. No wonder that Hildegard spoke of greenness as evidence of spiritual as well as physical wellness, wholesome activity and alignment with the divine life.

It is as a person, a living being, that I can see or smell a blossom. Indeed, it is an individual living thing that feels any delight or sorrow. It is particular people whose homes have been consumed by the wildfires in this era, scratched up in this blazing era, whose land is washed away by the thousand-year floods that are now happening many times in a decade, who die of despair when their farmland has become so dry the greenness cannot return of their time, not soon enough to salvage their lives and their living. So it is for every delight and every calamity that befalls any creature. Breath, nurture, protection, courtship, flight, exaltation, grief, and pain.

By contrast, corporations, governments, nations, and other idols cannot do these things:

> They have mouths but they cannot speak: Eyes have they, but they see not: They have ears but they hear not: Noses have they but they smell not: They have hands but they handle not : Feet have they but they walk not: Neither speak they through their throat. (Psalm 115, KJV)

Nor can they feel sympathy or guilt, and having no conscience, they are moved by calculation, and their calculations are in the service of the entity's purpose, expressed as procedures, processes, and budgets.

Many corporations and policy makers have invested heavily in teaching the public at large that, if you are moved by the need for action against climate change (for example), the right expression of this concern is in consumer choices that you make, household conservations, and what some politicians contemptuously relegate to personal virtue. Millions of dollars are spent in this tutelage, and it is deceitful and intentional misdirection. Individual choices and lifestyle changes cannot solve the great challenges of the Anthropocene—climate change, mass extinction, the pervasive influence and damage of industrial chemicals now so much a part of our life on earth that we take them in with our first taste of mother's milk. It is true that, if we are to avoid the worst that can be foreseen, coordinated action on a very large scale will be necessary—action that usually we are accustomed to accomplish through organizations such as governments, corporations, and alliances.

Things cannot act except by will of the people that constitute and operate them. It is policymakers, individual men and women, that license or forbid strip mines, subsidize oil companies and factory farms, direct resources in such a way that individuals must use cars and give them no alternative: individuals choose to require no prior determination of the effects of industrial chemicals; individuals choose to place few restraints on polluters of air, soil, and water. So we have come to a desperate situation in which collective action can be constructive and is necessary to the preservation of livable conditions for ourselves and other creatures in the next few years and beyond. At present, however, collective action is driving us in the wrong direction, and large resources are directed at ensuring that no change of direction will take place.

And yet, the individual is pivotal. Solutions to climate change cannot be made on the basis of individual choice even though it is individuals who suffer. Even though it is individuals whose consciences are led to choices. Why is it so easy to ignore that?

People being organisms find that their bodies are an inexhaustible source of impulse into desire. This renders them, from each new birth, a potential source of threat to the system. They may not naturally and without complaint subscribe to the worldview that's most supportive of the way our structures and systems work. Morever, when people's desires are informed by reverence, by the desire for peace, and the joy of mutual care, they are, to that extent, made more sensitive to the imperatives and temptations of greed, anger, isolation, and prejudice. Prophetic diagnosis can lead to prophetic speech and action.

The powerful understand that the operations of the market are a way to translate and contain desires they find disturbing to their place and to their peace. "To save the world, click here." Market forces and processes have been heavily theorized and studied so as to make them predictable and, in a world full of stochastic events, manageable. And much art and craft is aimed at teaching people that the way to act on their desires and needs is as consumers of products. People committed to education have long understood the importance of life-long learning. But much of what is pitched as educational is actually marketing or even propaganda. The powerful know that people have desires and reflections that could unsettle or even threaten the status quo. The most effective tools for control are mind-forged manacles.

It is a consequence of our society's illness that choice is so often construed as consumer choice. "Getting and spending, a sordid boon." This is a way to channel people's emotional reactions to damage and decay resulting from collective action, collective guilt, collective insight. Any culture or large human enterprise like a nation includes values instilled by those in power. While the hegemony may include some benevolent results, the systems include protections of privileges, and all the privilege of accumulated wealth brings many material benefits.[107]

One of the most effective tools for disarming moral response is the idea of "collateral damage," which gained wide visibility in the United States during the Vietnam War. If you say, "You can't make an omelet without breaking eggs," it doesn't sound so bad, but if you hear, "We had to destroy the village to save it," you might suspect that there is a need for closer examination. Yet it is a commonplace that the suffering of some people, the damaging of a landscape, the extinction of a species, or the pollution of the atmosphere is considered worth it because the benefits outweigh the costs for most people.

This collateral-damage thinking is, among other things, a way to deflect guilt or to diffuse responsibility—if I can be convinced that I am a beneficiary of some unjust action, I can be persuaded to overlook my responsibility for the injustice, especially if there are many of us benficiaries. Diffuse responsibility, related in complex ways to distributed causality, is both a balm to the individual conscience and a protection of privilege because it is taken to disarm or invalidate or supersede other moral values. Indeed, the system under which we live even sees fear or moral outrage as an exploitable resource, grist for the mill, and so products can be marketed as "green alternatives" even

---

107 A current example is "carbon footprint" which like other "greenwashing" has taken a true thing—the patterns of individual consumption and resource use have an important measurable impact on carbon and methane emissions—and has amplified and construed it in such a way as to divert attention or moral demand away from privileged and powerful actors (for example fossil fuel businesses). The extent to which evasion and impunity has been a conscious aim of corporations' "educative" activities has been documented in recent years, as proprietary secrets have emerged, see *Exxon: The road not taken* by N. Bannerjee et al. published by *Inside Climate News* (2015), also Solnit (2021) and Kaufman (2021)

when they are not because purchasing them can quiet or crowd out the small voice in which conscience speaks.

But the word of God (who knows when even a sparrow falls) to us is this: "Inasmuch as you have done it to these the least of my brethren, you have done it to me." The gospel life cannot overlook the plight of the vulnerable and unprivileged, the powerless and voiceless, or those who do not fit inside the categories that support the culture of exploitation. If we are followers of that Teacher, how can we not cast off habits and values that serve unfeeling, unseeing, unknowing idols, systems and tools that have been revealed to be anti-life and therefore against the Lord of Life? Once we see, we can only choose: Shall we remain in our sin, or shall we enact reconciliation?

An ordering of affairs that is consonant with the gospel, that follows the Word, calls us to the discovery of a radically different approach to our deciding and administering, rooted in reference and relying on the guidance of the Spirit of Christ rather than the spirit of the age or the *spiritus mundi*.

The unassailable foundation is love, which is also truth, the truth that frees from fear. So our decision-making or our building or reconstruction of culture and society must keep us always listening to that guide. So, the first fundamental test of our devices is, does it preserve an actual awareness of the spirit of love?

Such a test will ask us to address a range of challenges:

How do we understand the body of Christ (1 Corinthians 12) in a multicultural world, whose views of Christianity are colored by the excesses, perversions, and evils perpetrated by those who claim the name of Christ?

How do we balance the freedom of the Spirit with institutional memory and tradition, which are so important as resources for stability, pedagogy, and creativity?

How do we remember that order is not hierarchy? It does not mean designing and putting in place a grid or matrix or tree of power. Order rests on the identification of functions, placing individuals in a function, of support for the function, in support of the occupant, of truthful but charitable critique.

How do we stay flexible and so alert to the presence (or absence) of the love of Christ that we are not dismayed by diversities of approach?

How does a Christian live according to the gospel order in a shared coalition with others whose work is good to support, though they do it for different reasons than we might?

How do we accept and live with the fact that emergent order can't be all spontaneous? People need to use their minds. God is not the author of confusion.

How do we incorporate the fundamental duty of praying toward unity? This is needed for many reasons. First, each of us must focus our work within our own scale and capacity while encouraging others to be faithful in other ways. It is not enough to assert "many gifts, one Spirit." We have to be able to see—see it enough that we understand and feel so that our gratitude is warm and personal.

Now, you will say (and I have said myself) that this is too retail, too small-scale a response. But the ministry of Jesus began with a baby and ended with an execution. So, too, the stirrings in conscience and the experiments in seeking an order that reflects the gospel values, the prophetic values, the mandate to love: these have always seemed paltry and contemptible, even in the eyes of those who profess their faith. As James Nayler wrote,

> Many are ashamed at the Lamb's appearance, it is so
> low, and weak, and poor, and contemptible, and many
> are afraid seeing so great a power against him.

All this leads me now to the process of prophetic inquiry and action that Quakers have called the Lamb's War. By this, they encompassed both their inward struggles for personal liberation and their recognition, led by the Spirit, that one's progres toward full availability to the Holy Spirit must result in outward change.

The life engaged in the Lamb's War becomes tender and open to injustice and violence, outwardly as well as inwardly. The human soul, your soul, can be seen as a nexus, a confluence or focus of forces tending both to your good and ill. Some of the evils can be seen as external—sources of fear, oppression, or distraction. Others are apparently inward—anger, self-indulgence, and so on. Yet we are so constructed that we and our environment interpenetrate. Inward and outward forces activate or counteract each other. Because it is this kind of meeting place, the human soul is an appropriate battlefield upon which to begin the war against outward evils in the world. More than this—if the battle remains unfought in any soul, then in our unredeemed regions, seeds of sin and death lie as in an incubator from which they can spread abroad anew. The Lamb's War against the Man of Sin, in which we use the weapons of Jesus, acting at first upon our little, inward stage, is as well a social as it is, indeed, a revolutionary act.

The soul has its life cycle, just as the body does. We must claim holiness as our proper goal, but we can adopt for ourselves no outward attribute of it before, by grace, we come to it in truth, nor can we attempt what we are not prepared for by the Spirit's working. Whatever we may have seen, thought, or accomplished, we must seek always to participate in the birth of the poor Child.

If we seek for the light, dwelling in meekness, we see ourselves as we are, in both our weakness and beauty, as God's growing children. The encounter with the Light of Christ is judgment but also consolation: by accepting the former, we gain the latter. In both, we are brought closer to our brothers and sisters, empathizing in their judgment and reinforcing their consolation. This path of growth results from being teachable and faithful to a living God who is the God of the living. The counterfeit, which is the worship of the works of our hands (or constructions of our minds), has a very different result. Psalm 115 comments that those who worship such idols become like them, unhearing, unseeing, and unalive.

Reflection

Salvation lies in God's hand, not in our will. We so want to know the end before the beginning, to keep control of outcomes, to make good bargains and careful investments of ourselves. God's life will work transformation that is also fulfillment through choices, opportunities, and sorrows that we cannot arrange or predict ahead of time. We risk nothing by offering all.

Meditation: Nancy

As it does on every morning, the teacher's commute takes her past the long concrete walls topped with barbed wire, the watch towers, the blocks of faceless buildings within the compound. On this morning of all mornings she wonders about the people inside. No mission, no outrage, no message arises in her yet. The feeling is akin to curiosity, a little nudge, a little light and awareness play on that unwelcoming construction.

The women inside, still faceless, stay with her. In her contemplation, in the silence of her worshipping community, in the wordless activities of the garden or the kitchen, they visit her, and the little gleam of connection draws her toward doing something specific. Is there a way that she could get inside? What task or purpose might there be for a teacher who is drawn by a germinating relationship of relatedness to the women whose faces and names and conditions she does not know?

She finds someone to ask and discovers that, in the prison, there is a library. She offers to come there sometimes with new books or to have conversations or to lead discussions. Way leads on to way, and as she comes to know the people and the system, new openings to service suggest themselves and sometimes are permitted. The teacher who has rarely acted as advocate or apostle grows into the skills of negotiation, argumentation, advocacy, invitation, narrative.

When she's on this path, she feels the light of it; despite the anxieties, she feels the peace of it; despite her sense of insufficiency, she feels her power in it; and on the path, she learns to see and hear and interpret the glances and gestures and tones of voice that express acceptance, interest, resistance, rejection, opportunity.

All this while, her worshipping community makes encouraging noises and assures her of their love, but they don't really *know*. Her prayer, her opening, her sense of revelation are not yet taken into the contemplative life, the worship, the encounter with the divine in which she shares. The sense of distance is painful and perplexing, but since the service she is called to is for the women in the prison and not to educate her community, her new growth is not yet end-grafted into her community's life. Sometimes she will say, "Come and see."

The gift of response comes simply, when first one and then another of her brothers and sisters in the worship accept the invitation, enabled by love and relationship, to pass over the trepidations and doubts about what may lie ahead. She has learned and helps them see that, in the actual act, things are pretty simple: you go to the place, you enter the door, you speak to those who can give or refuse permission for entry, and if the door opens inward, in you go. Then you meet people, individual people, and if, as you come, you are teachable and simple, you find a way to spend time together.

Over the years, the teacher grows in her understanding, her scope in companionship; she becomes adequate to the challenges and opportunities offered her for service. Not always without doubt, not always without mistakes, not always without setbacks or anger or sorrow, yet a path keeps opening and grows wider as her understanding and her own inward dimensions grow.

In that growth, her community, in its measure, participates, and her example helps the community learn how to see the emergence of service in others and their community, other services, other needs and opportunities, other struggles. It is in such work that a worshipping community can become, in truth, a school of prophets, of servants under command who when the Lord says go, they go, and when the Lord says abide, they wait. In their listening and their doing, their learning and their transformation, they make their offering: a troubled and contrite spirit, a cheerful giver, a child of the light, each contributing to the common life that they do not own but in which they find their home.

Part Three: The Lamb's War—Worship, Praxis, and Proclamation for a Time of Climate Crisis

Meditation: Elephant Knowing

It is not only humans who know the world. Every bird or fish within its breeding territory, every animal within its home range, frames a part of the world, imagines it, and fills the imagination with knowledge, according to its nature. It defines and defends boundaries, perhaps, but it also knows the landscape intimately: vantage points, safe spots, water sources, the places where groceries may be found or lodgings. It comes to know where predators may be and learns its land as a network of pathways and possibilities. So well does it learn its place that it can quickly see the new and unusual and undertake an inquiry to understand it.

An elephant may live fifty or seventy years. Because it is of great size, it makes great demands upon its habitat, and the demands are all the greater because elephants are social animals. Over its long life-time, an elephant and its community encounter much variation from year to year—floods, droughts, fires, feasts, foes, famines, and oddities.

No wonder that memory matters, and an intelligence great enough to consider alternatives, evaluate possibilities, negotiate group decisions, solve problems, and remember the solutions. Diversity of personality matters: curiosity, sensitivity or irritability, reflectiveness, strategic thinking, docility, and decisiveness—all these contribute to the wisdom of the herd and make use of the knowledge of the herd. The matriarch leads and integrates the herd's wisdom with her own direct experience of the herd members and of the land upon which they live—its resources and the rhythms of the year, the trials and routines of an elephant's life.

The elephant, the honey bee, the hunting cat, the mole and finch, the vulture and the restless-minded primate—these each and all know the landscape in ways unique to themselves, just as humans do. If the Creator speaks sometimes in the language of organisms, each of them makes its own meaning of the common world, and it is only known by all these knowers together. How much we have to say to each other!

Letter Thirty: The Lamb's War

Dear friend,

Here is the opportunity that climate change offers us: to end at last our lukewarmness, our accommodation, and our complicity with the spirit of the age. We can, if we choose, finally grapple with the divine invitation to be transformed by the renewing of our minds, allowing ourselves to be conformed to the mind of Christ. This change in understanding is not only a preliminary to transformative action but also a consequence of experimental living in which contemplation and community responsibility provide a climate of attentiveness to the qualities, the nature of our acting or withholding action. I believe that the Quaker vision of the Lamb's War represents a way to concretely unify contemplation and worship, individual and community spiritual formation, and principled and prophetic action under the constraint of gospel love

Why the Lamb's War?

Every time I use the phrase, "the Lamb's War," I feel uneasy because of my revulsion against the evil and folly that is war and against the versions of "spiritual warfare" being used to design oppression and cultural-political injustice.[108] Yet, as William James **pointed out,** "war" is a powerful metaphor precisely because it has come to evoke not only images of its evils and folly but also the intense marshalling of intention, ingenuity, resources, and highly romanticized but often true accounts of war's power to evoke human characteristics such as courage, determination, and social cohesion.

The Lamb's War image arose among Quakers as they emerged in a time of social unrest, religious turmoil, and civil war—shaped in part by climatic changes in the preceding century, small in comparison with what we are facing but enough to reshape England's way of life.[109] It was a time of disorientation and for many a time of desolation in the loss of certainties and the questioning of values. The Anthropocene, even in its early years, promises such desolation.

The great early Quaker exposition of the Lamb's War was written by James Nayler around 1656. In that era, titles tended to present an abstract of the whole work and might well fill up much of the title page with statements of the key theses to be addressed. But here I want only to remind you of the first full declaration in Nayler's title: *The Lamb's War Against the Man of Sin.* The phrase, "man of sin," suggests much about the diagnosis of our times and therefore the challenge that Christians face.

The phrase comes from the second letter to the Thessalonians and denotes the great opponent of God's reconciling work. The Greek text speaks of the "person of lawlessness"[110] or "the lawless one," but the King James translation that Nayler would have used rendered this as "the man of sin." In any case, Nayler sees the man of sin as both a damaged inward condition of individuals and as the outward results in society and culture of this damage—results that are maintained and reinforced, in turn, by individuals' assent or consent to the perpetration.

---

108 Drayton 2024 The Lamb's War and "spiritual warfare": reflections on a dangerous metaphor. Amorvincat.wordpress.com

109 Geoffrey Parker has written *Global Crisis*, a deep study of climate change and its ramifications in the seventeenth century (Parker 2013).

110 The Gk uses *anthrōpos*, which like Latin *homo* just means a human being with no assertion of male sex.

> A king has soldiers, servants, messengers, lieutenants. He
> governs through his servants. Where are the servants of
> this—Anti-king? In our minds, lad. In our minds. The
> traitor, the self; the self that cries I want to live; let the
> world burn so long as I can live! The little traitor soul
> in us, in the dark, like the worm in the apple. (Ursula
> LeGuin, *The Farthest Shore*)

The work of the man of sin as Nayler sees it has several roots:
untruth, fear, love of power, over-consumption—all aspects of a kind
of idolatry that, holding nothing in reverence that does not reinforce
its illusions, easily reaches for violence to maintain its position and en-
force its preferences and its webs of deceit (some intentional and some
delusional). If we are to follow instead the Lamb that was slain by the
man of sin and yet is a living force in opposition, we need to recognize
that positive thinking and uneasiness (or even panic) at the signs of the
times are not enough.

Times ruled by the oppressions of untruth and violence favor the
emergence of prophecy in word and deed. Whose prophet, whose
messenger, will you be? And how can you or how can I engage in action as a free soul, free from the methods and aims of the oppressing
regime in which we are all participants? That is the Lamb's War.

The Scope of the Anthropocene Challenge

Violence, mendacity, and oppression are the hallmarks of the powers
currently making decisions about the welfare and treatment of humans and our necessary biosphere. Since the first detailed warnings
about climate change were widely published more than thirty years
ago, the collective response of humanity has hewed fairly closely to the
worst-case scenarios of carbon emissions from deforestation, fossil fuel
combustion, and other sources. Major oil companies knew—in the
1970s—what the consequences of continued and accelerating fossil
fuel use would be. (The trustworthiness of the scenarios, despite many
uncertainties, came from their being based on physics established
roughly a century before.) Nevertheless, the oil companies chose to
keep quiet and continue as usual. They and their allies have spent

millions of dollars propagandizing against the science and its implications and teaching by many methods that the way things have been done are natural and right and that the laws of economics (as construed by neoliberalism among other schools) are as unavoidable as gravity or thermodynamics.

At present, we have entered upon a climate that humans have never experienced during the existence of our species. The consequences are just starting to be felt. Because the climate system is actually made up of thousands of interacting systems, from local to global, the transformation of a pro-human climate to a much more anti-human climate takes a while to gain momentum (this is a good time to think about **exponential growth**, one of many ideas that matter.) Also, the changes build on each other. The one thing that's been a constant is that just about every milestone of climate impacts has come faster—much faster—than expected.

The power of denial (self- and other-) is strong in our species, in part because we live by stories and are in the grip of imagination.

> "Oh, what a lovely owl!" cried the Wart.
>
> But when he went up to it and held out his hand, the owl grew half as tall again, stood up as stiff as a poker, closed its eyes so that there was only the smallest slit to peep through—as you are in the habit of doing when told to shut your eyes at hide-and-seek—and said in a doubtful voice
>
> "There is no owl."
>
> Then it shut its eyes entirely and looked the other way.
>
> "It is only a boy," said Merlyn.
>
> "There is no boy," said the owl hopefully, without turning round."
>
> (from T. H White: *The Once and Future King*)

While frogs will not, in fact, sit in a pan of gradually heating water until they are boiled to death (frogs regulate their temperature by moving away from unacceptable conditions), because of our power of denial (spinning alternative narratives) people do things that fit the fable very well. This natural human response to unpleasant trends has been exploited by those who profit from the way things are, reinforcing with false claims and false hope the illusion that what we would like is the truth of the matter. As a result, the future is going to be pretty bad, and it's started to arrive.

The Relation Between Individual and Cosmic Welfare and Reconciliation: Beyond Tokenism

The broken relationship between humans and God also means a broken relation between humans and the material world. When a modern person reads a declaration that some social evil (poverty, oppression, hubris, war) arises from the lusts, as in the Epistle of James, it is hard to feel the logic, the intensity of the statement, because we don't read "lust" as something like "unbridled exploitation or consumption," which is part of what is meant. Any time a human desire or impulse is so indulged or exercised as to violate the constraints of love—of God and one's neighbor—lust is involved. This may be seen in an individual's conduct—or in a mindset, a shared attitude, which is accepted without reflection.

When such an unquestioned assumption is so widespread as to affect how wealth, resources, and power are used, then the individual becomes social and creates norms that reinforce and justify the error—normalize it. Slavery was such a norm; so also the view of women as chattels or subordinates to men or the exploitation of the many by the few that takes such forms as state capitalism (in the United States), Soviet-style command economies, and fascisms and racisms of many kinds. (Of course, none of these is really in the past, as anyone can see.)

It is part of the lust-dominated system we live in to somehow regard environmental crimes as not serious because to recognize them for their immorality would imply that the lust would need to be restrained or eliminated. Into this category fall such things as the unrestrained use of fossil fuels once their implications were understood; the relatively unrestrained poisoning and exploitation of fresh water, soil, and air; the wholesale destruction of natural systems like forests and grasslands in the service of short-term profits or the indulgence of unsustainable lifestyles.

You can't live centered in the conscious, intentional attitude of respect and justice that is at the heart of the love of the gospel and the greatest commandments (love of God and love of neighbor) and truthfully reconcile yourself to elements of a society—or of oneself—that are enchained by such lusts. Your behavior—my behavior—is part of the broader society, and participation without dissent (when insight comes) is to reinforce the norm.

To truly see one's complicity is to feel pain and be open to motions to change, to seek relief from that pain. So, just as I do in my own life, society finds ways to disperse responsibility and split hairs so as to insulate some kinds of evil against criticism. Thus it's no coincidence that lust has come to mostly connote sexual violations, though the earlier force of the word lingers in phrases used with little force, such as "lust for power."

And of course, the system of economics that rules us has evolved to protect privilege so that those who benefit (or long to benefit) from the way things are can continue to do so relentlessly. Consequently, even though the system is constituted of persons, it has such power and complexity that individual impulses to protest or live according to (even slightly) different values are likely to be crushed under the weight of the norm.

Thus, as acute moral reasoners in every age and culture have felt and said, the reconciliation of individual conscience and spiritual health is bound up with social and systemic ills—in effect, without some change of awareness, we are helping to maintain the prison in which we are held; we wear chains that we are taught to see as adornments, when they are truly signs of unfreedom: "mind-forged manacles."[111]

---

111   William Blake, "London": *In every cry of every Man,/In every Infant's cry of fear,/In every voice: in every ban,/The mind-forg'd manacles I hear*

The Nature of the Lamb's War

The Shepherd of Israel's revelation through Jesus gave us a human incarnation of the message of the prophets, in demonstration and in power. Disconcertingly, this first-born of many siblings fit few expectations, preaching as the Son of Man and announced by John the Baptizer as the "lamb of God." His miracles showed us that God is still present and sovereign in the very elements of earth—"even the winds and the sea obey him"— yet he exercised no earthly power beyond that of word and example. His healing and his teaching always carried also the message of inward wholeness, of reconciliation with God and neighbor. ("Your sins are forgiven....take up your bed and walk.") And his Gethsemane struggle and crucifixion in loyalty to his calling and to God laid open a way to see how God's power is perfected in our weakness. God's wisdom contradicts the vaunted wisdom of the powers and principalities with which we are to contend.

The testimony to God as Lord of the elements and the fruitful, teeming earth is expanded or deepened by the testimony of the disciple whom Jesus loved, to whose narrative the name John is attached in the opening hymn to *Logos*, the creating and healing message of light and life. Through this, we see that the Christ is engaged in a work of reconciliation that is the same impulse as the work of wisdom (Sophia) that has gone on since the beginning of things.

So the Lamb's War is conducted at every level of the personality, including our social life and the life of all our works and workings and embraces us as ecological beings as well as artistic, thinking, and passionate organisms. Nothing, in the end, can be excluded from the challenge, the wounding, and the healing of the Light. We are invited to live in the spirit whose "hope is to outlive all wrath and contention, and to weary out all exaltation and cruelty, or whatever is of a nature contrary to itself," and in that spirit to see the world whole. This is relevant to the climate crisis, which is so comprehensive and systemic in its scope, causes, and consequences, that we cannot any longer take some comfort in small personal gestures.

Research on climate change communication has shown that people are more willing to hear the truth of the crisis—the science and its implications—when they are also given information about some specific path forward, a way to act—"What can you do?" This helps people begin to wrestle with fear and despair. At this point, recycling and home insulation are useful but nowhere near an adequate response. Market solutions, to the extent that they possibly could have helped, are too slow and too voluntary to help now on their own. (And recent reporting keeps providing evidence that the captains of industry are not to be relied upon in this regard, despite their greenwashing rhetoric.)

As Naomi Klein wrote, "This changes everything." Half measures won't do as we struggle to live in this time when judgment is coming down on us, and the grapes of wrath are being gathered and pressed into a bitter vintage. How can we meet the challenges we face, accepting the powers against which we struggle—we who are part of the problem—while finding wells of hope and power to draw from? How do we speak both hard truths to power (even in ourselves), seeing and naming the sinfulness of sin and, at the same time, the love of God and neighbor?

The Epistle to Laodicea (Ironically) Speaks to Our Condition

In the third chapter of the book of Revelation, there are letters to several churches (meetings), and for years, I have been haunted by the letter to Laodicea:

> Thus says the Amen, the faithful Witness and true, the foundation of the creation of God: I know your behavior, that you are neither cold nor hot—If only you were cold or hot! But since it is the case that you are lukewarm, neither hot nor cold, I am about to spit you out of my mouth. Because you say "I am rich and have prospered, and I need for nothing," and you don't see that you are wretched and pitiable and poor and blind and naked.[112]

This diagnosis cuts me to the heart, and I stand convicted—but so I believe do most of us. It is so easy to be good enough! Yet we are

---

112 Revelations 3:14–17

called to be saints, we are called to be holy, in unity with the God of love.

What could it mean, not to be lukewarm? You know the answer, really.

> We would take seriously that we are to seek first the kingdom of heaven and its righteousness
>
> by following the promptings of truth when they come;
>
> by seeking to learn from others along the way—the afflicting teachers as well as the comforting—and seeing to embrace the whole gospel message (however we need to translate it into our individual spiritual language) from incarnation to resurrection;
>
> by telling each other with joy and trepidation what we are learning from and in the Spirit, however we name it;
>
> by seeking for the places where we know the fear of the Lord— the sense of awe that announces our deepest commitments and orientation;
>
> by placing expectations upon each other:
> - seeing people's gifts and urging and expecting each other to use them as fully as we can,
> - acknowledging our spiritual poverty,
> - recognizing where the Seed is oppressed in us and in others, and
> - learning to pray in spirit and in action to accept God's invitation to reconcilation;
>
> by growing so clear and confident about the power of our shared spiritual encouters that we have no hesitation in inviting people to join us in the experience of living with a living God.

In short, it would mean functioning, not as denominational organizations but as vital spiritual communities on quest. Such communities' entry key is the longing to travel together along a path tried, tested, and reconstructed over the past nearly four hundred years and in which good standing consists in putting in the time, day by day, alone and together in work that is at the same time mystical, prophetic, and practical. ("Yea, the work of our hands, establish Thou it!"[113])

Therefore, Climate Change Presents Us with an Opportunity

Climate change is going to change the meaning—the context and the consequences—of almost everything. Addressing it will involve a wholesale revolution in our relationship to the rest of creation. (Cherice Bock spoke at our yearly meeting of an ecological reformation, which captures much of the scale of the thing). As I have been arguing in this long series, it also requires of us a re-evaluation of our understanding of Christ and the gospel, seeing for the first time how indeed it is cosmic and how our individual acts of faithfulness relate to God's work, reconciling the world to Godself.

Now is our chance (not the first, and I hope not the last) for us to turn ourselves and all we possess into the channel of universal love and to grow into the understanding of the gospel and of spiritual growth that provides us a powerful, effective, and integrated method for growing into a true camp of the Lord and fellowship of the children of the Light. And for explaining what God is doing among us, rejoicing to see the Light break forth in any. It is our chance for freedom since the gospel, the good news, is the power of God for liberation.

And this is why I have come to feel that the Lamb's War is a meaningful way to think of how I, an individual in a community, can respond to the challenges of our time (with their roots in history and their seeds of the future). In the next few letters, I will explore some facets of this process and then conclude this series of letters.

Reflection

What is the community that you feel most loyalty to? In what ways does that community support you actively in seeking for a life of more clarity and courage? What resources for faithfulness does your community provide? Do you share your longing for a community that

---

113 Ps. 90:17 KJV

can welcome the Inward Teacher, the one who calls those who are listening to prophetic word and deed, reading the signs of the times?

Meditation: Exquisite Tunings

In May and June (spring in the nothern hemisphere), the horseshoe crabs swarm onto the beaches of Delaware bay. Their numbers are greatest, then, with the full tides of the new moon or the full moon. Not all wait for these highest of tides, but three of the animals' nine eyes are used to detect the ultraviolet light direct from the sun and reflected from the moon. This helps them track the lunar cycle; it may be that other eyes in the telson (tail) calibrate its biological clock with daylight. There is much knowing built into the design of the horseshoe crab, and who knows what a crab might learn over the course of its two decades of life?

The great aggregations at these tides culminate in the deposit of millions or billions of soft, yolk-rich eggs onto the wet sand.

Just as this crab convergence is going on, a large proportion of all the existing individuals of the eastern red knot (chunky sandpipers with robin-red breasts) arrive at the Delaware shores. They have been flying from as far away as Tierra del Fuego, and at Delaware are only two-thirds of the way to their summer nesting grounds in the Arctic Circle.

Before the knots headed north on this annual migration, they had built up huge fat reserves, gorging on mollusks and other seaside invertebrates. The fat fuels the long flight, and during that journey, their digestive system, including the muscular crop that enables them to crush and digest shellfish, atrophies. By the time they reach the mid-coast shores, they are depleted, but all their usual food sources are useless for them with thousands of miles of flying yet to come as they flee austral winter to raise their chicks in boreal summer.

For these few days, the horseshoe crab eggs, superabundant, digestible, and calorie-rich, take no effort to find. The knots are not the only predators gobbling them up, but if they arrive on time, there is enough for all (and the leftovers become the next generation of crabs). The knots rapidly bulk up—the largest known seasonal weight gain in proportion to body mass of any vertebrate.

The horseshoe crabs, if not over-harvested by humans for bait or pharmaceuticals, for the most part return to deeper waters after the eggs are laid, following patterns older than the dinosaurs. The knots head north and bring forth the next generation, making a less-dramatic journey to the south, arriving in time for southern spring.

The crabs need usable beach when the moon and tides converge in spring; the knots need the crabs' success. Flowers come forth when the weather invites, but their pollinators wait for other triggers; so flower and bee may or may not coincide. The warblers in my woods leave their winter homes in Central America in the faith that the springing of leaves will be so far advanced that the birds can feed their nestlings on caterpillars. As farmers and fisherfolk know in their bones, the world is full of exquisite tunings that interpret the polyrhythms of the changing earth, making possible abundant life and the fulness of joy for each according to its kind.

Letter Thirty-one: Watchfulness

Dear friend,

The foundation of participation in the Lamb's War is watchfulness. Watchfulness is a spiritual discipline known from many traditions around the world—especially watchfulness at the doorway to the heart (as the eighth century Hesychius the Priest puts it) so that one becomes aware both of what is entering one's heart and what is emerging from it into thoughts, words, or actions.

In his tract on the Lamb's War, James Nayler begins the section on "The manner of his war" with these words:

> ...that he may be just who is to judge all men and spirits, he gives his light unto their hearts even of man and woman, whereby he lets all see (who will mind it) what he is displeased with, what is with him and what is against him, what he owns and what he disowns, that so all may know what is for destruction, to come out of it, lest they be destroyed with it; that so he may save and receive...all who are willing to be set free, all that are in darkness and are willing to come to light...

> And as many as turn at his reproof he doth receive and give them power in spirit and life to be as he is in

their measure, (but all in watching), and wars against that which hath had them and now hath the rest of the creation in bondage, that he may restore all things to their former liberty.

All in watching. The first Friends were led from watchfulness as an individual practice to a corporate waiting worship that was not mere receptivity but a shared experience of presence and of visitation and, in that presence, of encounter with a living power with its own integrity and character. I frankly confess that this practice has its own pitfalls, and Quakers have observed many kinds of mishaps and mistakes that can make watchfulness a mere ritual or even a self-deceptive act.

Because we humans are so geared to action and yearn for the world's healing and our own, we can think of our waiting as a waiting to hear a message (for ourselves or others). It is good, though, to get down to first things and start by standing in the Spirit with no agenda, no expectation, but with open hands. In that experience, we can feel timelessness and understand something of the mystery in the words eternal life and the nature of God's love for us as creatures, like God's love for animals and plants, the changeable hills, the beautiful scarred moon, and the dust-filled vaccuum between the stars. Another way to say this is that, for those who seek a prophetic witness to the world or see the need for one, our watchfulness itself must be prophetic. But what does that mean?

William P. Taber Jr. once said that the work of the prophet consists in three elements: 1. to know the law (that is the will of God); 2. to point out the way to faithfulness; and 3. to make Spirit available.[114]

Much of what I have written to you so far has focused on the first point, that is, what is entailed in listening for the voice of the Shepherd of Israel wherever it is to be found—in Scripture, of course, but also in nature (creation), and in the tradition— not primarily in formulations about the tradition but the voices and lives of those who have found a practice of the Presence and allowed it to reshape their thinking,

---

114   Taber, William P., Jr.(1984) *The prophetic stream.*

feeling, and willing. You could say that, to understand the scope and challenge of the Lamb's War, you need to know the Lamb.

This results in an education about our alienation—the places where we are far from the love that "beareth all things, believeth all things, hopeth all things, endureth all things."[115] Moreover, our growing understanding of our alienation and our growing reorientation to the Light gives insight into how our alienation and that of other humans (and their institutions and practices) are akin—and the costs that they have to human flourishing and that of all creation.

Thus (to borrow Nayler's phrase), we learn "what we are to war against"—not against "the creatures" nor "flesh and blood" but against that very isolating, atomized, fearful, often cruel, and wasteful alienation. In short, we come to know the sinfulness of sin.

It also means that we can come to ever greater and more tender knowledge of the preciousness of the world in which we are placed, where our lives, including their spiritual aspects, are rooted and nourished. Accordingly, there can come a sharper and more comprehending recognition of why and how our own reconciliation with the love at the heart of things must necessarily transform our relations to the rest of creation.

It is in the tender places that concern can arise, the growing sense that I am required to attend to something (word or act)— required because, if I do not undertake it, I will move from reconcilation back toward alienation. Like a bolt of lightning, the connection builds both from the ground and the clouds, that is both from an opening urgency or attentiveness in ourselves and from a changed awareness or attentiveness to something out there—in society, in study, in nature—that calls for healing or relief. The electric connection is made, and we are required because our soul's peace remains shattered until we respond to the leading.

The origin of a concern, a sense of requirement, has many paths, and it often is felt first in such forms as curiosity or an ought (as in I really ought to find out more, or I really ought to do something) or an invitation from a friend. If we take these little nudges and intimations

---

115   1 Cor 13:7.

into our waiting, we may well find an answering witness within. The secret power of life is preparing you at a level before words—for relationship, for the growth of concern. Search for the stirrings of life within.

Curiosity and interest are not to be despised as the beginning of a leading. The eighteenth-century Quaker tailor and minister, John Woolman, made a visit to the Lenni-Lenape (Delaware) people living at the frontiers of the colony of Pennsylvania, and the story of this visit is full of instruction. It was nearly two years in the making, starting with an early sense of interest and then a lot of homework—gathering news, talking with travelers who knew the landscape and knew the Lenape (and, in this effort, making it known he was interested so that people thought of sending information or opportunities his way), speaking with Lenape people who happened to be in Philadelphia, and eventually beginning to speak of a possible shape for the concern—a journey west. Then began what the Quakers call a clearness process by which we mean examining a potential action to see if there is any stop or spiritual barrier to what is contemplated. For Woolman, this meant first seeking inward clearness, then clearness with his wife, and then with his meeting (the worshipping community) locally and at the regional level. Then came the planning and implementation. All this is condensed into his famous lines reviewing how he came to be in a tent, in a rainstorm, in the woods of central Pennsylvania en route to the Lenape settlement: "Love was the first motion, and then a concern arose." He had to wait to feel sure that love was the basic message and motivation for what he was feeling drawn to undertake before getting down to the practicalities.

The Quaker idea of "concern" is a profound one that repays some reflection. After all, we are making a claim that God is acting in the world by stirring you up to some service. Such a stirring is thus worth more than gold. If it is a true leading—borne out by its persistence, by its increasing clarity, by the concurrence of others who taste it and find a sweet and holy savor in it as the Witness is stirred in them in response—then it deserves the care, solicitude, nourishment, and respect that we accord any newborn from the first appearance to its fruitful maturity. Nothing more weighty and more encouraging can come to a Friend or a Friends meeting.

And one challenge is to dive appropriately into all the particulars of ways and means, while remembering that all of the busyness and logistics and learning had "love as the first motion"—and like John Woolman, we should make time to feel where that spring lies and flows in us.

Reflection

If we are to live with integrity the gospel life we are called to, our waiting must also probe such questions as these:

> Can I feel how this leading to action that I am feeling, at its base, is one more outflowing of God's love?

> Can I see, at least dimly, how that love sharpens and corrects my view of the people and things I am called toward?

If we wait to feel that, before we speak (even in worship) or act, the resulting integration of action with our love for the Light will be rewarded in unexpected ways.

Meditation: Life in the Depths

Let your mind imagine a journey downward from where you are toward the center of the earth. If you are sitting in a house, you pass through the layers of human nest-building, down further into the rock or soil, and eventually to the bedrock. There is layer upon layer of this, the crust of the world, cracked and fissured and porous. You do not have to descend too far to pass the reach of the deepest tree roots. If you are on the sea as you read this, the first part of your descent will be different, of course, and you will pass through unknown regions where dwell unknown creatures that endure and thrive in conditions instantly fatal to surface dwellers: bird, human, shark, herring. Only rare and rarely gifted creatures (whales, elephant seals) can commute to these places, and even they cannot approach the deepest abysses. Imagination can reach there to some extent, though limited by ignorance; the only other probes are sound waves and deep-probing drills

By either route, through the depths of water or the upper regions of the land, you come to crust. As you descend into it, the pressure grows, and so does the heat. In little over a mile, temperatures are climbing toward the boiling point, but water does not boil under the terrible pressure of the rocks. Oxygen exists here only in mineral compounds; organic matter is soon left behind.

282

Water is one of the most abundant minerals compounds in the solar system, and it is present here, parcelled out in smaller and smaller quantities, in cracks and pores thinner than a hair, interstices often undetectable by a human eye.

A century ago, geologists began to suspect that, as far down as they could probe with bore and drill, there were living creatures to be found. After nearly a century of tool-refinement, the evidence could be believed and some knowledge gathered. The rock beneath our feet for something like two miles down is full of life, as far as we can tell, unconnected to the biosphere above. It is microscopic and mostly microbial—bacteria and archeobacterial predominant here in the dark biosphere as they are in the light-driven world we inhabit.

These creatures extract energy and nutrients by ingenious biochemistry from the rocks around, and their living processes contribute to and shape their habitats in ways we can only guess at. They exist at temperatures and pressures so hostile to life as we have known it. So difficult of access are the raw materials for respiration (compounds of hydrogen, sulfur, iron, and other elements) and for metabolism that their lives are astonishingly slow—up to a million times slower than their counterparts in the upper world. It may be centuries or millenia before a cell can divide; there is no known age limit or lifespan for these creatures.

Yet this much now is known from samples brought up for study: the life locked in the rocks is wildly diverse, wildly inventive, and wildly abundant. Perhaps fifteen percent of all living biomass lives in these regions below our feet, passing lives that are to us of surpassing, astonishing strangeness.

Haldane said that the world is not only "queerer than we think, it is queerer that we can think." Our ignorance of this our home extends from your seat out across the world, through the cosmos, and downward to the smallest scales of our own bodies and the body of the earth.

Letter Thirty-two: Prompt Obedience

Dear friend,

Now let us suppose that in your watching, your waiting in the light of Christ, you have felt some movement to action at the point where awareness, the demands of justice, or grief are visited by compassion. If this has not happened yet, it will. No matter whether the grief or the anger or the love you feel is for the state of the planet or for humankind, emotion turns to motivation.

John Woolman's description of his experience of accepting one kind of service—the gospel ministry—is helpful here:

> I was afflicted in mind some weeks, without any light or comfort, even to that degree that I could not take satisfaction in anything. I remembered God, and was troubled, and in the depth of my distress he had pity upon me, and sent the Comforter. I then felt forgiveness for my offence; my mind became calm and quiet, and I was truly thankful to my gracious Redeemer for his mercies. About six weeks after this, feeling the spring of Divine love opened, and a concern to speak, I said a few words in a meeting, in which I found peace....From an inward purifying, and

steadfast abiding under it springs a lively operative desire for the good of others.

He had been stirred and felt moved to action but hesitated. Initially, his hesitation was from anxiety, from fear of getting it wrong. There might also have been reluctance at the prospect of beginning a work that would lead to unpredictable consequences, re-orienting his life in small or great ways. Sometimes we want to avoid taking on a new inconvenience or hard labor and other sources of resistance there may be, as well.

But the waiting also can be of another quality because it can come to focus us on our core commitments so that action we undertake will, more and more, bring them into reality. If we wait with intention, with expectation of guidance, and in freedom, waiting will not be stasis or avoidance of action but will help our acting be shaped by our values, our spiritual intent, and our understanding of our situation. In active waiting, we do not need to fear that we will not put our hand to good work; there are at least two factors that will move us to act.

The first is that humans are constantly generating ideas and impulses about things to do. Our species might well be named *Homo inquietus* (the restless earthling). People will act, especially when their interest, their emotions, their identity, or their needs are involved. In our acting as well as our waiting, we must learn how to act and when not to; when to speak and when to be still—itself an act of obedience and also sometimes a mercy to our weakness.

The second factor is that we are engaged with a living God whose work is (re)creative, whose Word is actively at work in the world "reconciling the world to himself." It is the Quaker experience that waiting is indeed waiting on—being still as preparation for service, doing the work needed to ensure that we do not run errands when we are not yet sent. Yet the Lamb's War entails love and obedience in action.

Prompt Obedience Is a Spiritual Discipline, a Spiritual Law

The outward fruits of inward life are cultivated by our accepting the Light we're given and acting on it in the smallest matters. When a command comes, however trivial, your soul's health is promoted by prompt obedience. Every command from the Light is given as bread for your nourishment and inward growth. "The just shall live by faithfulness." The inward disposition is good but only the beginning of new growth. "Faith without works is dead," says the epistle of James, and, "There is no time but this present time," as George Fox wrote to his parents. Another James, James Nayler, wrote:

> in this journey I have seen the slothful servant overtaken with a fault which he had once cast behind him, and never intended to join to again, of which the diligent servant is kept free, and I have seen the wages of each servant according to his diligence in that which he hath of God betrusted in him, and not by his own strivings in the thoughts of himself, his worth or wisdom. And in diligent hearkening and obeying of the Spirit have I found the right faithfulness towards God[116]

Ways and means. The urgency of the climate crisis and its intricate relationship with issues of justice, economic well-being, cultural integrity, earth-care, and more means that there is a wide field, a daunting range of opportunities offered to the awakened conscience, whose awakening has removed the first inertia that tempts to a false rest.

We are thus presented with continual challenges of imagination because each field of endeavor has its own appropriate tools, yet the Lamb's War demands of its advocates the weapons of the Spirit of Christ and a steady rejection of violence and terror. Nayler writes that the followers of the Lamb, the good Shepherd,

> war not against men's persons, so their weapons are not carnal, nor hurtful to any of the creation; for the Lamb comes not to destroy men's lives, nor the work of God, and therefore at his appearance in his subjects, he puts spiritual weapons into their hearts and hands: their armor is the light, their sword the Spirit of the Father and the Son; their shield is faith and patience; their paths are

---

116 *What the posession of the living faith is*

prepared with the gospel of peace and good will towards all the creation of God. Their breastplate is righteousness and holiness to God; their minds are girt with godliness, and they are covered with salvation, and they are taught with truth.

This is not idealism. It is directly aimed at the kinds of change that will be needed if we are to address climate change and its interconnections: changes of mind and, yes, heart, as well as behavior. Of course, it is great if we can get people to modify their behaviors right away without any change of mind—but the changes needed are so dramatic and pervasive that, if they are not to be ensured by coercion, they must be supported willingly.

As a society, we face not just the loss of the ease and comfort of the subsidized petroleum empire and the uncertainties of transition to new forms of energy and transport. We also must confront and replace the assumption of exponential growth of economies and the forces and strains that lead to and follow from the unequal distribution of wealth and power. The alternative to increasing immiseration of the majority of the world is a very different system for the generation and distribution of well-being that is less focused on wealth and more focused on well-being.

All this is radical and will demand a revolution in understanding about what the good life looks like. If it is to be implemented with justice and maintained by mutual consent (though dissenters and critics will always be present and necessarily so), then it will be a nearer approximation to the ethos of "love thy neighbor as thyself" than most societies have yet approached. Though there will be many ways of articulating the frame-shift, here is a Christian phrasology:

> The light says, Love your neighbor as yourself: This the first birth cannot do,... the creature must give up that to death that he may come to the meek Spirit, for the power of that life and obedience that has righteousness in it; and the creature drawing his mind and affections, and faith from the first, who has words without power, and giving these to the second, the first falls, withers, and dies in that

> vessel, and as the mind is diligent in the second, he rises
> in the faith, and Christ raises the power of obedience in
> that vessel.[117]

So the Lamb's warrior, working in the world with others of good will, must engage with the tools of science or persuasion or politics or education, always under the constraints of the love of Christ and the weapons appropriate to it.

Yet despise not the day of small things. Our path must begin with the smallest openings, the simplest leadings, the weakest of visitations. This is true in the Lamb's War as in the spiritual life. There is an infancy in the work that may seem unpromising and even ridiculous in the face of the great challenges before us. But recall that this is the life in which the Messiah rides on a donkey and washes the feet of his students. Power looks different, and maturity also. Isaac Penington writes,

> the great deceiver of souls lifts up men's minds in the
> imagination to look for some great appearance of power,
> and so they slight and overlook the day of small things,
> and neglect receiving the beginning of that, which in the
> issue would be the thing they look for. Waiting in that
> which is low and little in the heart, the power enters, the
> seed grows, the kingdom is felt and daily more and more
> revealed in the power. And this is the true door and way
> to the thing: take heed of climbing over it.

We must be wary of the temptation to postpone action until something really worth our effort comes along. If we wait deeply enough, we will find that our anxiety about impact will be lifted from us because we can see that the fundamental message is the love of God as we can embody it, and this is at work in many lives and many places. "To those who have, more shall be given."

A warning. To act in love, in urgency, and faithfulness, using the weapons of the Lamb, is very likely to require us to change deeply. To meet this challenge so that our witness reaches the Witness in others' consciences, we need to be about the work of getting clear. How

---

117 from J. Nayler *Milk for Babes and meat for strong men.*

faithful am I? How truthful is my life? How grateful and unwearied in well-doing? How long-suffering and humble am I? What do I need to do to get down low enough to receive the presence and welcome the life of the Lamb and prophesy of the ocean of life and light that flows over the ocean of darkness in all our ways and works?

To summarize, the second task for you—and me!—in responding to climate change as part of the Lamb's War against the systems of oppression, death-worship, and alienation from God, from each other, and from the earth is this: out of waiting and watching, act promptly on what the Spirit truly gives you to do. It may be big or, by your measure, it may be tiny. The key thing is that you have stepped into and are moving with the prophetic stream. As you follow it along, your strength will grow, in part by the addition of others', and in part through your own growth in grace and wisdom. Start now! Seek diligently, and act diligently, turning the whole of your life into the "channel of universal love":

> ... let your food be in the life of what you know, and in the power of obedience rejoice, and not in what you know, but cannot live, for the life is the bread for your souls, which crucifies the flesh, and confounds that which runs before the cross.
>
> So let your labor and diligence be in that which... seeks a conformity to Christ in obedience of what you believe, and hearken in love to that...So in receiving His commands in that which loves to be like Him in life, your faith works by love. That faith works obedience, quickness and willingness, it works out the old, and works into the new (Nayler, *Milk for Babes*)

Reflection

Do you make time to sit quietly so that you can feel where your conscience may be stirred?

If something persists in claiming your attention so that you feel, "I think I must do something about this," do you test it against the requirings and the constraints of love? As you consider the action you are moved to take, does it come with a feeling of wholesome freedom or feel like an opening way?

Do you dare to share your leading with a few wise people from your spiritual community? If they raise questions, do you need to reach more clarity about your motive? The specifics of your course of action? The timing or scale of the action?

As you begin to move forward, how will you ensure that you incorporate space and time for contemplation and reflection—both on the work you are undertaking and on the love and wonder that are the grounding of your work?

Meditation: Ant Farm

The caterpillars have spent all night grazing throughout the oak tree. As dawn and the sun's heat approach, they travel back down the trunk, accompanied by red and black ants who fend off predators and examine and clean the caterpillars as they descend.

At the base, the caterpillars and their shepherds pass through round openings in a structure that the ants have constructed and maintain. Inside, the caterpillars gather in dense groups, in chambers that are dark, cool, and moist, and there they rest. The ants attend the caterpillars, cleaning off specks of fungi and protecting them if need arises. Ant workers come and go through passages that connect the byre to their huge nest, visble as a mound perhaps fifteen to thirty inches in diameter, rising perhaps two feet above the forest floor.

The ants maintain the clearing in which their mound rises, and as its population grows, satellite mounds are raised and excavated. To enlarge the clearing or protect it from the probing roots of surrounding trees and bushes, the ants inject formic acid into the roots and stems, killing them. Debris is cleaned away.

The mound area and its environs support far fewer spiders than a comparable area chosen at random in the forest. Spiders are the caterpillars' most important predator, and the ants eliminate them within the perimeter of the nest and the oak trees nearby where the caterpillars are found. Larger visitors, such as skunks or inquisitive naturalists, are chased away by a prompt assault by thousands of workers emerging from the numerous openings that dot the mound.

The ants, for all their energetic site management and hunting prowess, subsist for the most part on nectar and other sweets. This is why they house and protect the caterpillars, each of which has a gland near its tail-end that exudes a distillate from the night's grazing: honeydew, which nourishes the ants and maintains the covenant between sheep and shepherd. When the caterpillars pupate, for a time becoming unresponsive capsules, the ants protect them. The final exchange, the renewal of the deal, comes when the butterflies emerge. Soon after taking wing, they mate and deposit eggs on the oaks where they were hosted and maintained.

Letter Thirty-three: Suffering and Folly

Dear friend,

Our response to climate change and other aspects of the Anthropocene—the nature of it, its effects on us and creation, and the whole system of interests and fears that drive climate denial and defend the regime of exploitation and consumption—is an integrated, necessary part of the Lamb's War in our day.

I have tried to explain some aspects of participation in this struggle. The first two are waiting or watchfulness and prompt obedience. Now I come to two that are likely to be less appealing: suffering and proclamation. These are perhaps more closely related than might appear at first, but I will treat them separately, starting with suffering—and folly. How are these part of the spiritual opportunity presented by our present age?

One Source of Suffering: The Brutality of Power and of Unreason

Making a witness for the Lamb, using the Lamb's weapons, can draw repressive acts from the subtle to the brutal. Let us first hear James Nayler's voice (from the *Lamb's War*)

> What They Are to War Against: and that is, whatever is not of God… whatever the god of the world hath begotten in men's hearts to practise or to plead for, which God did not place there. All this the Lamb and his followers war against, which is at enmity with it both in themselves and wherever they see it.
>
> … So their wars are not against creatures, they wrestle not with flesh and blood which God hath made, but with spiritual wickedness exalted in the hearts of men and women, where God alone should be.

Nayler here is echoing an important idea from the Gospels (and heard elsewhere, of course, including in gnostic writings), about the contest between the true God (God of Truth) and the God of this world. Because of the state of sin in which humans are mired, the sinful part offers its allegiance to evil and worships it in one of its many forms.

One kind of incense that these powers and principalities love is the anger and alienation stirred up on their behalf, as well as the fear that they can inspire, and these are the base notes in many great manipulations and oppressions. Direct physical and psychological punishment is always either an implicit or explicit tool of power (whether power actually established in social structures or aspiring to be so).

As with many gods, the false god can appear in various guises. Indeed, this false god takes so many shapes, attuned to human desires or weaknesses, that one can believe themselves to be faithful followers of the true God while actually serving the false. Jesus was pointing this out when he remarked that you can't serve two masters, God and Mammon (Matthew 6:24) or God and Caesar (Matthew 22:22). A key work of the prophet is to recognize and name the self-delusion that we are all so liable to:

> I hate, I despise your feast days, and I will not smell in your solemn assemblies. Though ye offer me burnt offerings and your meat offerings, I will not accept them: neither will I regard the peace offerings of your fat beasts.

Take thou away from me the noise of thy songs; for I will not hear the melody of thy viols.

But let judgment run down as waters, and righteousness as a mighty stream. (Amos 5:21–4 KJV)

Mind Games

We are engaged in a conflict of worldviews. One is comforting and affirming to those who are at ease with the way things are working and who are convinced that their ease is evidence of their correct view of the world. The prophetic voice, by contrast, sees what the ruling order wishes not to: that though you congratulate yourself that you are right with God, that your prosperity is affirmation of your virtue, your heart is far from God's. (As Thomas Merton wrote, "The satisfaction that comes from being in tune with our times is certainly not a charism, still less a sign of supernatural life.")[118]

After all, a God who can say, "Inasmuch as ye have done it unto one of these the least of my brethren, ye have done it unto me," must see the world very differently from those who uphold the present order. It is no wonder that, to some extent, the upholders of the present world system must avoid certain facts about the world. The age of climate change is characterized by an extravagant commitment by the powerful and their loyalists to deny facts that disturb their repose and self-satisfaction—deny them on such a scale and on so many fronts as to make the habit of lying or denial a normal practice, buttressed by well-rehearsed patterns of action and rhetoric and supported in more and more settings by the use of coercion and violence.

The Age of Feeding on Wind

We often hear about how new technologies get developed first for war (or space flight) and then become everyday contributors to our way of life. (Indeed, sometimes such spin-offs are used to argue for spending more money on the war machine). You may not be aware that one of the main spin-offs from World War I was the modern science of marketing built upon wartime research on propaganda. (Edward

118   Thomas Merton *Contemplation in a World of Action*

Bernays, the father of public relations, said as much in 1928, in his ground-breaking book , *Propaganda*.)

Since then, of course, the manufacture of consent (as Walter Lippman called it) has, like everything else, become a major industry. Its arts and techniques, enriched and refined, have been allied with the power of massive corporate wealth to reinforce consumers' loyalty to key pillars of the way things are—to regard such matters as constant economic expansion, unrestrained exploitation of people and other natural resources, and the socialization of costs and risk as part of modern capitalism. (That is, the public bears the costs and risks as much as possible while sharing the wealth created as little as possible.)

Thus, it is not surprising that vast sums have been (and are being) spent to prevent any serious action on climate change—not just in the past thirty years since it's been a matter of public interest but for almost two decades before then, when scientists in the oil industry correctly diagnosed the dangers of fossil fuel emissions and predicted the implications for our future climate. The oil industry first acknowledged and then buried the science.

Why Do the People Imagine a Vain Thing?

For many reasons, there is a widespread antagonism against expertise and the whole enterprise of the discovery and verification of knowledge. Climate denialism took its place in the increasingly powerful movement to undermine the credibility of science in many fields, often enlisting the same experts in a wide range of causes, many related to public health and limitations on corporate accountability. The movement, indeed, also includes various kinds of pseudo-science that are not primarily driven by business interests. (Anti-evolution is a venerable example.) The overall effect, however, is to create, maintain, and protect an image of the way things are supposed to be, which can ensure that the control and uses of power and wealth (powerwealth) remain in the right hands.

They That Call Evil Good, and Good Evil; That Put Darkness for Light, and Light for Darkness

The powerful in our society are playing cynically with disinformation, social alienation, and anxiety for the quite evident ends of power and wealth. While such methods have long been translated into violence and oppression in foreign lands or specific oppressed groups within the nation's borders (I speak generally because what we see in our times has been seen before), increasingly the tools of suppression are being deployed on anyone who objects to the way things are supposed to be. A recent crude form has been the appearance of laws intended to protect from prosecution people who injure protesters by driving through the crowd.

So it is no wonder that wisdom cries out in the streets but may well be scorned and rejected cruelly by those whose lasting welfare she seeks. The organization and mind of our society is designed to protect the powerful and those who take refuge in their identity.

The Spirit of Truth is a standing threat to these established structures of mind and organization, and those who bring its message in their measure become the outward and visible targets of assault and rejection—though what is being rejected is an inward and spiritual reality. But the powers are against any reality that they cannot control. It would be folly to oppose the wisdom of the rulers of the world: "All they that see him, laugh him to scorn." Christ has ever been seen as foolish and unhelpful, though silent Christs, fabricated Christs, and distant Christs will often be expedient. Since his life continues in his body, the church, we, acting as its members, may receive the continued wrath of his opponents.

Another Source of Suffering: Disruption of Your Life

Here, another word from Nayler; some of you reading this may have stories like this to tell of yourselves or others and find some kinship with James in your measure:

> I was at the plow, meditating on the things of God, and suddenly I heard a voice saying unto me, "Get thee out from thy kindred and from thy father's house"—and I

had a promise given in with it. Whereupon, I did exceedingly rejoice, that I had heard the voice of that God which I had professed from a child but had never known him.... when I came at home I gave up my estate, cast out my money.

But not being obedient going forth, the wrath of God was upon me, so that I was made a wonder to all; and none thought I would have lived. But (after I was made willing) I began to make some preparation, as apparel and other necessaries, not knowing whither I should go.

But shortly afterward going a-gateward with a friend from my own house, having on an old suit, without any money, having neither taken leave of wife or children, not thinking then of any journey, I was commanded to go into the west, not knowing whither I should go nor what I was to do there; but when I had been there a little while I had given me what I was to declare; and ever since I have remained, not knowing today what I was to do tomorrow.

When the voice of our prophet, Christ, comes, even in its gentlest, meekest appearance (as the babe in the manger), a true receiving of the invitation will make us see our lives and certainties with different eyes. To make room for the newborn, our plans and habits may well need to be altered or even overthrown: you who have been parents (or who have been overcome by a new love) can attest to this! Such an upheaval may be small at first yet bring with it anxieties and uncertainties which before we had protected ourselves against in some degree—but which are among the costs of creativity and of new growth. Moreover, this is a continuing revolution: as the newborn grows and gains power and agency, so we must as well, and our stewardship may be costly of time or treasure, though we pay the costs in love.

Exile Among Our Own: Disconcerting Our Friends

Taking the step that is given to us and not outrunning our Guide, we will find that our inward process, now incarnated in our action, has consequences close to home. These can include reactions (in ourselves or others) that are unpleasant and discouraging; suffering can take many forms, visible and invisible, more or less understandable to others, and tolerable or intolerable to one's self. Even in a religious society, a new appearance or commitment to faithfulness may take forms that make our friends uneasy or even disparaging of our experiments in piety.

These may engender a spectrum of pains and afflictions, ranging from self-doubts and questioning to puzzlement or ridicule within our community, to inconvenience and complications in our outward affairs, to much more serious threats or pains. These sufferings may weigh on us and perplex, even if we are at the same time able to keep in touch with the joy that is rising as we move forward in a true leading. Woolman writes in his *Journal,*

> As I lived under the cross, and simply followed the openings of Truth, my mind from day to day was more enlightened; my former acquaintance was left to judge of me as they would, for I found it safest for me to live in private and keep these things sealed up in my own breast.

We need to listen to questions, to recognize that it is possible we may be wrong, to stay teachable, but the consequences of our earnest and loving attempts to be faithful will be both lesson and reward. Our friends can help us sort through it all, and that may be part of the nourishment that comes. But each of us bears our own cuts and bruises, and the healing, in the end, comes from within.

Suffering as Symptom, as Consequence, as Evidence: "It Was in the Cross to My Will"

There are kinds of spirituality that see suffering as evidence of the rightness of one's leading or actions. It was not uncommon for Friends, for example, to put most trust in a leading that was against their natural inclination. This can develop into a sort of warped scruple—it must be good for me because it tastes so bitter. (To quote Bilbo at the Council of Elrond, "I have never known you to give me pleasant advice before," he said. "As all your unpleasant advice has been good, I wonder if this advice is not bad.")

Yet, if one can avoid false asceticism, the experience of inconvenience, disturbance, or even fear at the prospect of assent to the divine promptings can be a way to test the leading and learn better and better how to follow the Guide's true direction.

> The cross is to the carnal part, which is the ground of images, the ground of the seducers, and the ground of the false prophet...the cross is to that ground, to the root and life of it. This being minded, which is pure and eternal, it makes a separation from all other lovers, and brings to God, and the ground of evil thoughts comes to be opened, and the cross is to that ground; which Cross overturns the world in the heart. Which Cross must be taken up by all who follow Jesus Christ...Where the world is standing, the Cross is not lived in. But dwelling in the Cross to the world, here the Love of God is shed abroad in the heart, and the Way is opened in the inheritance, which fades not away."[119]

Opportunity in Desolation

A spiritual challenge is one which requires us to grow because it is hard to integrate with our prior spiritual beliefs and habits. It demands some definite change in the way we act on and interpret the world and our condition; and it may require us to seek and use spiritual, intellectual, community, or physical resources to guide and feed the growth required. If we engage with such a challenge wholeheartedly, we will know we have met it for the time being by the reward of peace or sense of inward reconciliation, by a sense of clarified understanding, by a removal of some fear and sense of insufficiency, and by a renewed understanding of and faithfulness to our most essential spiritual commitments.

Our challenge in these times (as it was for the early Quakers, and for the first Christians before they experienced Christ's return) is desolation. There is grief and alarm at the loss of much that is beautiful and valuable in itself and at the consequent increase of suffering that

---

119 George Fox, Epistle 51.

will accrue to our ever-more-numerous human family. The changes we have set in motion will take decades to fully unfold, and it will be centuries before a new equilibrium is reached. Even if dramatic measures are taken in the next few years, we will only be able to somewhat soften the blows that are coming. The temptations to self-preservation at all costs, to competition and exclusiveness, will only rise because these are the most natural responses to crises that are already underway and, indeed, accelerating. Moreover, our political systems by and large have developed in such a way that they are now best suited to serve a few powerful interests rather than the common good.

*   *   *   *   *

Paradoxically, we are called, I think, to move toward a kind of folly, armed with all the wisdom that science can offer us. It is a kind of folly to turn more deeply to worship, to allow ourselves to be drawn into prayer and service and witness and suffering for the cause of love, to follow the Light with abandon. It requires us to accept that we are ignorant of much, that we have much to overcome in ourselves as we seek to speak or enact truth ever more clearly. We will disconcert or disappoint ourselves or our friends or family. We will have to contravene in all humility our culture's commitments to inequality, to injustice, to waste, and to control of one another.

Here, Paul, that great, flawed apostle, is a good model, living with ever more freedom and experimentation, seeing only in part, prophesying only in part. But in his clear moments, he felt the unity in the Spirit that is ours to live and felt that the life-blood of that unity and of the often painful growth in the Spirit was rooted in love and enacted by faith, and the fruit of these is hope. He put it clearly here: "Be not shaped to fit the world, but allow yourselves to be reshaped by the renewing of your minds." The Lamb's War is first and foremost waged in the theater of purposes and intentions, minds and hearts. It creates anew, it divides us more and more from the powers and the purposes that serve death, not life. To those powers, the Lamb and his followers seem ridiculous, and the power of their compassion and their resilience is inconceivable.

I conclude with a few words from Erasmus, whose dame Folly says:

> [Christ] seems to have been in the highest degree delighted with children, women, and fishermen. Moreover, among the animal kind, those seem most to please him, which are farthest from a fox's subtlety. And he preferred to ride sitting on an ass, though he, if he pleased, might have sat on the lion's back without harm. And that Holy Spirit chose rather likewise to settle down in the seeming of a dove, rather than of an eagle or a kite.
>
> ...Add to this, that his own people, destined for etermal life, he calls sheep— of all creatures the most foolish. Yet Christ proclaims himself the shepherd of such a flock, and even more, he himself is delighted by the name "lamb," with John the Baptist pointing him out saying, Behold the Lamb of God, of which there is much mention in the Apocalypse.
>
> ... in some sense Christ himself, although he was the wisdom of the Father, when he came to succor mortal folly, when he was found in the human predicament, having put on human nature, in a way was made in some measure a fool... Nor did he will to heal us in any other way than by the folly of the cross, than by the foolishness of the cross, and through ignorant and dull-witted apostles—, to whom, indeed, he earnestly advised folly, warning them away from wisdom, when he commends to them the example of children, lilies, mustard, and little birds.[120]

Can we dare to follow such a Shepherd?

Reflection

Think of a specific action (however small) that you believe arises from a good root, which you are avoiding. Ask yourself: What prevents me from acting on this leading right now? Is it the tangle of tasks and duties that hinders? Is it distraction or fatigue? Or is there in it some

---

120 *Moriae encomium* [Praise of Folly] pp. 187-8.

little chance of suffering or folly that you are shying away from? These stops or roadblocks may be the next thing to address in your inner exercises. It may be that, once you name the inhibitor, to yourself and perhaps to a trusted other, it will seem no real hindrance at all in comparison with the act you are called to, and so it will dissolve like frost in morning sunlight.

Meditation: The Two Great Commandments and Care for the Earth

Thou shalt love the Lord thy God with all thy heart, and with all thy soul, and with all thy mind, and with all thy strength: this is the first and great commandment, and the second is like unto it: Thou shalt love thy neighbor as thyself. On these two hang all the law and the prophets.

Whether of the two horns of the great commandments you choose, you are bound to care for the earth.

If in your present condition you incline to choose the love of God as the door to more abundant life, then you are loving the Spirit who owns the wild beasts, the cattle on a hundred hills, and the hills themselves, for "the earth is the Lord's and the fulness thereof," that is, all that is in it.

Remember and acknowledge that the Word, Christ, the Wisdom of God, is the means of creation and delights in the creation. All through the gospel stories, Jesus gives thanks for the blessings of the natural world and the fruits of agriculture and describes the kingdom he invites us to as one of abundance. Nowhere does he condone abuse, nor would he differ from the prophets in his disapproval of over-consumption and the ruin of the land. Would it not be a radical and wicked rejection of the blessings of creation to make seed-time and harvest impossible or to eliminate the creatures that are of God's making and objects of God's love?

So, if to be a Christian is to imitate Christ, thanks to a transformation or re-shaping of our understanding so that we can become doers of the Word, that imitation must include gratitude and deep reverence for the earth, God's footstool and great work.

If, on the other hand, you are more moved by the challenge to love your neighbor as yourself, then, once again, an appropriate care for the earth is a necessary consequence. For "the earth" is not just a collection of objects, and "the fulness thereof" includes living things (including ourselves), and these are in process, in dynamic interaction with each other and with the materials of the planet. Moreover, the inter-relationship of living and non-living things is such that life shapes the seas, the rocks, the air, and the soil in ways that support life's flourishing. As the science of natural history and ecology has shown ever more clearly over the past two hundred years, it is really impossible to say with any certainty where biosphere ends and other spheres (litho-hydro-, atmo-) begin.

Therefore, for your neighbor to flourish as well as yourself, a healthy, functioning earth is indispensable. Further, it is indisputable that one of the major ways in which love has failed is in the despoliation and fouling of the resources needed for abundance of life.

And if you are a skeptic and look askance at arguments from first principles as found in the Scriptures, then I leave you with the following reflection from a historian of ecology:

> Environmental conservation becomes, in the light of this historical awareness, an effort to protect...the biological world from incompatible changes going on within our economy and technology. It is not a program of locking nature up within a museum case, freezing it for all time. Rather, it is a pattern of behavior based on the idea that preserving a diversity of change ought to stand high in our system of values, that promoting the coexistence of

many beings and many kinds of change is a rational thing to do.

The pace of innovation in computer chips may be appropriate to a competitive business community, but it is not appropriate to or always compatible with the evolution of a redwood forest. Some things take longer to grow or improve. Some things cannot adapt as fast as others. These are differences revealed by the history of nature and society.

Today, historians of every sort can no longer claim that there is a single universal narrative of change that all species, all communities, all places must conform to. "History" has given way to "histories." Each of those histories needs space in which to play itself out, to unwind its narrative.

That is precisely what the modern idea of conservation must aim to do: provide the space, either set aside in large discrete blocks, or protected within the interstices of the landscape, so that all the many earthly histories can coexist—the history of a coral reef alongside the history of a coastal city, the history of a tropical rainforest, alongside the history of a political struggle. Such a strategy of trying to conserve a diversity of changes may seem paradoxical, but it is founded on a crucial and reasonable insight. We may have to live with change, may even be the products of change, but we do not always know—indeed, we cannot always know—which changes are vital and which are deadly. [121]

---

121 *Nature's economy: a history of ecological ideas. 2   ed.* by Donald Worster. pp 432–433.

Letter Thirty-four: Proclamation

Dear friend,

I think I have said almost all that I can offer you in explaining my mind—I hope you have at some points been encouraged and challenged. For my part, your companionship along this way has been a comfort, a pleasure, and an instruction to me. The act of putting meaningful things into words is itself a quest, and (if done in the right spirit) it is a way of seeking companionship—and also a way of discovering and explaining who I am when I am singing this song.

One central part of enacting the Lamb's War is proclamation. This is, after all, one possible result of watchfulness and of prompt obedience to the leading of the Spirit—and proclamation, speaking out, can result in suffering of various kinds, both inward and outward. There is no doubt that verbal acts are acts: they can have an actual impact in the real world, and to the extent they are truthful but not part of the conventional wisdom, they involve risk-taking.

It is not surprising that, these days, many (including many Friends, my own community) have a hard time with proclamation, the publishing of Truth. In our diversity of belief, we are reluctant to be too definite lest we impose on others. Is this not sometimes also rooted in a dislike of being imposed upon by others' certainties? It seems safest to speak in unpressing generalities and mystical or mystic-like language that refers as much as possible to one's own condition without requiring the hearer to engage for themselves. Best of all is to "let our lives speak" and avoid words that draw lines or exclude or harm.

There is much to be said for this carefulness, and Quakers have always warned each other about the dangers of speaking too freely about the things of the Spirit. Indeed, from the beginnings of the Christian movement, heralds of the gospel (including Jesus and Paul) have felt free to trim their words to reach the individual condition of their hearers in order that they might be drawn into more abundant and more robust life in God. The letters of Paul and Peter speak of nourishing the new Christian with milk, as a baby's first food, until their growth enables them to digest more challenging food for the soul. Spiritual guides are careful not to break a bruised reed or quench the smoldering flax.

But you can be smothered by feathers as well as by sand. The same George Fox who recommended that we should "let our lives preach" also wrote from prison:

> be a terror and a dread to all the adversaries of God, answering that of God in them all, spreading the truth abroad, awakening the witness, confounding the deceit, gathering up out of transgression into the life, into the covenant of light and peace with God. Let all nations hear the sound by word or by writing. Spare no place, spare no tongue, nor pen; but be obedient to the Lord God.

Indeed, even the famous nonverbal act of "going naked as a sign," in which someone calls on others to wake up to an emergency by an unconventional act, was in seventeenth-century Quaker practice not nonverbal.[122] It was by no means silent but was accompanied by powerful testimony [often both spoken and written] to make clear the meaning of the sign. William Simpson, who frequently was called to undertake this kind of action, wrote, "My body hath been temporally naked in many places in England, as a sign of the nakedness and shame that is coming upon the Church of England who live in oppres-

---

122 For more on this practice, see https://amorvincat.wordpress.com/?s=going+naked

sion and cruelty…a necessity was laid upon me from the Lord God of life and power to be a sign."

This kind of sign was a remarkably compact expression of several important ideas—that God still speaks and calls people to a fundamental critique of their times; that the ears of the many are so filled with the habitual and the conventional that Truth has a hard time gaining entrance; that to go with a word from the living God so as to break in to hearts and minds, contrary to custom and expectation, cannot be done only by conventional means, customary channels, the marketplace of ideas, and all the other ways by which unruly or inconvenient spirits are regulated.

Confronting climate change, as we still are not doing as a society, requires a change of mind, a reordering of priorities, a rethinking of life-ways, habits of consumption, relationship with each other and with the creation—and with actions that result from the change. Yes, you can get people into new ways of thinking by getting them to act differently (the nudge theory of social engineering[123]), but the wholesale changes that face us will require some level of understanding and assent. This is work that involves ideas and attitudes, and that means work with words: content and rhetoric, fact and image, dialogue and poetry. And if we hope to speak (from our growing experience and hope) of a changed worldview that is rooted in reverence so that it can endure, drawing on spiritual resources beyond our own strength and will, then we have to learn to explain where we are coming from.

> How then shall they call on him in whom they have not believed? and how shall they believe in him of whom they have not heard? and how shall they hear without a preacher?[124]

Our times need voices of warning and of teaching so that many take part in the recognition of the state of the world and the forces that are at play, set in motion by humans as participants in the global climate system. By all means, as many as can should be learning some of the science and history of our predicament and the possible technologies and other elements of mitigation and adaptation. Some of us

123 Thaler and Sunstein, 2008.
124 Romans 10:14

will be drawn to the causes, some to the impacts on humans, some to the implications for the natural world, some to the engineering or policy. Each of us can find some piece of the elephant to grasp; all views are needed for this most comprehensive of problems. But this kind of response can be hoped for from every member of our society.

Beyond this, however, we need to be alert to the spiritual damages and dangers that have resulted in our present crisis, in all its complications. The witness against social injustice upheld by many traditions has always included an understanding that the perpetrators of oppression are also victims, and their healing must be part of the ultimate transformation that frees the oppressed and removes the roots of the evil both in outward structures and in the minds of the perpetrators and the complicit. Quakerism and other traditions have developed a rich vocabulary of diagnosis and analysis to help connect people's inward dispositions with outward conduct and social structures and to place individual cases and structures of oppression or deceit in the context of the long story of salvation, of reconciliation between God and humankind. As we awaken to our condition, I hope some people in every tradition will find what their tradition offers in this area and make it freshly useful for our times.

The climate crisis will require people at large to "be transformed by the renewing of their minds," and it is thus an opportunity for Christians to see the message of the gospel freshly and in terms that the gospel-allergic may be able to connect with (this has been the hope behind this long series of posts). In my own community, we need to recall that original Quakerism was a movement, not a sect, and in understanding what that meant, we can make a distinctive contribution, both in our ways of action and our ways of thinking—reconciling with our Friends of the past and drawing authentically and with power on our historic practices. Other movements will have their own contributions to make, and that is as it should be. The gospel order grows from within and will move along the paths of diversity in this astonishing and diverse world.

Proclamation and Thanksgiving Among Ourselves, Too

We need to speak among ourselves about our experiences upon the way, as we learn, experiment, fail, and grow. This is for the feeding and strengthening of the soul beyond the instruction of the mind. As Isaac Penington wrote,[125]

> The end of the ministry is not only to gather, but also to preserve and build up what is gathered, even to perfection. And the soul being (especially at first, if not for a long time) weak and babish, not so fully acquainted with the measure of life (having had but some touches and demonstrations of it, but not being gathered fully into it, nor rooted and settled in it); I say, the soul in this state, hath as much need of the ministry to preserve, direct, and watch over it in the truth, as to gather

What a gift it is when someone tells us how their concern arose, how they learned about it, prepared for it, what it took to feel, how it was love at work, what journey they were taken on (however humble).

We need that witness, those stories, more than any other because they kindle the life in us and give us the hope that comes from truth enacted.

We need to help each other give thanks for any step forward upon this way. We need to help each other practice telling the story—the whole story, from inside out and outside in. If you act on a true concern in love, you have changed the world in at least two ways: you have done your task, but you also had to be changed to be able to do it—just as Penn wrote about the First Publishers, "They were changed men themselves, before they went about to change others."

And so it is also important that we encourage and nurture gifts of proclamation and teaching, as many as appear, large and small, building up a servant ministry that invites and urges to more abundant life, that reflects the divine life at work in us all, and that helps us do the work each of us is called to, which is unique and precious.

---

125 *Works*, vol. 2:368

*   *   *   *   *

There is a time to set all policy, contrivance, and technology aside for a moment and think of meanings and foundations. The Divine One, seeking to come to birth and full growth in each and all, comes anointed with the sap of growing things. Its blood is the life in my blood; its battlements and its forests of transformation, its playgrounds and flowing thoughts are all around us. Christ teaches that the human form is adorned and uplifted by its power to embrace our neighbor, by rightly ordered labor, by the opening hand and yielding heart, the mind that seeks for clarity and service, the tongue that speaks truth and praise, asks questions, sings.

But however powerfully that life can run, it is tender, humble even, in exaltation, available for service—and so the un-reverent, the scattering, the scornful, the over-reaching, the wayward, the self-serving, the cruel—we feel how these strike at that sweet life, wound it, drawing a cry of recognition and a call for healing in truth and long-suffering.

Sometimes what is needed is a time to be awake and to awaken others; then, awakened, strength can be accepted, and we can work and politic and argue and organize—spending heart, soul, strength, and mind under the sweet Spirit's direction. In such an awakening, the pain of truth and the delight and joy at the heart of things are one and the same.

Seek First the Kingdom of Heaven and Its Righteousness

In these times, amidst these crises and fears, our seeking will reveal to us the works and words we need for our part in the work of reconciliation in the whole order, among and with the earth and all that lives therein.

Joy, Your Birthright as Children of the Light

In these times of stress and change, if we take the opportunities for inward growth that are offered us and take up the Lamb's War against evil under the banner and with the equipment of love, we will infallibly find, amidst and through our grief and fears, a path opening to more abundant life. The Christian life, when authentically lived, is one of trial, of painful transformation, and of emergent joy that is not cheap, nor a denial of sufferings and uncertainty but a transformation of them, "tears the very wine of blessedness." On the night he was betrayed, Jesus promised his followers joy, drawing on the depths of the divine delight. That joy, the joy of the Creator and of us, the Creator's children, is the ground-note of our message.

Reflection

One of the ways that the gospel stretches us out of our comfort zone is that it teaches us that, while we are each responsible for our own faithfulness, we are also bound into a common life. Part of the work of the Lamb's War is to develop a feeling sense of the one Spirit whose operations may take many forms.[126] A frequent attention to the community and a waiting to feel where the unity stands (beneath all our diversity) is a gift to oneself and one's meeting. The kind of prayer I am advocating is one in which our selves and all the parts and actions of our spiritual body are held lovingly and are known at bottom to be deeply connected. As we make this kind of attention or attentiveness a steady thread of our practice, we can find our way experimentally into an understanding—and an ability—to see and then to live in unity in some measure. We may well lose sight of the unity, but once we have had the taste of it, we know that it can be found and felt again.

---

126   The following lines are drawn from a letter sent to Multnomah meeting and reprinted in Drayton, B. (2021) *Messages to meetings*. San Francisco: Inner Light Books.

Meditation: World Tree

In a woodland, on a town green or on a hill overlooking a close-cropped pasture, an English oak draws the eye with its twisted, unique shape, its personality, and its evident great age. Such trees, living for hundreds of years, teach unmistakeably the uniqueness of the individual, as a leaf of grass or passing butterfly cannot. Yet an English oak is both frame and element in a remarkable association of living things.

Recent studies have identified 2,300 species of birds, animals, fungi, invertebrates, and plants that reside within or upon a mature oak. More than three hundred of these live nowhere else, and another two hundred or so prefer oaks for habitat or forage.

The oak ages with the hills, and in each year, it grows in generosity and intricacy. The creatures that live from, on, and within it shape and mark it over their generations, while the oak persists.

The heartwood, which as in all trees is the residue of previous years of active growth, is host to heart-rot fungi, which, as they grow and consume the tree's core, leave interior chambers and cavities open to the outside.

The rotten wood piles up inside and spills out through gaps in the living shell. The fungus has taken nutrients from the wood and, in the process, made them more available to other creatures. Fungi and detritivores move in to inhabit and consume the developing compost. So rich is this material that the tree itself extends roots inward from the trunk to draw nourishment from its transformed heart.

Letter Thirty-five: Another Reason Why Climate Change Theology Matters

Dear friend,

Like many others, I have been trying to identify how climate change relates to Christian understandings (theology, you can call it, or "giving account of the hope that is in us" to use Paul's phrase), and at times, it can feel like a pointless enterprise. But theology is relevant if it helps us weave together the disparate parts of ourself into a whole and speak the truth we discover in that process. And theology includes the doing of the truth. After all, God's Word (narrative message) is spoken as light, starts, earth, creatures, and the Spirit walking among and within them all.

Recently, I've been thinking about political developments that have theological dimensions: governments and large corporations (their conjoined partners) have responded to protests against the continued hegemony of fossil fuels and in favor of a future that avoids the worst cases of climate change by essentially criminalizing such protests.

The Ohio legislature, for example, recently passed such legislation, and the bill—if approved—would authorize substantial financial penalties, not only for protesters using any of a number of tactics but also for organizations, including religious groups that provide any support or encouragement. As the *Huffington Post* reports:

> Any organizations that "knowingly direct, authorize, facilitate, or encourage a person to commit any of the following offenses or provide compensation to a person for committing any of the following offenses" can be "punished with a fine that is ten times the maximum fine that can be imposed on an individual." Companies that operate critical infrastructure could then sue those same organizations in civil court, too.

The bill includes fossil fuel facilities and pipelines among the items of critical infrastructure. In addition to physical damage or human injury, crimes may also include such broad offenses as "to interfere with the use or enjoyment of the property of another."[127]

Now there are a lot of Christians—and others—who are feeling moved to what our tradition would call prophetic witness. The climate movement, with its growing emphasis on justice for the victims of climate change who so often have contributed little to its causes, represents a more serious challenge to the way things are. In other areas, such as refusal to participate in war, the mainstream has treated the variance represented by small dissenting sects as an annoyance that is excluded from their definitions of free exercise of religion.

Legislation that is designed to inhibit or repress these movements of protest and warning about environmental disaster makes a similar prouncement about permissible morality. On the one hand, this can be seen as an example of the narrowing in American religious discourse of the nature of sin so as primarily to focus on sexual activities; the culture does not now consider gluttony or usury or envy or acedia as sins to be avoided.

On the other hand, much rhetoric around variant theological views treats minority positions almost like consumer choices. Opposition to abortion, in this view, is absolutely central to Christian

---

127   In the past two decades, legislations across the United States have considered dozens of other bills, some of which have been enacted into law, designed to restrict, prevent, or punish dissent.

belief, whereas opposition to war or reverent treatment of creation are considered eccentric add-ons. If I make you violate those strictures, I am not causing you any serious spiritual damage, whereas if, for example, I make a law that forces a health professional to treat a trans person like anyone else or prescribe a Plan B One-Step emergency contraceptive, I am endangering their souls, interfering with their religious practice in a way that they claim the Constitution forbids.

Something like the Quaker stance against participation in war and war preparation,[128] however, claims that opposition to war is an unavoidable mandate and shifts the center of moral decision making away from its current mainstream fixation on body issues. It is a shift that can be hard for the mainstream to understand and even harder to accept as valid.

I remember when I was standing before my draft board, arguing my case to be classified as a conscientious objector. My draft board was deeply skeptical about my position because I claimed a religious motive based on arguments from the Scripture and such figures as Erasmus and John XXIII. I was not yet a Friend and so not a member of a recognized peace church—so I was outside any box they recognized. They peppered me with the sort of questions that many COs got back then.[129]

The thing is that, though this was an intimidating and even scary experience, I found my fears taken away when I remembered why I was standing there. I'd filed as a supporting document a copy of the gospel of John, and when I kept the commandment to love in mind and Jesus' dialogue with Nicodemus, I felt grounded—not confident in myself but deeply rooted and prepared to take what came. I was strengthened to make my case and succeeded.

---

128   Shared in some form by other Christian groups such as the Anabaptist tradition and the Jehovah's Witnesses

129   "Wouldn't you have taken up arms in the American Revolution? What if Earth were being invaded by aliens? What if you saw someone raping your grandmother? And you happened to have a pistol? And you happened to be able to use it effectively?" and so on.

When I later came among Friends and read the "Peace Testimony" statement from 1660,[130] I felt that I was among a people who understood the gospel more fully than my former communities had, and I was surrounded by a cloud of witnesses to instruct and strengthen me.

So with climate change and earth care and the need in our times for prophetic words and acts. If we understand that the Spirit of Christ is expressed also in God's engagement with and love for the creation, then we cannot separate that testimony from our other testimonies about worship, marriage, war, justice, etc. The responsibility to stewardship of creation, as an expression of love of God and love of neighbor, is consequently unavoidable, inalienable from our understanding of the gospel. It is, therefore, not an option or a consumer choice or a political fad.

This can strengthen us individually and as communities in times of struggle and social conflict around these issues when the powers seek to crush dissent from their hydrocarbon idolatry—but it also gives us an additional way to appeal to the witness in others, including those who profess Christianity or who claim to defend the sanctity of conscientious action. And so our theology can equip us to fully make our case—not only acting as the Holy Spirit directs but putting it into words and perhaps images and songs as well as deeds, using many channels to convey how the story of God's love is taking, yet again, uncomfortable shape, bringing turbulent peace on the Dove's wings of *metanoia* and transformation and how this story is our story.

Reflection

In any era, individuals seeking for faithfulness will find their spirits drawn to more than one kind of issue. Some will most strongly feel

---

130 *We utterly deny all outward wars and strife and fightings with outward weapons, for any end or under any pretence whatsoever. And this is our testimony to the whole world. The spirit of Christ, by which we are guided, is not changeable, so as once to command us from a thing as evil and again to move unto it; and we do certainly know, and so testify to the world, that the spirit of Christ, which leads us into all Truth, will never move us to fight any war against any man with outward weapons, neither for the kingdom of Christ, nor for the kingdoms of this world.*

George Fox: Journal, ed. John L. Nickalls 1952, pp. 399-400

a concern for racial justice, some for the plight of children, some for protecton of oceans, and so on. Yet consider that all these responses are manifestations of God's calling to reconciliation. In what ways does your theology (or other fundamental moral commitment) support your search for authentic action in these days of challenge? Can you connect your feelings and intentions around climate change with others' leading concerns?

Meditation: Wonder

The sun is pouring down on Pacific waters, the surface of the gentle swells ruffled and sparkling, echoing the Chilean mountains standing along the shore.

From the deck of the sailboat, you look down through the glare and glitter to the green-gray interior. Within the fluid world, you can make out improbable things: massive forms, as if a submerged forest, motionless. Broader at the upper end, tapering downward till the flukes flare wide. Five, six, eight—spaced across the seascape, about a bodylength away from its companions. The body is otherwise bulky, an undulating surface—though almost halfway down the length there is a small, oval, enfolded eye.

As you watch, holding your breath, from time to time, little clouds of bubbles flow up from the heads, silvery against the dark matrix in which the whales exist. They are sleeping, with half their brain awake and half asleep for perhaps fifteen or twenty minutes. Their voices are still, and their bodies are still—majesty in silence. And then they awaken with all their power and unguessable intelligence, mysterious in ocean.

Letter Thirty-six: Complicity, Conviction, & Creation, Divine Invitation to Renewal

Dear friend,

You may know that Quakers from the beginning have spoken of their encounter with the light, which is a human faculty but integrally related to (and identified with) the Christ alive and at work among us. It was most often in terms of the light that Friends described and made sense of their transformative encounter with the living God.

But maybe in our day something additional is emerging. I was struck years ago by a passage in "A short catechism for the simple-hearted" by Isaac Penington (emphasis mine):

> Q. Why dost thou call him the light? Are there not other names every whit as proper, whereby he may as well be known?
>
> A. Do not thus set up the wise and stumbling part in thee; but mind the thing which first puts forth its virtue as light, and so is thus first to be known, owned, and received. Yet more particularly, if thou hast wherewith, consider this reason: *we call him light, because the Father of lights hath peculiarly chosen this name for him, to make him*

known to his people in this age by, and hath thus made him manifest to us. And by thus receiving him under this name, we come to know his other names. He is the life, the righteousness, the power, the wisdom, the peace, &c., but he is all these in the light, and in the light we learn and receive them all; and they are none of them to be known in spirit, but in and by the light.

The statement that "the Father hath particularly chosen this name.. to make him known…in this age" made me wonder: Is there some other name by which we are being called to God in this age? This question has driven much of my search into spirituality and climate change because it raises the possibility that God is offering opportunities for us to grow inwardly as children of the Light by paths particular to our time and place. Note that, as Penington taught it, receiving God under one name enables us to know all the other names as they are given to us. So my question is not a rejection or abandonment of the Light but an openness to an alternative path toward the Light, which, being specially suited to our times, can reach people's hearts in a fresh and stirring way.

How would we recognize this path? In Quaker theology, the Light (that is the light of Christ inwardly perceived) is seen to have quite specific effects, the first of which is to reveal sin. For example, Penington goes on:

> Q. How may I…find the light in the midst of the darkness of my heart, which is so great, and this seed so small?
> A. By its discovering and warring against the darkness. There is somewhat which discovereth both the open and secret iniquity of the corrupt heart…This which thus warreth against the darkness, to bring people off from all false foundations to the true and living foundation, this is the light; and thus thou mayst find it, at some time or other, at work in thy heart, if thou mind it.

"Sin" is, of course, a problematic word. We repeat endlessly that "the New Testament word for 'sin' actually means 'missing the mark.'" This makes most everyday humdrum sins feel more like peccadilloes;

we can't understand why there can be any real harm or danger when the actual thing being abhorred is a mere aim-and-a-miss

Well, one could point out that there are several (some people count 6) words for sin in the Greek Scriptures, so the simple metaphor of poor aim is perhaps not the whole story. We tend, with miss-the-mark language about sin, to avoid the sense of revulsion or uncleanness. There is also an overtone of inadvertence about such language and thus a downplaying of responsibility. This is very modern.

Certainly, in all ages, it has been recognized that people offend without intent or unintentionally do harm (sometimes through carelessness): the Psalmist says (Ps. XIX), "Who can understand his errors? cleanse thou me from secret faults." For such things, one may be inclined to feel regret but not to feel that one's basic spiritual health is in question.

On the other hand, there are sins of actual commission—I chose to act thus, but now I see that it was not only error, a wandering away from the path, but in fact a real harm or offense or even (morally speaking) a crime or wound inflicted. This is a fact with implications about my worldview, the motives and values by which I make my choices. "Jesus said to them, If you were blind, you would have no sin: but now you say, We see; therefore your sin remains."

This leads me to a second reflection on the way that the Light makes sin visible to us: though it may start with an insight about a particular event or attitude, it does not stop there. If we are receptive to its teaching, we can come to see a wider picture—the ground or fabric of attitudes, history, and fears from which sinful acts come. This broader view is obscured by the shooting at/missing the mark way of thinking about sin (though it is not necessarily incompatible with it). Thus, God opens us to the recognition of sin and, beyond that, an insight about sinfulness. The point is the revelation of a posture or orientation.

> ..the Lord said...this people draw near me with their mouth, and with their lips do honour me, but have removed their heart far from me, and their fear toward me is taught by the precept of men:

Isaiah here points out that we can understand the root or ground of our distance from the Spirit's life in relation to the first and great commandment, the love of God (which may be felt in you most poignantly as love for your neighbor). The prophets understood that, if you are not worshipping (giving allegiance to) God, your loyalty and values are derived from elsewhere. The prophets in every age know that the smallest acquiescence with evil, even in its most diluted form, can, if unchecked, grow strong and resistant to change. If my friend and I stand side by side and turn so that the angle of our walking will be even 1 degree different—we start out side by side, but in a few paces, the distance has widened to yards, and eventually we will be out of sight or earshot of each other. The difference was a tiny angle compounded by persistence on the path taken.

If you come to a realization of this kind, it may in turn reveal a need to change, to make a course correction so as to seek for a path toward a reconciliation with the Witness that is accusing merely by its presence and visibility to you. It is a motive or opening and the beginning of a change of life (*metanoia*).

But how does this relate to climate change and encountering the Witness in some other form than light, accepting revelation as it comes to us from the Word of Wisdom?

Many of us, as we have come to understand the nature of climate change and the future that may be unfolding, have felt grief and fear. Beyond that, though, as we come to recognize the ways that humans have triggered this crisis, our grief is accompanied by guilt and self-reproach—we have all, unwittingly, contributed to it, as have our parents and grandparents. The realization is the more bitter because the system in which we are embedded does not allow us to free ourselves from continued complicity. Your individual efforts to reduce your carbon footprint are good but make little actual impact on the unfolding disaster. Our economic order, which plays such a central role in the definition of our society and our ideas of well being, is the concrete representation of a disrespectful and exploitative relationship with creation.

No wonder there is widespread denial or (among those who do not deny) a resignation or even despair. It is hard not to hear the echoes of Paul's lament in the letter to the Romans:

> For the good that I would, I do not: but the evil which I would not, that I do. Now if I do that I would not, it is no more I that do it, but sin that dwelleth in me. I find then a law, that, when I would do good, evil is present with me. For I delight in the law of God after the inward man: but I see another law in my members, warring against the law of my mind, and bringing me into captivity to the law of sin which is in my members. O wretched man that I am! who shall deliver me from the body of this death?

Thus, when we take seriously the revelation of Christ, the wisdom or reason of God in creation, we feel convicted. As we grow in our understanding of the complexities of the great system in which we live, we can come to feel powerless, insignificant, and (perhaps more importantly) misdirected. As when we stand in the Light, we come to see not just our specific misdeeds or failings.

Beyond that, this way of encounter with creation reveals to us our unhallowed mind. In climate complicity, we can see how small things contribute to great evils and are in continuum with them—so the seed of evil is an evil in itself, just as the seed of the Light is a power if we regard it with the clear spiritual eye. Our complicity can be haunting, an ugly smear that we cannot expunge—expiation is the only response, true action that is true because it reflects an inward transformation, even if it is partial.

Moreover, we must accept the real possibility that, no matter how faithfully we respond to this new sense of what is hallowed and what is contrary to the wisdom and light of Christ, restoration or reconciliation will not look like the world from which we are moving. God's salvation is built on love and justice, but it is creation and re-creation, and this always means the breaking down of certainties and verities: a new order. Guided both by the Shepherd of souls and shaped, too, by what we have learned about the world and our right role in it, we can shape our sphere according to the order of the gospel, the power of God in which the world has been unfolding from the beginning. The change will not be comfortable, but the blessings will be astonishing even if they may not at first appear so. We must expect to be confounded, even as we are born into a new life.

> Wherefore the Lord said, Forasmuch as this people draw near me with their mouth, and with their lips do honour me, but have removed their heart far from me, and their fear toward me is taught by the precept of men: Therefore, behold, I will proceed to do a marvellous work among this people, even a marvellous work and a wonder: for the wisdom of their wise men shall perish, and the understanding of their prudent men shall be hid. (Isaiah 29:13–14)

Reflection

Charles Péguy famously said, "Life holds only one tragedy, ultimately: not to have been a saint." What can this mean to you? As you consider the signs of the times and your participation in the work of reconciliation, what do you feel stirring in your heart? What might be the next step in following those hints, those nudges of compassion?

Meditation: Horse Chestnut

The tree towers upward like a thunder cloud building, green and brown. The early summer blooms, white and pink flowers whose arrangement seemed to echo the shape of the tree, have long ago yielded to the burred seeds. With autumn now coming in, the splayed hands of the leaves are drying, twisting, and falling, making rustling piles, child's playground and squirrel's workplace.

Beneath the dry starfish hands of the leaves, sea-urchin husks, prickly and drying green to yellow to brown, open up hour by hour. Squirrels and deer help with paws, hooves, and prying teeth.

Seeds come out, deep reddish-brown, glossy/silky to the eye and to the touch. How can you not collect them, fill your hands? They roll and skitter out, which invites you to do it all over again, fill your pockets, fill your hat. For what? Holding them is a delight all by itself, like hoarding seashells in your walking meditations by the sea.

What else? Count them, throw them, string them for games and ornaments. Like gems, shells, ceramic, a polished wooden spoon, prayer beads, the nuts speak to the eyes and the finger tips. They are only for delight—they will not be processed, roasted, saved: they glow, sit quietly on the windowsill, bringing the woods inside; and met with outside, they are familiars in the dying year.

Letter Thirty-seven:
Atonement as Homeostasis

Dear friend,

I started thinking about the issues that have resulted in these let-ters when I realized that, in order to grapple with the spiritual issues of the Anthropocene and to respond to them with integrity out of the Christian witness, I had to understand and accept in a deep way the implications of our status as earthlings, as beings of earth whose spiri-tual health is inseparable from our actions as living creatures.

Having got that far, I began to realize that this has meant seek-ing to connect this realization with the nature of the work of Christ. In a simple-minded way, I wanted to understand as concretely as I could how the atonement, the reconciliation, actually works. I was not and am not satisfied with the idea I was taught as a child that God required the blood sacrifice of his son, an innocent victim, to somehow redress human sinfulness. Nor did other stories about the atonement make sense to me because it has been clear from the be-ginning of Christianity that Christians are not freed from sin by the crucifixion: the evidence is quite clear that we all keep sinning just as before, and over the centuries, we have developed (individually and as institutions) all kinds of rationalizations to disguise our continued thralldom. Jesus, the first-born of many brethren, opened clearly for us the path to freedom in God's love, yet we must complete Christ's sufferings with our own (Colossians 1:24). Just as creation has been a process that continues until today in each particular of the *kosmos*, so, too, the atonement is a timeless and pervasive work in which Christ guides us in finding our way and in enabling us to follow as we grow into fullness in and through the Spirit.

When the early Quaker leader, James Nayler, was tried for blasphemy in 1653, he was asked about his understanding of Christ's work. I found the exchange from the trial very striking (emphasis mine):

> *Col. Brigs:* Didst not thou write a paper wherein was mentioned, that if thou thinkest to be saved by that Christ which died at Jerusalem, thou art deceived?
>
> *James:* **If I cannot witness Christ nearer than Jerusalem, I shall have no benefit by him**; but I own no other Christ but that who "witnessed a good confession before Pontius Pilate"; which Christ I witness suffering in me now.

As I have pondered Jesus' teachings, I have come to see things in a way that makes sense to me as a naturalist and may also make sense to you as a fellow earthling.

In the gospel narratives, Jesus evidently expected that people would need to follow their own individual paths to reunion with God. The common feature, of course, is that we are each of us to deny ourselves and take up our cross and follow him, laying down our lives daily for our neighbors. "Denying self" can only mean "Set aside your agenda, and wait for instructions from God."

His replies to people who ask for direction are notably individual, and the implication is that each of us will have our own path, our own challenges, and our own transformations to undergo. Of course, some he did invite to drop everything and follow him. The rich young man was urged to sell his possessions, give the proceeds to the poor, and follow the master. But he did not tell Mary and Martha to sell their hospitable home; nor Peter's mother-in-law; nor Nicodemus, Joseph of

Arimathea, or the woman at the well. The most common command is "sin no more." His advice is often coupled with a searching question: "What does the law say? How faithful are you to the teachings already given?" If they reply that they're doing what the commandments require, he says, in effect, "Great, you're on your way!"

Jesus also taught that his friends were a community, indeed that they shared a common life rooted in their unity with him: "I am the vine, you the branches." The same life flows through all, but the mere fact of this intimate linkage does not mean that further cultivation will not be needed if all are to yield fruit. Paul later develops this sense of active unity—one in which each has a place to belong and a service to provide—in his image of the church as the body of Christ with Christ as the head, animating and directing all the members, whose unity does not erase their differences in gifts and functions.

But Jesus clearly also saw that, within this community, there would be conflicts. The eighteenth chapter of Matthew always repays reflection and clearly teaches that even Jesus' most committed followers would have further work to do. In this chapter, there is a clear expectation of conflicts within the community. Sometimes the community would need to help in the resolution of issues between members, and Peter is told that people have to be prepared to foregive, not just seven times but seventy times seven.

Moreover, the community, when they are gathered in Jesus' name (and his presence), is empowered to adjudicate so that what they bind or unbind may be taken as God's will for that purpose in that community.

Since each one is called to their own faithfulness, each one must find out what is required of them to become free children of the Spirit, which is the Spirit of Christ. This search, involving the whole self, is what goes on in true worship when we make sincerely a whole offering of ourselves, our souls and bodies. It is all we have to bring to the manger, to the altar, to the mercy seat, and so, as Paul says, it is a perfect, living, and holy sacrifice.

Jesus' death on the cross was revelation and an indispensible prophetic sign of the rigors that the path of gospel love requires. Each of us must experience the death of much that we cling to or that has been ingrained by culture or by our personality, which prevents us from breaking free—free of our commitments to that which leads to spiritual death, to capitulation to the ways of injustice, exploitation, and self-interest in their many idolatrous forms.

This is what it means to deny self, and that can be a bitter experience (though sometimes it is accompanied by a sense of relief and quick delight). We are wounded in many ways, and these wounds need to be bound up. Sometimes the Healer must cut deep, as the keeper of the garden must prune the vine before new life can take shape. And the first step is to see the need to change: *metanoia*, a renovation of our understanding.

Thus, atonement (at-one-ment, reconciliation, renewal) as a process seems to me to be most comparable to the physiological processes of the body—healing, growth, and homeostasis—the monitoring of inward health and the response to imbalance by a marshalling and redirection of resources for continued abundant life.

In the body, as in an ecosystem, part of the (anabolic) dynamic of building and rebuilding includes also (catabolic) processes of dismantling, of death, of recycling. The upbuilding cannot continue without the death and recycling to enable new life. And in that up-building, changes can take place to better fit the organism's current condition and challenges and to realize its own kinds of joy and generation.

So it seems to me that our souls and the spiritual life of our community partake in organic processes that are deeply available to us as participants in the mysteries of creation, the cross, and the renewal. Our integration in the Spirit of Christ commits us to reconciliation with the creation life, since Christ the *Logos* and *Sophia* of God, with whom we are invited to be in unity, works to maintain and renew that whole creation, and our healing and liberation are just one aspect of that universal work.

Reflection: Climate Change and the Anthropocene as Spiritual Opportunity

1. Climate change, with its current and future consequences, presents us with a spiritual challenge unprecedented in human experience. A full recognition of the situation is bringing many to despair, which is life-killing, or to its twin, apathy. It can, however, rather bring us to the experience of desolation, a desert in which revelation becomes visible because habits and defenses are stripped away, though not without lamentation. Over the centuries, many movements of Christian renewal, Quakerism among them, had their roots in just such desolation, an echo of the despair of Jesus' disciples on the day after the crucifixion. Yet the promise of abundant life is there for us, just as it was for them: we, too, can find the seeds of the gospel of peace in that low, stark place.

2. The challenges of climate change invite us to enlarge and refresh our understanding of the the work of Christ in and through all of creation of which humans form one element. In the desert, after his testing, Jesus was ministered to by angels in the company of the wild things. We, too, accepting our condition as the light

reveals it to us, can be ministered to by the Spirit in its many forms and by the wild things who are our fellow creatures. Then, like Jesus, we can proclaim the presence of the holy order ("kingdom of God"), see more and more how it touches all of life, and learn our role as stewards and dependents of it.

3. In body, mind, and soul, we are integrated with the rest of creation; this is why we can draw spiritual as well as physical refreshment and healing from nature—we are in it and also of it.

4. However, in using our capacities of imagination, art, thought, and technique, humans have altered our physical habitat in profound ways, and these alterations are founded on a mental habitat that places humans at odds with the rest of the creation (nature) in the service of an ideal of human flourishing that is based on endless economic growth. This worldview is symbiotic with human alienation from the spirit of love and truth—and alienation from each other on many levels.

5. We have always been called to a reconciliation with, in, and through the Spirit that many call the Spirit of Christ, comforter and life-giver, "without whom nothing was made that was made." This Spirit, however named, invites and enables each of us at a point where we are available to a prophetic challenge, that is a challenge to our worldview that is coupled with an invitation to transformation or enlargement in love, power, and joy.

6. The Wisdom of God, which encompasses all the complexity of creation, will disconcert us, refuse to conform with social conventions, and often present as numinous paradox. An important part of the revelation through Jesus is just this kind of challenge.

7. The essential task of worship and of the daily practices that emerge from worship is to keep our eye on the place where the disconcerting Comforter is at work and to follow where it draws us. We do this by a worship founded in encounter with the Living One, a worship that does not allow supports for that encounter to substitute for the experience itself.

8. The Lamb's War is one way to express the unity among worship, judgment, personal transformation, and outward witness and

action. This dynamic, toward a freedom constrained by love, develops as we fall into the hands of a living God whose job is not to appease or flatter us but to renew our minds under the strictures of truth and of love.

9.   The message of the reconciliation offers us the chance and the power to dwell more fully in the world in all its abundance, beauty, terror, and uncertainty. The message of unity does not remove struggle, but it frees from fear and toward full availability and faithfulness to the Spirit. This power, which is the good news Jesus lived in and preached, is the gospel: not a dogma or dead text but a life and a process still unfolding: discovery, *metanoia*, metamorphosis through will-death to more abundant life. It is a plain but arduous path, whose trailhead can be found at every threshold and along which we have a guide and many companions from across the generations.

10.   We are given life. But we are also challenged to choose life or death, to decide to live either toward despair or toward hope, to keep on the chains of fear, or rather don the creative constraint of love. In a world of gathering ecological overturning (catastrophe) in which we earthlings are both victimizers and victims, how and by what story shall we live?

Letter Thirty-eight: Joy at the Root

Dear friend,

I find that I have one more thing laid on me to write to you: the spring from which, in these days of challenge and even desolation, we can drink to renew our strength, our love, our courage, and our sense of justice is the font of joy. Joy, indeed, is the natural air of the Reconciler and Sustainer, of Wisdom and her children. When one seeks to follow the guidance of that Holy Spirit and to take action in the world following its lead, our strength is renewed, and our vision cleared when we pause until we can find again the taste of that joy whose other names are Love and Truth, Life and Light.

But what joy is appropriate to the hard work ahead of us in which grief and doubt are our daily companions? The equation of joy with mirth has, I think, caused a good deal of discouragement down through the ages, when committed souls find themselves struggling and experiencing pain and doubt and unable to maintain a steady state of cheeriness. Does that represent a failure to live in joy?

My quest to understand the nature of joy, for one seeking to live a life rooted in the gospel, that is, the power of God to salvation, was set off by my trying to understand the passages about joy in the Gospel of

John. Most especially in the farewell discourses delivered on the very night before the crucifixion, Jesus speaks of joy.

Now I do not know what your understanding is of how Jesus understood his nature and his mission. But I do not think that one needs to attribute any divine foreknowledge to Jesus to believe that he knew he was on the edge of catastrophe. If nothing else, Jesus was an acute observer and shrewd enough in his understanding of human motivations and the signs of the times, as any prophet is. Reading those signs and knowing what is in the human heart, he must have had a sense that the radical and paradoxical nature of his vision as a messenger of God's revelation was about to be made manifest by a climactic encounter with those who embody the conventional wisdom and the structures of power. The cross is the final revelation of just how unexpected his messiahship was.

At this pivotal moment in the fifteenth chapter, Jesus says, "These things I have spoken unto you, that my joy might remain in you, and that your joy might be full." He emphasizes that his experience of joy and that of his disciples is of an unconventional kind, when, in chapter 16, he says, "ye shall weep and lament but the world shall rejoice; and ye shall be sorrowful, but your sorrow shall be turned into joy."

Already the questions and temptations and grief and fear of Gethsemane must have been gathering upon him. Already he knew very well how incomplete, how unfinished the work of transformation was in the hearts and wills of his apostles, his closest friends, and successors. Given how people reacted to his preaching about the relationship between God and humanity, about the mystical bond of life and substance that flows through and within all those who participate in his body, he must have known that the prophetic sign it was about to enact would reach very few, at least at first. He must have wondered what the plan might be or, in modern parlance, what was God's theory of action? Although he knew God's power for transformation, although he had experienced the intensity of presence in the transfiguration experience, although he knew mercy and forgiveness and the welcome which his message had received in many hearts and minds, at the time of the last supper, the weakness and folly of the reinterpretation of history that his messiahship represented must have been a heavy burden.

And yet, at this point, he spoke of joy and comfort at the same time that he spoke of persecution and the powers of darkness.

Now, the two commonest words for joy in the Christian Scriptures are *khara* and *agalliasis*. *Agalliasis* appears typically in the context of an event, such as a wedding or a sudden realization of good fortune, when being persecuted or dancing before the ark of God—an expression of jubilation. *Khara,* on the other hand, is the word that's used in the passages from the Gospel of John that I have quoted already. You might say that *agalliasis* represents "acute joy," "rejoicing," while *khara* represents a "chronic," underlying condition, which may or may not be evident in outward expressions of rejoicing.

In the Gospel of John, Christ is first identified with the *logos.* As I have written, this word is full of complications, but one of its nuances comes from its use in Stoic philosophy (probably transmitted and flavored by neo-Platonists such as Philo). By *logos,* the Stoics meant something like the sense at the heart of the chaotic universe. Well, the Stoics also used a word to describe the condition of one who perceives the *logos* and is in harmony with it. That word was *khara,* the same word that John uses for the joy that Jesus wishes for his disciples and indeed promises them in defiance of the world's judgment. It's the sense of being at home in the universe, sort of like their version of enlightenment. It's also related to the word for "grace" and also "thanks"—*kharis.* That's the word that Jesus uses and promises to his disciples in defiance of all the powers arrayed against them and on the night of Gethsemane.

Mystics such as Julian of Norwich or Francis of Assisi and the numberless others who have have sought to understand the mind of Christ over the centuries have come to know Christ's joy in the time of testing in Gethesmane and at Golgotha, which includes both a deep participation in the beauty and wonder and order of creation and at the same time a deep and undeniable suffering.

We are challenged, when we speak of Christian joy in the wilderness of this world, to take note of people who participate fully in the complexities of the world and who do not deny the ocean of darkness and death, the pain and tribulation that is attendant upon mortal life, testifying to joy and often rejoicing. They remain undismayed because of some fundamental assurance that they have come to. Yet it's promised to all of us and therefore within the reach of all of us if we can find our way there. I am only a stumbler along this path, but I need to make my testimony to you for your encouragement.

Ever since I began trying to penetrate the heart of this mystery, which in some sense is deeply part of the mystery of incarnation, the mystery of the divine that is achievable through and in human life, it has seemed important to seek out the places where a joy is found which is not celebration. A joy that, in some sense, feels like participation in God's love and a fundamental affirmation of the person, the individual, and the traveler who explore and witness.

How have I been doing it? There is not much technology or technique here: I have slowly developed a habit of stopping whenever I can—it's happening more and more often—to see whether I can feel something which flows below—like an underground stream of cool water—or around—like the air we draw in and release constantly in rhythm with our heartbeat—whatever else is going on. I go through fads, trying things that help me remember to check in, "to mount the watchtower."

As I've tried from time to time to seek for a place of chronic joy (*khara*) in many different conditions, I have come to feel that if I accept joy as a query, I may also come closer to understanding the paradoxes embedded in the Christian message—how it is that the meek shall inherit the earth, how it is the merciful obtain mercy, how those who hunger and thirst for righteousness can be satisfied, how one can find in the folly of Christ's revelation a glimpse of the wisdom of God and thereby see the folly at the heart of the wisdom of the world, that is the world from which God has been excluded or in which God is perhaps no longer sought.

I would like here to hold up some faces of joy, which are paths to it and evidences that it is present

Delight

One element of joy is certainly delight, an intense, very often sensual feeling of well-being. Mirth can come from it, of course, but it's more than that. We are drawn, for example, to feel kinship with nature, and in that space, our sense of alienation from others (even perhaps ourselves) falls away, leaving us free. This is a condition in which we hear the echoes of the days of creation, when as evenings and mornings began their cycles, God saw that it was good—very good. It is a place of innocence and freedom. When we are in this place, the creatures, among whom we take our place and feel it blessed, teach us compassion, endurance, resilience—which for me are the tracks of the joy I am looking for.

Freedom from Fear

We are fearful of a lot of specific things, but at bottom, there are two, existential fear and social fear—what I think of as fear of not being and fear of not counting. Many of the things that trigger fear involve both—if I lose my job, I worry about how my family and I will be sheltered, fed, and stay healthy, but I also may feel personally rejected or feel a failure and suffer from a loss of structure and purpose through which I find much of my identity. Often the things that are disturbing to us seem far removed from existential challenges, but nevertheless, trigger deep alarms. Maybe this is the source of some of the anger that we find rising up unexpectedly with no recognizable source. Deep down inside, a primordial response says, "Death!"

In the place where joy abides, I am not afraid. There are fewer and fewer things that I am afraid of. It seems a bit arrogant to say so, but what I want to emphasize is that it works. One can grow into this joy, and indeed many can testify to such growth—it's what we're invited to and led to if we will.

At the same time, we can feel free to acknowledge our limits and even more of our limited nature. I find that I can even look with love at the fact that my life in this body will end and accept that there are things I will never know or understand, tasks I will not complete, things I don't have the strength or wit to do.

Freedom to Compassion

Sometimes the first opening we have to freedom is in fact a motion of love, a sense of identification with another. It's related to the delight, the innocence of nature, the freedom from fear. In the feeling of this opening beyond our own isolated selves, accompanied by a perception of the respect due the other or even kinship with the other—joy comes in there, and in time, the respect and kinship can be transformed or enriched by a reverence that can live side by side with clarity of judgment and with truthfulness.

Willingness To Be Used

The actions of the Inward Teacher or what Friends used sometimes also to call the Inward Monitor—instructing, prompting, restraining, guiding—these are perhaps the most tangible signs of the Living God present and at work—Christ come again in the bodies of his saints and preparing the way to the kingdom life. Those engaged in the frequent encounter with this inward activity that comes from beyond the self—and yet, in measure, cleanses, prepares, and consecrates the individual—experience, in the words of Father Mapple, "topgallant joy."[131]

Reverence Is Also a Face of That Joy

All these are characteristics of chronic joy, but they are also paths toward it. Another path toward it, which can help us recognize it in a nonmystical setting, is:

Right Work

Our culture has glorified creativity, but many of us can testify that there are many kinds of work, which, when we are absorbed in it, are paths to joy. Psalm 90 (KJV) begins with a burst of praise at a cosmic level: "Lord, thou hast been our dwelling place in all generations. Before the mountains were brought forth, or ever thou hadst formed the earth and the world, even from everlasting to everlasting, thou art God." But it ends with the prayer, "Establish thou upon us

---

131 *Moby Dick*, Chapter 9: The Sermon.

the work of our hands; yea, the work of our hands, establish thou it." There is great joy in exercising your skill. The work of the craftsman, the teacher, merchants, and even rulers and bureaucrats (remember Joseph?) receive Biblical notice: the challenge is to do them honorably and wholeheartedly and enjoy the appropriate satisfactions that come from meeting a need, exercising a skill or gift, balancing what was incomplete, capturing some aspect of experience in a form (of words, material, motion, music) that invites and enables someone else to participate in it for themselves and be nourished by what you have done.

In all these places or experiences related to joy, we are vulnerable, open, and available to the work of the Living God, whose work is going forward endlessly, and we are called to take our part. Take any path that works in your quest for this kind of joy that leads toward compassion, reverence, freedom—each of us can just start at the nearest opening, the most accessible pathway. It is bread for our journey and nourishment that we can share with others along the way. As we taste, digest, and share our morsels with others, the endless subtleties of its flavor and substance, which are all the tastes of the living earth and the Spirit of the Lord, open for our refreshment and the kindling of our spirits. Active, unpossessive love becomes possible again. This life is our gift, the promise and the commission for our work. Therefore, let us choose life!

In Christian love, your friend,

Brian

Acknowledgments and Thanks

Words can only begin to express my gratitude to Darcy Drayton, whose love, wisdom, and creativity have recreated my life in ways large and small for the past half-century. It has been a delight to have her participate in the creation of this book.

I have been accompanied for the past two years by what Quakers call an oversight committee, whose role has been to read, respond, challenge, pray, think, and wonder with me: Sarah Gant, Doug Gwyn, Ken Jacobsen, and Darcy Drayton. I am daily grateful for their insight, friendship, searching honesty—and sheer endurance.

Finally, I am very grateful to Michael Knotts for his work in preparing images of Darcy's drawings; and to Erin Farwell, who was generous with her time and attention in supporting Michael's work with Darcy.

I am grateful for the careful and sympathetic editorial and design work of Eric Muhr and Barclay Press. I am glad also to acknowledge the support of New England Yearly Meeting's Obadiah Brown Benevolent Fund, and the Mosher Book and Tract Fund, which contributed to the costs of production and distribution.

Bibliographical Notes

For Further Reading

The following are some books that have been most helpful to me—note that some science references relating to climate change are to be found in the appendix.

About early Christian thinking about creation and its relation to the revelation of scriptures, the Holy Spirit, and science, see Blowers, P.M. (2012) *Drama of the Divine Economy: Creator and Creation in Early Christian Theology and Piety*. Oxford: Oxford University Press. For an exploration of a Christian contemplative encounter with nature and climate change: Christie, D.E. (2013) *The Blue Sapphire of the Mind: Notes for a Contemplative Ecology*. Oxford: Oxford University Press. On the "two books" doctrine, see also Heyden, K. (2019) Liber creaturae und sacra scriptura: Zur Bedeutung der Naturkunde für die Bibelexegese der lateinischen Kirchenväter. in Gorsky, Z.B und R. Hirsch-Heipold hrsg. *Christus in Natura: Quellen, Hermeneutik und Rezeption des Philologus*. Göttingen. 163–177. Finally, I cannot recommend highly enough Elizabeth Johnson's (2018) *Creation and the Cross: The Mercy of God for a Planet in Peril*. Maryknoll, NY:

Orbis Books; and *Laudato Sí: On Care for Our Common Home*, Pope Francis's encyclical letter from 2015.

Special Topics

Studies of Erasmus and his radical view of the gospel message are very numerous, but aside from his own writings, I keep returning to two books: Fitzpatrick, S. (2012) *Erasmus and the Process of Human Perfection: The Philosophy of Christ*. Dunshaughlin, Co. Meath (Ireland): Stauros. and Screech, M. A. 1980. *Erasmus: Ecstasy and the Praise of Folly*. London: Penguin Books.

On the topic of the Lamb's War and gospel order in Quaker thinking, see Gwyn, D. (1995) *The Covenant Crucified: Quakers and the Rise of Capitalism*. Wallingford, PA: Pendle Hill Publications. Also Gwyn's (2014) *A Sustainable Life: Quaker Faith and Practice in the Renewal of Creation*. Philadelphia: QuakerPress. About Sophia, the literature again is vast. A valuable study that points to many other sources is Pramuk, C. (2009) *Sophia: The Hidden Christ of Thomas Merton*. Collegeville, MN: Liturgical Press.

Appendix: Climate Change and Biodiversity Loss

There are many excellent books and websites that provide information on the nature of human-induced climate change and the loss of biodiversity. At the end of this appendix, I will list a few with comments about each; there are other citations that can be found in the full reference. Here, though, I will just mention some key scientific findings.

Let me begin by noting that climate change and biodiversity loss are closely connected, and if you find yourself drawn to work on biodiversity issues, you are also thereby working on climate change—and vice versa. A website that articulates this link is "Biodiversity for a Liveable Climate" (https://bio4climate.org). Note also that justice, including indigenous rights, is a central concern to be addressed in understanding climate change's causes and our future. Most of the references recommended below pay attention to the justice connection.

Climate Change

1. Already by the mid-nineteenth century, scientists had understood the physical mechanisms by which an increase in atmospheric

carbon dioxide (CO_2) would lead to climatic warming. By the 1890s, the consequences were predicted with some accuracy, and already by the 1950s, some scientists in the petroleum industry were predicting disturbing impacts on a global scale. Why?

The insulating effects of the small amounts of CO_2 in the atmosphere are what keeps the earth's climate hospitable for life as we know it. A surprisingly small increase, however, significantly slows earth's loss of heat so that the average temperature rises. The earth's geography and its dynamic nature mean that this average temperature will be reflected in complicated ways. At the beginning of the industrial revolution, which is also the beginning of significant and sustained use of fossil fuels, CO_2 constituted about 285 parts per million (ppm) of the atmosphere. At the time of writing, the present levels are above 420 ppm.

2. There is a time-lag in the effects that come from thickening the atmospheric blanket with more CO_2. The global temperature has risen about 1.3° (C) so far, owing to the rapid injection of CO_2 into the atmosphere in the decades up to about 1930. There have been exponential increases in CO_2 emissions since that time—more than 50 percent of CO_2 added to the atmosphere has been added since 1990. Because of the time-lag, we are therefore already committed to at least 1–2 degrees (C) more warming, even if we ceased all CO_2 emissions right now. It is very likely, given the slow pace of political and economic action, that we cannot avoid reaching 450 ppm or even higher. This might commit us to an increase of perhaps 6° F (3°C) by the end of this century; the difference between our current climate and the last glacial period is about 9°F.[132]

3. I am writing this in June 2025. The ten warmest years (global average temperature) in recorded history have occurred since 2014; 2024 was the warmest year yet. Over the last several decades, each ten-year period has been hotter than the decade preceding it: The 1980s were hotter than the 1970s; the 1990s were hotter than the 1980s; the decade from 2000–2009 was hotter still. The current decade will be the hottest so far.

---

132   See the 2025 *Global Energy Outlook* from the International Energergy Agency: Https://www.iea.org/reports/world-energy-outlook-2025.

4. Because of how the weather system distributes heat, the Arctic is warming faster than anywhere else. While New England has warmed about 2° (F) in the past forty years, the Arctic has warmed 8–10° (F). As the ice has melted, the ground and sea, darker than ice, have absorbed more heat, thus speeding the melt. The melting permafrost has started releasing its vast reserves of frozen plant matter as CO_2 and methane, another very powerful greenhouse gas. This is speeding the warming. If we do not dramatically decrease human-caused CO_2 emissions, the natural emissions from these and other sources will soon increase so swiftly that they will become the most important factor in the CO_2 imbalance, and human activity will not be able to prevent the earth's tipping into a new, stable operating condition, dramatically warmer than anything humans have ever had to deal with.

5. Ocean levels are rising as the water warms (about 80 percent of the excess heat trapped by the enriched atmosphere has been absorbed by the oceans), and as ice-caps and glaciers melt. While reaching unprecedented temperatures, seas are also absorbing CO_2 and becoming more acidic at a rate that is astonishing and alarming researchers. Plants and animals are changing their ranges or altering behavior or going extinct. Deserts are spreading in Africa and Asia. The great ice cap of central Asia is melting fast; this is serious because it supplies the Ganges and many other major rivers supplying water to China and South Asia.

6. Weather patterns are becoming more variable. In many cases, dry places are getting drier, and moist places are getting wetter, though some critical regions (such as Amazonia) are drying out, with consequent transformation of ecosystems. Both precipitation events and droughts are becoming more extreme. Indeed, increased variability is a central expected outcome of global warming because the increasing heat intensifies important weather processes like evaporation and cyclone formation. The *New York Times* columnist, Thomas Friedman, likes to refer to "global weirding" instead of "global warming."

7. Widespread biological changes are taking place as a result of climate change. I mention here just some of the many kinds of changes being seen: species displaced (including millions of human

climate refugees) with habitats degraded or lost; species extinguished; disrupted seasonal rhythms such as blooming, insect emergence, bird and bat migration and reproduction; changes reported in average size of some species, including fish, lizards, and birds. Diseases are emerging, and disease vectors (e.g. insects and ticks) are shifting their range.

8. While the most important variable under human control is CO_2 emissions from carbon combustion and deforestation, there is at present no evidence that humans are responding at a speed and scale to prevent dramatic and indeed catastrophic changes in our climate that will last for at least a thousand years, affecting food supplies, biological diversity, and many other ecosystem functions essential to our welfare. The best scientific analysis suggests that the worst case can still be avoided if we take concerted action within the next five to ten years.

Biodiversity Loss

Biological diversity has been shown to be an essential contributor to ecosystem health and resilience and also to the health of the human psyche and spirit. As species in an ecosystem make maximal use of the solar energy available to them, they partition, use, and recycle nutrients and other resources, keeping them available to the living creatures of all kinds and transforming the chemistry, physics, and even the shape of landscapes.

The study of biodiversity, once a central focus of biology and one of the most important areas of science, has long been underfunded and under-appreciated with the result that we currently inhabit and exploit a world that is unknown to an astonishing and alarming degree. The total number of named species is around 1.3 million (the number is approximate because new species are being discovered every year). Because new species continue to be identified, we do not yet know how many species actually exist. Scientists have used many different approaches to estimate the number of species still to be found. A recent, widely accepted estimate is that the total number of species is likely around 8.75 million (Wiens 2023; Mora *et al.* 2011) . Thus, we know only about 20 percent of all the species on earth. ("Know" in this case means "have enough information to assign a name and taxonomy." This does not mean that much is known about most species' biology or ecology—much is unknown about even very familiar species, such as the American robin.[133]) Species vary in their detectability (Cruickshank *et al.* 2016), which requires a large amount of natural history research on species of interest to allow for the likelihood that a species might be (un)detected.

Nevertheless, it is clear that a sixth mass extinction is under way (Kolbert 2014, Wiens 2023). The data show a loss of species in many taxa at rates much higher than the background rate of extinctions. A precursor to escalating extinctions is seen also in the evidence of dramatic reduction of individuals within many species: populations of vertebrates show a 25 percent average decline in abundance since 1500; two-thirds of monitored invertebrate populations show an average 45 percent decline in abundance (Dirzo *et al.*); similar dramatic reductions are seen in aquatic populations around the world (salt and fresh). Moreover, a high proportion of new species being discovered must be seen as threatened or endangered, reinforcing the conjecture that very many species are going extinct without our knowledge, with potential implications that will only be intensified by climate change.

For Further Reading

The science is moving fast and on many fronts so that blogs and websites are often the best way to find out the latest developments. The books listed here provide valuable context and background.

There are several blogs that are good sources of reliable information and a gateway to many other sources of information. As with everything on the web, things change rapidly, but here are a few with which to get started, each of which has links to further information on the science and its social and other impacts:

Skepticalscience.com (from Australia) provides up-to-date science news, including biological and human impacts. It has also compiled a very accessible and reliable discussion of most-used climate myths.

---

133   For example, much remains to be discovered about the American robin's life during migration and in their winter territories.https://www.audubon.org/magazine/fall-2020/scientists-are-unraveling-american-robins

Climate.gov was for many years a reliable source of climate science, well organized, regularly updated, and nonpartisan. I regret to say that the Trump administration has closed this site and sought to eliminate all government research or reporting about climate change.

Talking climate with Katharine Hayhoe at www.talkingclimate.ca features Dr. Hayhoe, a widely respected climate scientist and an evangelical Christian. Her Substack newsletter provides "clear-eyed and hopeful look at climate science and solutions...weekly climate updates, good climate news, event information, ideas on things to do and ways to join the conversation."

Insideclimatenews.org provides information and current investigative journalism relating to science and solutions with attention to justice, health, energy, and the economy.

Yaleclimateconnections.org offers wide-ranging scientific and social information and useful links. See also Yale Climate Communication https://climatecommunication.yale.edu, reporting research and analysis about attitudes and understanding of climate change in the US and around the world.

Books

Climate Central (2012) *Global Weirdness: Severe Storms, Deadly Heat Waves, Relentless Drought, Rising Seas and the Weather of the Future.* An excellent, step-by-step primer on the basic science and some of the possible solutions for climate change.

Hanson, James (2010) *Storms of My Grandchildren.* Hanson was the first prominent climate scientist to sound the alarm about the reality of climate change.

Klein, Naomi (2014) *This Changes Everything: Capitalism vs. the Climate.* Trenchant, deeply researched, and passionate examination of the challenges before us with special attention to social and economic factors.

Kolbert, Elizabeth (2006) *Field Notes from a Catastrophe.* Lucid, challenging, and engaging science writing about the science and impacts of climate change. Originally a series for the *New Yorker*.

Kolbert, E. (2014) *The Sixth Exinction: An Unnatural History*. Groundbreaking journalism and still an excellent starting point.

Macy, Joanna and Chris Johnstone (2012) *Active Hope: How to Face the Mess We're in Without Going Crazy*. A powerful guide for engaging with the work that reconnects. Draws on the authors' years of despair work and other faces of the spirituality of healing wounded spirits.

Mann, Michael (2021) *The New Climate War*. A distinguished climate scientst on the science, the politics, and the social impacts of climate change.

McKibbin, Bill (2010) *Eaarth: Making a Life on a Tough New Planet*. Concrete and passionate about our present situation and the challenge of responding constructively. McKibben has written a number of other books, starting with *The End of Nature* and most recently *Here Comes the Sun*, which are a good source of information about science and policy.

Rathe, T.T. (2023) *Extinction in a Human World: The Environmental Cost of Human Progress*. Good journalistic overview of current state of biodiversity and extinction science and extensive current bibliography.

Seidl, Amy (2009) *Early Spring*. An ecologist's moving and well-informed exploration of the way that climate change affects the life and culture of New England.

References

This list is probably not exhaustive but offers a range of resources for further exploration of many of the topics that appear in the book and that do not appear in the notes at the end of the book. Some specific resources on climate change and extinctions do not appear here but are in the appendix. Questions or comments welcome: Brian Drayton (drayton.be@gmail.com).

Aland, K. M. Black, C.M. Martini, B.M. Metzger and A. Wikgren (1975) *The Greek New Testament* 3rd ed. New York: American Bible Society.

Alberts, E.C. (2022) Global biodiversity is in crisis, but how bad is it? It's complicated. https://news.mongabay.com/2022/04/global-biodiversity-is-in-crisis-but-how-bad-is-it-its-complicated/.

American Psychological Association (2009). Psychology and Global Climate Change: Addressing a Multi-faceted Phenomenon and Set of Challenges. https://www.apa.org/science/about/publications/climate-change

Arendt, Hannah (1958). *The Human Condition*. Chicago: Chicago University Press.

Bacon, K. & Swindles, G. (2016). Could a potential Anthropocene mass extinction define a new geological period? *The Anthropocene Review* 3, https://doi.org/10.1177/2053019616666867.

Bainton, R. (1969). *Erasmus of Christendom*. New York: Scribners.

Ball, P. (2006). *The Devil's Doctor: Paracelsus and the World of Renaissance Magic and Science*. New York: Farrar, Straus and Giroux.

Barbour, H.S. (2006). Quakers, Quarks, and Queries: A Process Theology of the Spirit. in Birkel, M. ed. *The Inward Teacher: Essays to Honor Paul A. Lacey*. Richmond, IN: Earlham College Press. pp. 26–44.

Basil of Caesarea (1857). *Hexaemeron*. in Migne, J-P. *Patrologia Graeca* 39. pp 3–208. https://books.google.com/books?id=O-Q8RAAAAYAAJ&printsec=frontcover&source=gbs_ge_summary_r&cad=0#v=onepage&q&f=false.

Bauer, E., W.F. Arndy, and F.W. Gingrich (1979). *A Greek-English Lexicon of the New Testament*. 2nd ed. Chicago: The University of Chicago Press.

Blowers, P.M. (2012). *Drama of the Divine Economy: Creator and Creation in Early Christian Theology and Piety*. Oxford: Oxford University Press.

Boyle, M. O. (1977a). *Sermo*: Reopening the Conversation on Translating JN 1,1. *Vigiliae Christinae* 31:161–168.

Boyle, M. O. (1977b). *Erasmus on Language and Method in Theology*. Toronto: University of Toronto Press.

Brannon, P. (2019). The Anthropocene Is a Joke. *The Atlantic*. https://www.theatlantic.com/science/archive/2019/08/arrogance-anthropocene/595795/.

Bromley, G.W. (1985). *Theological Dictionary of the New Testament (G. Kittel and G. Friedrich), translated and abridged in one volume*. Grand Rapids, MI: William B. Eerdmans Publishing Company.

Cardinale, B. J., et al. (2012). Biodiversity Loss and its Impact on Humanity. *Nature*, 486, 59–67. doi:10.1038/nature11148.

Chadwick, H. (1980). *Origen* Contra Celsum. Cambridge: Cambridge University Press.

Chantraine, P. (1977). *Dictionnaire etymologique de la langue Grecque; Histoire des mots*. Paris: Les Éditions Klincksieck.

Charry, E.T. (1997). *By the Renewing of Your Minds: The Pastoral Function of Christian Doctrine*. New York: Oxford University Press.

Chesterton, G. K. (1987). *St Francis of Assisi*. New York: Image.

Christie, D.E. (2013). *The Blue Sapphire of the Mind: Notes for a Contemplative Ecology*. Oxford: Oxford University Press.

Colledge, E., O.S.A. and J. Walsh, S.J., eds. (1978). *Julian of Norwich: Showings*. New York: Paulist Press.

Cook, B. (2007). The Uses of *Resipiscere* in the Latin of Erasmus: in the Gospels and Beyond. *Canadian Journal of History* XLII(4):397–410.

Crossan, J. D. (1991). *The Historical Jesus: The Life of a Mediterranean Jewish Peasant*. New York: HarperCollins Publishing.

Dandelion, P., D. Gwyn, and T. Peat (1998). *Heaven on Earth: Quakers and the Second Coming*. Birmingham, UK: Woodbrooke College.

Deignan, K. (2007). *Thomas Merton: A Book of Hours*. Notre Dame, IN: Ave Maria Press.

Dewey, John (1988a). *The Public and Its Problems*. in Boydston, Jo Ann, ed. *The Later Works of John Dewey, 1925–1953. Vol. 2*. Carbondale: Southern Illinois University Press. pp. 235–372.

Dewey, John (1988b). *The Quest for Certainty*. in Boydston, Jo Ann, ed. *The Later Works of John Dewey, 1925–1953. Vol. 4*. Carbondale: Southern Illinois University Press.

Dillon, J. (2011). Protreptic Epistolography, Hellenic and Christian. *Studia Patristica* LXII. pp. 29–40.

Dillon, J, R.B. Stevenson, A.E.L. Wals (2016). Introduction to the Special Section: Moving from Citizen to Civic Science to Address Wicked Conservation Problems. *Conservation Biology* 30:450–455.

Dirzo, R., H.S. Young, M. Galetti, G. Ceballos, N.J.B. Isaac, B. Collen (2014). Defaunation in the Anthropocene. *Science* 345 (6195): 401–406.

Drayton, B. (2024) The Lamb's War and "Spiritual Warfare": Reflections on a Dangerous Metaphor. Amorvincat.wordpress.com.

Drayton, B. (2021). Functions of Nature in the Colloquies: Erasmus Birthday 2021. Amorvincat.wordpress.com.

Drayton, B. (1994). *Selections from the Pastoral Writings of James Nayler With Biographical Sketch and Notes*. Mosher Book and Tract Fund of New England Yearly Meeting of Friends.

Edgerton, F. N. (1973). Changing Concepts of the Balance of Nature. *The Quarterly Review of Biology*, Vol. 48, No. 2, pp. 322–350.

Emerson, R. W. (1983). *Nature*. In *Emerson: Essays and Lectures* (15th printing). New York: Library of America. pp. 5–49.

Erasmus, Desiderius (1979) *Moriae encomium, id est Stultitiae laus*. In *Opera Omnia: Ordinis Quarti Tomus Tertius*. Amsterdam: Elsevier.

Erasmus, Desiderius (2003) *In euangelium Ioannis annotationes*. In *Opera Omnia: Ordinis Sexti Tomus Sextus*. Amsterdam: Elsevier. pp. 29–17.

Erasmus, Desiderius (1706). *Periphrasis in evangelium Marci*. in LeClerc, J-B ed.*Opera Omnia Des. Erasmi Roterodami*, VII Leiden: Peter van der Aa. pp.157–272.

Erasmus, Desiderius (1990). *Paraclesis* In Welzig, W. ed. *Erasmus von Rotterdam Ausgewählte Scriften*. Band 3: Darmstadt: Wissenschaftliche Buchgesellschaft. pg 12.

Fitzpatrick, S. (2012). *Erasmus and the Process of Human Perfection: The Philosophy of Christ*. Dunshaughlin, Co. Meath (Ireland): Stauros.

Fox, G.. (1831/1990). *Epistles*. In *Works of George Fox*, vols vii and viii. State College, PA: New Foundation Publications.

Fox, M. ed. (1987). *Hildegard of Bingen's Book of Divine Works*. Santa Fe, NM: Bear & Company, Inc.

Funk, Robert W., Roy W. Hoover, and the Jesus Seminar (1993). *The Five Gospels*. New York: Macmillan Publishing Company.

Geertz, C. (2000). "Common Sense as a Cultural System." In *Local Knowledge: Further Essays in Interpretive Anthropology*, 3rd ed. New York: Basic Books. pp. 73–93.

George, E.P. (1979). Robustness in the Strategy of Scientific Model Building. In *Robustness in Statistics*. (Launer, RL & Wilkinson, GN, Eds.). New York: Academic Press. p. 202.

Giese, R. (1935). Erasmus and the Fine Arts. *Journal of Modern History* 7(3): 257–279.

Gilford, D., Moser, S., DePodwin, B., Moulton, R., and Watson, S.(2019). The Emotional Toll of Climate Change on Science Professionals, *Eos 100*, https://doi.org/10.1029/2019EO137460.

Gwyn, D. (1995). *The Covenant Crucified: Quakers and the Rise of Capitalism*. Wallingford, PA: Pendle Hill Publications.

Gwyn, D. (2014). *A Sustainable Life: Quaker Faith and Practice in the Renewal of Creation*. Philadelphia: QuakerPress.

Harvey, A.E. (1979). *Companion to the New Testament*. Cambridge: Oxford University Press, Cambridge University Press.

Heine, R.E. and K.J. Torjesen, eds. (2022). *The Oxford Handbook of Origen*. Oxford: Oxford University Press.

Heyden, K. (2019) Liber creaturae und sacra scriptura: Zur Bedeutung der Naturkunde für die Bibelexegese der lateinischen Kirchenväter. in Gorsky, Z.B und R. Hirsch-Heipold hrsg. *Chrisus in Natura: Quellen, Hermeneutik und Rezeption des Philologus*. Göttingen. 163–177.

Hoffmann, M. (1994). *Rhetoric and Theology: The Hermeneutic of Erasmus*. Toronto: University of Toronto Press.

Holmes, M.W. (2007). *The Apostolic Fathers*. 3rd ed. Grand Rapids, MI: Baker Academic.

Johnson, E. A. (2018) *Creation and the Cross: The Mercy of God for a Planet in Peril*. Maryknoll, NY: Orbis Books.

Johnson, E. A. (1993) "Wisdom was made flesh and pitched her tent among us." in Stevens, M., ed. (1993) *Reconstructing the Christ*

Symbol: Essays in Feminist Christology. New York: Paulist Press. pp. 95–117.

Jones, J.D. (2012). A Theological Interpretation of *Viriditas* in Hildegard of Bingen and Gregory the Great. *The Portfolio of the Dept of Music and Ethnomusicology, Boston University.* Vol, 1, https://www.bu.edu/pdme/jeannette-jones/.

Jones, R. M. (1936). *The Testimony of the Soul.* New York: The Macmillan Company.

Josephson-Storm, J.A. (2017). *The Myth of Disenchantment: Magic, Modernity, and the Birth of the Human Sciences.* Chicago: University of Chicago Press.

Kaplan, M. (2008). Researchers Sneak up on Sleeping Whales. *Nature.* https://doi.org/10.1038/news.2008.613.

Kaufman, M. (2021). The Carbon Footprint Sham: A Successful "Deceptive" PR Campaign. https://mashable.com/feature/carbon-footprint-pr-campaign-sham.

Kelly, T. (1941). *A Testament of Devotion.* New York: Harper & Row.

Klein, N. (2014). *This Changes Everything: Capitalism vs. the Climate.* New York: Simon & Schuster.

Kohls, E-W. (1966). *Die Theologie des Erasmus.* 2 Bände. Basel: Friedrich Reinhardt Verlag.

Kugel, J.L. (2012). *How to Read the Bible.* New York: Free Press.

Küng, Hans (1994). *Great Christian Thinkers.* New York: Continuum Publishing Company.

LeGuin, U. K. (1968). *A Wizard of Earthsea.* Berkeley, CA: Parnassus Press.

LeGuin, U. K. (2001). *The Other Wind.* New York: Harcourt Brace & Company.

Leonard, W.E. and S.B. Smith, eds (1942). *T. Lucreti Cari: De Rerum Natura libri sex.* Madison: The University of Wisconsin Press.

Leopold, A. (1993). *Round River.* New York: Oxford University Press.

Liddell, H.G., R. Scott, and H. S. Jones (1977). *A Greek-English Lexicon.* 3rd ed. with Supplement. Oxford: At the Clarendon Press.

Lollar, J. (2013). *To See into the Life of Things: The Contemplation of Nature in Maximus the Confessor and His Predecessors.* Tournhout, Belgium: Brepolis Publishers.

Maximus Confessor. *Ambigua ad Iohannem,* in *Patrologia Graeca Cursus Completus* 91:1061–1417.

McDonnell, M.J., S.T.A. Pickett, G.E. Likens and W.J. Cronon, eds. (1997). *Humans as Components of Ecosystems.* New York: Springer.

Merton, T. (1963). Hagia Sophia. in *Emblems of a Season of Fury.* New York: New Directions. pp. 61–69. Also reproduced in Pramuck (2009). pp. 301–305.

Merton, T. (1965) *Conjectures of a Guilty By-stander.* New York: Image Books.

Merton, T. (1998). *Contemplation in a World of Action.* Notre Dame, IN: University of Notre Dame Press.

Metzger, B. M. and M. D. Coogan, eds. (1993). *The Oxford Companion to the Bible.* New York: Oxford University Press.

Miles, M., M. Huberman, & J. Saldaña (2013). *Qualitative Data Analysis: A Methods Sourcebook,* 3rd. ed. Thousand Oaks, CA: Sage.

Mora, C., D.P. Tittensor, S. Adl, A.G.B. Simpson, and B. Worm (2011). How Many Species Are There on Earth and in the Ocean? PLoS Biol. 2011; 9:e1001127. https://doi.org/10.1371/journal.pbio.1001127 PMID: 21886479.

Morries, G.P. (2010). *From Revelation to Resource: The Natural World in the Thought and Experience of Quakers in Britain and Ireland 1647–1830.* Doctoral dissertation, University of Birmingham. Available at: https://etheses.bham.ac.uk/id/eprint/631/. Downloaded ca. 4/1/2022.

Moser, S. C. (2009). Communicating Climate Change and Motivating Civic Action: Renewing, Activating, and Building Democracies. In *Changing Climates in North American Politics: Institutions, Policymaking and Multilevel Governance,* eds. H. Selin and S. VanDeveer, 283–302, Cambridge, MA: The MIT Press.

Moser, S. C. and C. Berzonsky (2013). There Must Be More: Communication to Close the Cultural Divide. In O'Brien and

E. Silboe, eds., *The Adaptive Challenge of Climate Change*, Cambridge University Press. http://susannemoser.com/documents/Moser-BerzonskyChapter_RevDraft10-21-13.pdf.

Moser , S. C. and L. Dilling, eds. (2007). *Creating a Climate for Change: Communicating Climate Change and Facilitating Social Change.* Cambridge: Cambridge University Press.

Moulton, P.P. (1971). *The Journal and Major Essays of John Woolman.* Oxford: Oxford University Press.

Murray, W.A. (1958). Erasmus and Paracelsus. *Bibliothèque d'Humanisme et Renaissance*, T. 20, No. 3:560–4.

Nayler, James. (2004–9). *Works.* Volumes 1–4: Glenside, PA: Quaker Heritage Press.

Nickalls, J.L., ed. (1952). *The Journal of George Fox.* Rev. Ed. Cambridge: Cambridge University Press.

Nuttall, G.F. (2003). Love's Constraint? A University Sermon. In Nuttall, G.F., *Early Quaker Studies and the Divine Presence.* Weston Rhyn: Quinta Press. pp. 265–272.

Nuttall, G.F. (1967). "Unity with Creation": George Fox and the Hermetic Philosophy. In *The Puritan Spirit: Essays and Addresses.* London: Epworth Press. pp.194–203.

Nuttall, G.F. (1966). *The Holy Spirit and Ourselves.* London: Epworth Press.

Parker, G. (2013). *Global Crisis: War, Climate Change, and Catastrophe in the Seventeenth Century.* New Haven: Yale University Press.

Pelikan, J. (1993). *Christianity and Classical Culture: The Metamorphosis of Natural Theology in the Christian Encounter with Hellenism.* New Haven: Yale University Press.

Pelikan, J. (1986). *The Vindication of Tradition.* New Haven: Yale University Press.

Penington, I. (1995–7). *The Works of Isaac Penington, a Minister of the Gospel in the Society of Friends.* Vols. 1 to 4. Glenside, PA: Quaker Heritage Press.

Peterson, A.W. (1950). Backward Swimming of the Muskrat *Journal of Mammalogy*, Volume 31(4):453.

Pickett, S,T.A., J. Kolasa, and C.G. Jones (2007). *Ecological Understanding: The Nature of Theory and the Theory of Nature.* Burlington, MA: Elsevier Academic Press.

Pramuk, C. (2009). *Sophia: The Hidden Christ of Thomas Merton.* Collegeville, MN: Liturgical Press.

Primack R.B. (2014). *Walden Warming: Climate Change Comes to Thoreau's Woods.* University of Chicago Press.

Rahlfs, A. and R, Hanhart (2006). *Septuaginta. Ed. alt.* Stuttgart: Deutsche Bibelgesellschaft.

Reuther, R.R. (1993). Can Christology Be Liberated from Patriarchy? in Stevens, M., ed. *Reconstructing the Christ Symbol: Essays in Feminist Christology.* New York: Paulist Press.pp.7–29.

Rittel, H.W. J. and M. M Webber (1973). Dilemmas in a General Theory of Planning. *Policy Sciences* 4(155–169).

Rupp, E.G. and P.S. Wilson (1969). *Luther and Erasmus: Free Will and Salvation.* Philadelphia: The Westminster Press.

Sanchez-Bayo, F. and K.A.G. Wyckhuis (2019). Worldwide Decline of the Entomofauna: A Review of Its Drivers. *Biological Conservation* 232 (4): 8–27.

Sandmel, S. (1978). *Judaism and Christian Beginnings.* New York: Oxford University Press.

Screech, M. A. (1980). *Erasmus: Ecstasy and the Praise of Folly.* London: Penguin Books.

Seidl, A. (2009). *Early Spring: An Ecologist and Her Children Wake to a Warming World.* Boston: Beacon Press.

Seidl, A. (2011). *Finding Higher Ground: Adaptation in the Age of Warming.* Boston MA: Beacon Press.

Solnit, R. (2021). Big Oil Coined 'Carbon Footprint' to Blame Us for Our Greed. https://www.theguardian.com/commentisfree/2021/aug/23/big-oil-coined-carbon-footprints-to-blame-us-for-their-greed-keep-them-on-the-hook.

Stevens, M., ed. (1993). *Reconstructing the Christ Symbol: Essays in Feminist Christology.* New York: Paulist Press.

Strona, G. and C.J.A. Bradshaw (2018). Co-extinctions Annihilate Planetary Life During Extreme Environmental Change. *Nature Scientific Reports* 8:16724. DOI:10.1038/s41598-018-35068-1.

Swim, J., S. Clayton, T. Doherty, R. Gifford, G. Howard, P. Stern, E. Weber (2009). *Psychology and Global Climate Change: Addressing a Multifaceted Phenomenon and Set of Challenges. A Report by the American Psychological Association's Task Force on the Interface Between Psychology and Global Climate Change.* http://www.cred.columbia.edu/pdfs/publications/APA_climate-change_2009.pdf. Accessed 5/14/10.

Taber, W.P., Jr. (1984). *The Prophetic Stream*. Pendle Hill Pamphlet #256. Wallingford, PA: Pendle Hill Publications.

Terborgh, J., and J.A. Estes, eds. (2010). *Trophic Cascades: Predators, Prey, and the Changing Dynamics of Nature*. Washington, D.C.: Island Press.

Thaler, R. H. and C. B. Sunstein (2008). *Nudge: Improving Decisions about Health, Wealth, and Happiness.* New Haven: Yale University Press.

Therrien, M.E. (2022). *Cross and Creation: A Theological Introduction to Origen of Alexandria*. Washington, D.C.: The Catholic University of America Press.

Thomas, Dylan (1971). *Collected Poems*. New York: New Directions.

Thompson, C. R. (1965). *The Colloquies of Erasmus*. Chicago: University of Chicago Press.

Tolkien, J.R.R. (2005). *The Lord of the Rings*. New York: Mariner Books.

Tolkien, J.R.R. (1988). *Tree and Leaf*. London: Unwin Hyman Ltd.

Traninger, A. (2017). Erasmus' *Personae* between Rhetoric and Dialectics. *Erasmus Studies* 37: 8–22.

Urs von Balthasar, H. (2003). *Cosmic Liturgy: The Universe According to Maximus the Confessor.* tr. B.E. Daley, S.J. San Francisco: Ignatius Press.

Urs von Balthasar, H. (1984). *Origen: Spirit and Fire. A Thematic Anthology of His Writings*. Washington, D.C. The Catholic University of America Press.

Urs von Balthasar, H. (1991). *The Glory of the Lord: A Theological Aesthetics. V: The Realm of Metaphysics in the Modern Age.* San Francisco: Ignatius Press.

Whitlock, J. (2023). Climate Change Anxiety in Young People. *Nat. Mental Health* 1, 297–298 (2023). https://doi.org/10.1038/s44220-023-00059-3.

Whitman, W. (1982). *Poetry and Prose.* New York: Library of America.

Wiens J.J. (2023). How Many Species Are There on Earth? Progress and Problems. PLoS Biol 21(11): e3002388. https://doi.org/10.1371/journal. pbio.3002388.

Wilken, R. L. (2003). *The Spirit of Early Christian Thought: Seeking the Face of God.* New Haven, CT: Yale University Press.

Wills, Christopher (2013). *Green Equilibrium: The Vital Balance of Humans and Nature.* Oxford: Oxford University Press.

Wilson, E. O. (1984). *Biophilia: The Human Bond with Other Species.* Cambridge, MA: Harvard University Press.

Wilson, G. H. (1990). Restoring the Image: Perspectives on a Biblical view of Creation. *Quaker Religious Thought* #74 Vol. 24(4):5–21.

Worster, Donald (1994). *Nature's Economy: A History of Ecological Ideas.* 2nd ed. Cambridge: Cambridge University Press.

www.ingramcontent.com/pod-product-compliance
Lightning Source LLC
Chambersburg PA
CBHW011100280526
45786CB00008B/2767